MW01053205

$ IU.7U

DOS Beyond 640K

Third edition

DOS Beyond 640K

Third edition

Jim Forney

Windcrest®/ McGraw-Hill

New York   San Francisco   Washington, D.C.   Auckland   Bogotá
Caracas   Lisbon   London   Madrid   Mexico City   Milan
Montreal   New Delhi   San Juan   Singapore
Sydney   Tokyo   Toronto

THIRD EDITION
FIRST PRINTING

©1994 by **Jim Forney**.
Published by Windcrest, an imprint of McGraw-Hill, Inc.
The name "Windcrest" is a registered trademark of McGraw-Hill, Inc.

Printed in the United States of America. All rights reserved. The publisher takes no
responsibility for the use of any materials or methods described in this book,
nor for the products thereof.

Library of Congress Cataloging-in-Publication Data
Forney, James.
    DOS beyond 640K / by Jim Forney.—3rd ed.
      p. cm.
    Includes index.
    ISBN 0-8306-4351-6 (H)   ISBN 0-8306-4350-8 (P)
    1. Operating systems (Computers) 2. MS-DOS (Computer file) 3. PC
-DOS (Computer file) 4. Random access memory. I. Title.
QA76.76.063F644 1993
004.5'3—dc20   93-10184
                                                                              CIP

Acquisitions editor: Brad Schepp
Book editor: Kellie Hagan
Production team: Katherine G. Brown, Director
                Susan E. Hansford, Coding
                Wendy L. Small, Layout
                Kelly S. Christman, Proofreading
                Jodi L. Tyler, Indexing
Design team: Jaclyn J. Boone, Designer
                Brian Allison, Associate Designer   WU1
Cover design and illustration: Sandra Blair, Harrisburg, Pa.   4356

To Sheila

Contents

Part three: Real-mode DOS

Acknowledgments

With each edition, the list of companies and individuals who have contributed to this book has grown longer. And this time, as with each past edition, I've made new friends who, even beyond their contributions of time, expertise, special knowledge of the subject, and on occasion even special hardware and software, have made the project all the more a pleasure.

I would especially like to thank Martin Hewitt and Cliff Laney (IBM DOS Brand division) and Terry Gray and John Webb from the IBM OS/2 development team in Austin. And special thanks again this time around to Gary Saxer of Quarterdeck Office Systems (Desqview) and Bill Brown at Qualitas (386max).

And thanks to the following companies, though only a part of the many that contributed. They not only played important roles in the research for and preparation of this book, but helped shape its direction:

ALL Computers Inc.
AST Research
Borland
Digital Research, Inc.
Fifth Generation Software, Inc.
Hauppauge Computer Works
Helix Software Corp.
IBM
Intel
Intelligent Graphics Corp.
Kingston Technology

Newer Technology
Novell
JDR Microdevices
Lotus Development Corp.
Phar Lap
Qualitas
Quarterdeck Office Systems
Software Link, Inc.
Stac Electronics
Theos Software Corp.

Preface

This book changed in midstream because the world of DOS turned upside down somewhere between the day I started writing it and when it finally went to press. For this, I can say only "thank goodness for computers" and the way a project like this can be pulled apart, reorganized, rewritten, and put back together finally in some completely different form. Which is what happened as I tried to put the changes in perspective—considering both the immediate needs of today and the impact they'll have on how you live and work tomorrow—or at least as far into tomorrow as the crystal ball can see.

This, then, is not so much a new edition as a new book. And having said that—before we jump right in—let me say a bit about the way I put this book together. As with previous editions (and other books I've done), I relied heavily on personal, hands-on experience, not only in selecting products for inclusion in this book, but in rating them.

Rating, of course, is a largely subjective study in itself because what works or doesn't work for me might not reflect what will or won't work for you. In order to reduce the likelihood of my findings being influenced by hardware differences and possible incompatibilities, I ran most of the software products discussed in this book on two or more quite different 32-bit systems with as little as four and as much as 16 megabytes of installed RAM. And, where applicable, I ran some in 16-bit environments as well.

You must understand that, with the exception of MS-DOS 6, much of this work was done with prerelease software. As a result, some of the data and some of the conclusions might not exactly coincide with certain details in the final, released form of these products. I have, however, tried to take this into account and tried, right up until this went to press, to update and/or to confirm any data I felt was suspect. Still, I cannot guarantee that some things didn't escape my notice, or that your results will match my own.

As a matter of general interest, the three machines on which most of the work was done were all configured around the use of the OS/2 2x boot manager. Although part of the OS/2 2x package, the boot manager is really independent of it and an absolute gem whether you ever use OS/2 or not. With it, I was able to install up to four different operating systems, each configured individually, on each machine at any given time. I was also able to give each the benefit of its own partition and, in the case of NT and OS/2, the special high-performance file systems these operating systems work best with.

Because so much has happened, several subjects I explored in depth in earlier editions were omitted this time to make more room for issues more directly related to memory management. With the exception of Windows—

which itself raises a number of specific memory-management issues—there is not a detailed look at multitasking. Nor are hardware issues covered other than the one that's so key to everything we do these days: more memory and how to get it.

I've tried to call them as I saw them, wherever possible eliminating products that, in my opinion, didn't measure up—because there were plenty more that did. There will be those who won't agree, perhaps, but I've done my best to present the information fairly. I can only hope the results will be as rewarding to you who read this as the experience of writing it has been for me.

Introduction

This is a book that bridges two distinct DOS eras: the age of real-mode DOS and a new age that has come upon us quietly—hardly noticed even by the great majority of users, but which has already changed the way a great number of us work with DOS today.

It's a book that tries to define DOS at a time when DOS, in fact, has reached a parting of the ways; a point at which the philosophical differences between both the near- and long-term strategies of Microsoft and IBM and Novell are increasingly apparent. And nowhere is that philosophical split more apparent than in the way these two new DOSs look at memory, particularly memory beyond 640K. Within the context of this book, it's also a time of new proprietary management technologies— as in the past, mostly by third-party developers—that do the seemingly impossible beyond 640K.

Today there's more than one kind of DOS. And by that I don't mean the DOS from Microsoft *versus* something from those other guys—whatever other guys you want to talk about. Today, DOS lives in real mode as it always has. But it also—and increasingly—lives now in the protected mode as well; a place that didn't even exist when DOS was first conceived. DOS *thrives* in protected mode, in fact.

Not all DOSs are the same

But having said that, I must make a distinction between the DOS you've always known—DOS that could be run on any member of the 8086 family from the 8088 PC on up—and a new breed that can, at least in certain cases, run only in protected mode.

Theoretically, *any* recent, decent DOS—real mode, protected mode, or otherwise—should be capable of running any software written for DOS. And indeed, for the most part this is true. With remarkably rare exceptions—most often the result of poor programming practices—all DOS software cares about is seeing an environment that *looks* like real-mode DOS. In other words, a block of (typically) 640K of address space that appears to begin at 0000h that provides a standard set of I/O services. It doesn't matter if the address space is real or virtual—or even if the machine that's running it is real or virtual.

Sometimes DOS software needs a little something extra like expanded memory, extended memory, or high memory, and sometimes it needs to use upper memory in order to free up enough traditional 640K memory to do the job effectively. But, as always, the common denominators of 640K and a standard I/O interface to system resources are the heart and soul of DOS.

Unfortunately, this same comfortable commonality does not apply when you begin to move beyond 640K. In real-mode or protected-mode DOS, software can access extended and expanded memory, the HMA and upper memory, but the tools it takes to provide these services—services now considered basic—are different. And different tools mean different ways of working, even to run the same DOS software you've used for years.

Taken at face value, then, using the old "if it ain't broke, don't fix it" logic, there might seem little reason you should bother with anything other than plain old real-mode DOS. Unfortunately, it just isn't all that easy. In the last couple of years a lot of people have started using Windows. Windows does things differently, and using Windows as a shell to run DOS programs runs DOS in protected mode, which, the way Windows does it, is a whole lot different than the way it's done in OS/2, Windows NT, or Novell's DOS 7. Or in DESQview—yes, even the first successful DOS multitasker, DESQview, runs DOS sessions in protected mode on 386 and higher systems.

Even if you don't use Windows, DESQview, or a host of other applications that work best with lots of memory, times have changed and the chances are you'll need to use whatever memory you have more carefully and more effectively than you did in the past. And for anyone running on anything other than an 8088, there's no escaping DOS in protected mode.

Almost every protected-mode DOS or DOS emulation deals with memory in at least a slightly different way. And then there are the hybrid situations such as taking an ostensibly real-mode DOS—any version you happen to like—and running it under something like OS/2 2x. Again, the rules of memory management beyond 640K are different.

A time of change The only thing that's certain as you try to look ahead is change. It's true because it's always been that way. Looking back, it's hard to imagine that the first edition of this book was written mostly on an old 8088 PC upgraded to an 80386 with an accelerator card that also sported two whole megabytes of RAM (256K chips). It would have been hard to imagine that after such a relatively short span of two DOS generations, this book would be written on a new machine with nearly ten times that much installed RAM. And even that much—16 megabytes—isn't enough to run the latest prerelease version of Microsoft's new Windows NT operating system.

Who would have dreamed, even a scant year or so ago, that IBM would come out with a highly credible new DOS distinctly different from Microsoft's. Or that Windows would finally become a major force. Or that OS/2 would really have an impact, turning even some of its most vocal detractors—like John Dvorak—into born-again believers.

Until now the change was mostly gradual, but with the new DOS 6s from arch-rivals IBM and Microsoft, suddenly the issues have come into sharp focus. This is in part because these two new DOSs so clearly define the split between Microsoft's heavily Windows-oriented view and that of IBM which, while supporting Windows, focuses on DOS itself, giving special attention to the needs of users who have 8088 machines.

Now, though, with the emergence of Novell's DOS 7.0, a DOS that does far more in protected mode than in real mode—coming on the heels of OS/2 2x's surprisingly strong showing, Windows NT poised to make its bid, and Microsoft reportedly working on a brand-new 32-bit DOS—protected-mode DOS operations have taken on a whole new meaning. All of these support or emulate the DOS environment, even to the extent of providing emulations of extended and expanded memory, etc. But with all of them, you must approach the world beyond 640K quite differently than with DOS in real mode.

More than just a time of change, it has been a time of great excitement, too— and plenty of surprises. Companies once major players in the memory game have faded from the scene with many disappearing altogether, while some have moved on to other, seemingly more inviting markets. And others have carved new niches for themselves, hardly making my job any easier. It has certainly been more interesting, though, and certainly more challenging.

So there is a lot of ground to cover, more now than ever. In the immortal words of Sherlock Holmes, then, "Come, Watson. The game is afoot . . . ."

Part one
The issues

1 The central issue: memory

Memory: that's what it's all about. It's what this book is all about, and what computing is all about. Memory: an infinite collection of what has to be the world's most elemental building blocks, all just alike—at least in principle—and each one capable of only two alternatives. You flip a light switch and the light goes either on or off, depending on which way you flip it. This is simple and the only logic known to computers.

On or off. A single simple switch is all it takes to either light a room or darken it. But take a lot of simple switches, turn some on and others off, and you can set up a pattern that can recreate the words of Shakespeare—the entire unabridged works if you have enough switches. All by just interpreting a lot of ons and offs—or, in computer parlance, 0s and 1s. Inscribe that pattern onto something that retains it, and you have memory.

Letters, numbers from 2 through 9, and symbols—even the symbols used in higher mathematics—don't exist in memory. Just a lot of 1s and 0s. It's a tough job—really dull, just turning on and off—but someone's got to do it. Do it often and do it fast. And that's what memory—computer memory—is all about.

In computers, you basically have two kinds of memory. One kind is for long-term storage—called *nonvolatile*, it includes such things as floppy disk, hard drives, and CD ROMs. The other kind is what we're concerned with here: *volatile*, which means that whatever information it contains exists only while the power is on. Yet this is where you keep running code and data while you work, this very temporary kind of memory called *RAM* (random-access memory).

All for one,
& one for all
Notice I've made no distinction between different kinds of memory: conventional, extended, expanded, etc. That's because there isn't any. The memory—the random-access kind itself—is all alike. Any differences are for the most part artificial, products of a technology that grew too much too fast (see FIG. 1-1).

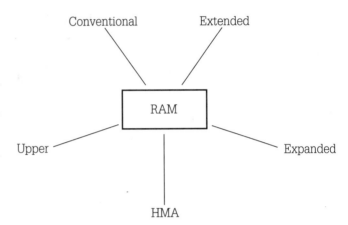

1-1
There's really only just one kind of memory in our computers, and except for things like special-purpose blocks like caches on some CPU chips, it's all interchangeable. The only difference is in how we manage it.

Logically, since the computer memory you use is all alike, it should be treated that way—all of it together in a single block. Logically, whatever memory you have or any part of it should be available to any function that needs memory—none of this conventional, extended, and expanded stuff, each with a different set of operating rules. Most of it, in point of fact, is *outside* of DOS, believe it or not.

Most of the original IBM PCs were shipped with only 32K of memory (RAM)—which, at the time, was really quite a lot. As users started adding floppy drives (the first PCs were diskless) and the need for RAM exceeded 32K, IBM redesigned the motherboard for 64K chips, and out they rolled with 64K soldered to the board and sockets for three more 64K banks. These were upgradeable all the way to 256K—Wow!—but DOS (version 2.1 by then) was still so small that both it and some of the first crude applications software could be run in only 64K.

It was this 64K world that DOS was really meant for. DOS (which stands for disk operating system) wasn't even needed for those old diskless 32K boxes. The only operating system they required was on the ROM chip installed at the factory; it contained a keyboard interface and some elementary video instructions, among other things. Early ROMs didn't anticipate the luxury of anything as fancy as a floppy drive (cassette tape recorders were the most popular and affordable mass-storage devices at the time), so the ROM (read-only memory) operating system didn't provide a floppy interface.

DOS, then—DOS as it was originally intended—was really nothing but a patch, a kluge to get around the fact that PCs didn't have a built-in interface for floppy drives. The concept of a true operating system for PCs—more than just some pretty basic I/O functions—had yet to emerge. And, due to design limitations, the 8088 chip around which the PC was designed could go up to only one megabyte (1024K)—and there was no way that could ever change. That was the top of the world. Except it really wasn't, if the truth be known.

Technology isn't born overnight, and even as the fledgling IBM PCs first saw the light of day the 80286 was on the drawing board: a chip that could accommodate as much as 16Mb of RAM. Reportedly, those privy to this information were warned repeatedly that a disk operating system should not be limited to only one megabyte. Some people just don't listen.

Unfortunately, however, once the die was cast—once the basic rules of DOS were formulated and that formulation based, short sightedly, on Intel's 8088—it was too late. DOS was limited to just one megabyte of address space—a flaw, fatal seemingly, of such a nature that it couldn't be fixed. Not then. Not now. Not ever. In fairness, in a world that seemingly could live quite comfortably in just 64K, the 640K the 8088 could handle after deducting 360K for system use was almost mind-boggling. It wasn't long, however, before the only thing that boggled was how anyone could live in *only* 640K.

Fortunately man is an ingenious creature, and from the collective genius of a host of hackers, users, and assorted entrepreneurs—with the occasional snake-oil salesman thrown in—a lot of ways emerged to get around the problem. But it's no credit to the short sighted few who stuck us with the problem in the first place that DOS lives today. Not only lives but thrives, still gaining new adherents at a far faster rate than Bill Gates can lure them into Windows and away from all the kluges and the fixes and patchwork that is DOS today.

In the process of creating the crazy quilt-like DOS environment we work with now, memory has become increasingly fragmented, with one piece called *expanded memory* and another called *extended memory*. And then there's something called *upper memory*, and something beyond that called the *high memory area* (HMA). Each one is different and each has its own set of rules.

All have one important thing in common, however: all are memory, collections of the little on/off switches called RAM. Imagine these individual switches shrunk and shrunk again until, if you could look inside the bug-like plastic blocks that house them, you would have to use a microscope to see them. Deep down inside those little plastic bugs called *chips*, you could conceivably have one switch serving as extended memory, the one beside it as expanded, and the ones to either side of those as upper memory—or conventional memory, the stuff below 640K in DOS where it all began.

Call it what you want, there's really only one kind of memory in your computer, and except for things like the special-purpose blocks like caches on some CPU chips, it's all interchangeable. At least electrically—the different kinds of packages it comes in might not be, but, broken down as far as you can break it down, it is.

Understanding this becomes especially important when and if you leave the world of DOS and suddenly have only one kind of memory—it doesn't even have a special name, just memory. And you don't have to look that far past DOS to find it.

But alas, there is still DOS. And as long as there is DOS you have conventional, expanded, extended, and upper memory . . . and, oh yes, that other something called the high memory area.

Extended memory

The 80286, with its ability to support as much as 16 megabytes of memory, brought more than just the promise of more memory than most of us could ever imagine. It brought the promise of a new and different kind of memory— still RAM, the same old chips we always had, but different.

The promise was for a kind of memory that was continuous, no longer broken into clumsy 64K segments. This new kind of memory would start just out of reach of DOS—1 megabyte + 1 and up. There were just two problems:

❑ There was no suitable operating system that supported anything beyond 1 megabyte.
❑ Intel had goofed when they designed the chip and there were flaws in it that couldn't be corrected any more than DOS could ever work beyond 1 megabyte.

By the time it was apparent just how badly flawed the 286 chip was, Microsoft was busily developing an operating system tailored to it, something called OS/2. This was to be a true 16-bit operating system because the 80286, unlike the 8088 (which, though it could handle 16-bit instructions, contained two 8-bit processors working in tandem), truly was a 16-bit chip. It could have up to 16 megabytes of RAM. And it would operate in something called *protected mode*, a special mode designed to guarantee that each of several programs loaded concurrently in that vast amount of memory (using a task switcher, for instance) would have a protected space to run in—something not really guaranteed in real mode.

Other than the fact the 80286 chip didn't work the way it was supposed to, history gets murky at this point. Microsoft just never managed to pull OS/2 together as a truly viable product. Admittedly, the failure of the 286 to live up to expectations dashed a lot of hopes, but Intel already had another chip, the 80386. As we all know, the 80386 chip *did* work, not only solving the problems of the ill-starred 286, but offering a host of other powerful new features as well.

The 80386 chip was a 32-bit chip, however, which immediately cast doubt on the viability of any 16-bit operating system. A 16-bit OS/2 would certainly run on 32-bit CPUs—as would DOS. But just as DOS could never unlock the power of the 80286 even if it had worked properly, no 16-bit operating system could ever unlock the truly awesome power of 32-bit 80386 (see FIG. 1-2).

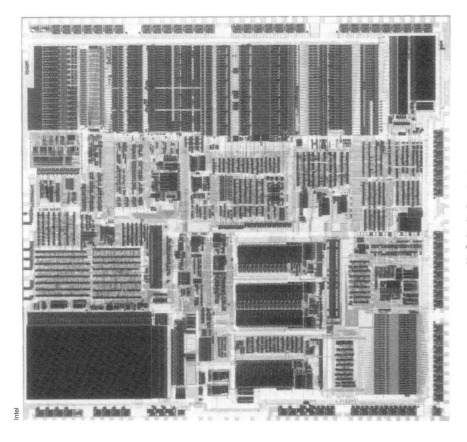

1-2
The internal structure of modern CPU chips is incredibly complex. The Pentium, for example, contains the equivalent of several million transistors.

In the meantime, Bill Gates had somehow become enamored with the concept of a graphical (rather than character-based) user interface. Xerox had developed one but never tried to market it. Apple had adopted the idea and IBM had toyed with it unsuccessfully in something they called Top View—a scheme that had died dismally. But Gates was fascinated. So much so that ultimately, when Microsoft was either unable or failed to develop a 32-bit OS/2 to meet the needs of IBM (trying to push Windows instead), IBM took back the task of OS/2 development. And from that point, relations between IBM and Microsoft have steadily deteriorated.

In the meantime, DOS goes on. And on.

Meanwhile the world couldn't wait for another operating system or for a chip that really would support extended memory. There was an immediate need for more than just 640K to work with. Lotus spreadsheet users were among the first to feel the pinch and scream for something more—or at least the first who had a company to listen to them.

There was a technique already in use on some machines outside the DOS world that allowed banks of additional data-filled memory to be switched in and out of a relatively small block of address space as needed. Lotus, Intel, and Microsoft got their heads together and, with at least the tacit approval of IBM, adopted the technique for DOS. The technique involved using a portion of the address space IBM had reserved for system use—everything in DOS's megabyte above 640K—as a "frame" through which these extra little (four 16K) blocks of RAM could be accessed.

Because of the nature of the 640K barrier—space set aside for video usage—this page-frame memory was never contiguous to DOS's main block of memory (which came to be known as *conventional memory*) and for that reason it was generally usable only for data storage. However, since the page frame lay within the megabyte of address space that DOS commands, whatever bank of memory was switched into it was fair game for DOS applications—which could easily be programmed to use it if available or live without it if is not.

As originally implemented, the amount of additional RAM—called *expanded memory* in DOS parlance—had a theoretical limit of about 8 megabytes, though as a practical matter the maximum was somewhat less initially. Nonetheless, it was enough to revolutionize the world of DOS and give the operating system a new lease on life though both Microsoft and IBM officially ignored EMS memory (expanded memory specification) up until DOS 4x. Even after offering minimal expanded memory support beginning with DOS 4—and then only for 80386 and higher systems—Microsoft never used it in any of their applications software (see FIG. 1-3).

Subsequent development of the technology—most notably by AST Research, then one of the leading vendors of plug-in memory expansion cards—extended the use of bank-switching technology to more than just the page-frame area and paved the way for full-fledged multitasking (aka DESQview).

Ultimately, this led to an extension of the EMS specification (4.0) to include a number of additional features. Officially known as the LIM 4.0 EMS specification, it was in fact derived directly from the pioneering work of AST Research and their EEMS specification (although not only was AST never officially given credit—in fact they weren't even consulted—but even Lotus failed to implement the features it afforded in subsequent releases).

EMS expanded memory, while still the only memory beyond 640K for 8088 machines, has a number of inherent limitations, not the least of which is the

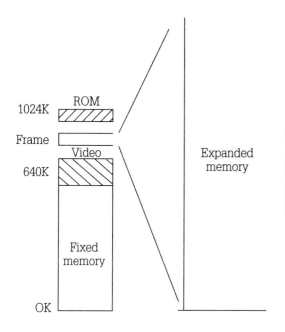

1-3
A traditional pre-EEMS/LIM 4.0 EMS system with both fixed conventional memory and expanded memory, as first implemented under the original LIM specification.

limit DOS puts on the maximum size of program code that can run at any given time. Multitasking or no, that plus DOS and typically much of an application's data must still fit and run within a 640K environment. This is as opposed to extended memory, in which a single program and its data can have up to as much as 4 gigabytes—more than 6000 times 640K—to run in. Not to say you really need that much for individual programs, but it's there— and many even now far exceed the 640K in size.

And so you have conventional and expanded memory, and something called extended memory (theoretically at least).

AST's EEMS expanded memory—which allowed whole running programs to be switched in and out—then led to multitasking. But multitasking itself added overhead, which put a squeeze on what was left to run applications. On an 8088 there wasn't anywhere to go to ease the squeeze, but on an 80286 . . . Even though the chip was badly flawed, it at least had the capability to address more than just 1024K—DOS's miserable megabyte. And desperate for a place to hide at least some of the overhead imposed by multitasking, Quarterdeck discovered something interesting.

One thing leads to another

DESQview's developers discovered that although DOS works in 64K segments, segments don't have to start at any special place in memory. In fact, with a little experimentation, they found that they could start a 64K segment just inside of DOS's megabyte and run it even though the bulk of it was hanging out beyond one megabyte, invisible to DOS but yet addressable by any chip that had the capability of going past one megabyte—and in fact it didn't even require going into protected mode to do it.

The computer press picked up on this, referring to this extra 64K as if it was something that had been there all along but only just discovered. There was—and is—a little more to it than that. In fact, even Microsoft didn't know it was possible to squeeze this little extra out until Quarterdeck shared the secret with them. Called the HMA (high memory area), it was subsequently codified in Microsoft's XMS memory specification (although Quarterdeck had already been shipping DESQview, which had used it for some time by then).

The HMA didn't use expanded memory as the source for DOS's secret extra 64K segment. Rather, since the memory it used had to be contiguous with the little stub (about 16 bytes) that anchored it below 1 megabyte, it had to reach up and borrow from what otherwise would have been extended memory. And since DOS, with its absolute 1-megabyte limit, could access this extra 64K segment only by way of the little 16-byte stub it could see, this now meant an entirely different set of rules.

So then there were four: four kinds of memory and four sets of rules. But it still wasn't over. Not by a long shot, because there was still all the overhead that just kept squeezing down that precious block of memory below 640K—and not just multitasking overhead, either. There were device drivers, and almost everyone had Sidekick or other pet TSRs chewing pieces out.

We were fast running out of space, but there was still one more place . . .

UMBs The 80386 (and later chips) have a number of unique memory-management features, not the least of which is the ability to "map" memory to every bit of address space in DOS's purview, where it becomes something called *upper memory*, with blocks of it called UMBs (upper memory blocks).

This upper memory area—governed by still another set of rules—typically includes any otherwise unused address space above 640K. Mostly this lies above C000h, but often includes (typically) smaller unused portions of address space reserved for video as well. Above the video address space but below the system ROM (usually starting at F000h), or below the page frame (typically) to the 128K below E000h, this address space is often fragmented by network cards and other hardware ROMs and interfaces.

While there are usually several small blocks of unused address space up in this area, the size of the smallest usable block is dependent on the size it takes to load the smallest TSR or driver you want to load. This, though, isn't the size after loading but the space required during initialization (loading), which is often several times the size the loaded TSR or driver needs. This often leaves some tantalizing bits of unused real estate. It's a fact of life, however—or at least it was.

Given the press for more and more not only mappable but usable space above 640K and competition between the top contenders in the memory-management department, a number of increasingly innovative techniques have been found for using every scrap of address space above 640K. The most notable of these are contained in the following programs:

BlueMax from Qualitas   Mapping over certain portions of the system ROM region (especially on PS/2s that have a 128K ROM that, with a little clever manipulation, can be squeezed into something more like 64K).

386max with Flexframe, from Qualitas   Borrowing from the page frame during the initialization phase to allow larger TSRs the space they need just during that phase, then freeing the page frame area for EMS use.

QEMM386 with Stealth, from Quarterdeck   Locating the page frame in an area that largely overlaps the system ROM, but providing a mechanism for putting the page frame aside, allowing access to the covered ROM when needed.

Netroom with Cloaking, from Helix   Replacing the ROM and often the video BIOS with all-new software BIOS, most of which is actually located outside of DOS in protected memory.

Another trick that can be used in many cases, which adds an extra 64K (sometimes up to 96K) of genuine conventional memory when running only character-based software, is to simply map RAM to the usual video graphics area (A000h to AFFFh or in some cases B7FFh).

Unlike the HMA, which must draw on what would otherwise be extended memory, it doesn't really matter where you borrow from to fill the little nooks and crannies in the area between 640K and 1024K. You can use extended or expanded; in fact, it has been down both ways—though with the world moving increasingly to what is termed "pooled" memory, the distinction is often blurred. As is the issue of which address space is mappable, which makes this the most hotly contested address range there is.

Altogether, the RAM you use with DOS is broken into five distinctive categories, each one governed by a different set of rules—and not all of them are even under DOS. Extended memory—the biggy—isn't under DOS. DOS doesn't even know it's there. It can't, because by definition it all lies beyond one megabyte—beyond the realm of DOS.

Five different sets of rules

In fact even the memory DOS sees as EMS expanded memory is not DOS memory. It, too, is actually memory that lies beyond the reach of DOS except for those often brief moments when, with just a little hocus pocus, the EMS manager makes them appear at page-frame addresses.

Then there's that spooky region called the HMA, which is and isn't DOS. You can have an HMA only if you have:

❑ Some memory installed beyond one megabyte
❑ An XMS driver that provides extended memory
❑ DOS software that provides specific features to make use of it

Upper memory is a totally amorphous bunch of bits of address space that bend to suit so many different sets of rules, depending not only on whose memory manager you use but how effectively you use it. It's ironic in this age of gigabytes that so much effort should be expended on just that first 384K above 640K. But as long as there's DOS, or as long as we use DOS, this is likely the most important little piece of real estate you own.

And then, of course, there's what's called conventional memory, which is the stuff that DOS is really made of—not only a product of DOS but the very reason there *is* DOS, without which all the rest is academic. And I haven't even mentioned *virtual memory* yet, the stuff that is but really isn't—the memory of last resort that we'll look at in some detail later.

In any case, no matter how you rate them in importance, the engine that has driven the computer world—more so even than the latest CPU and sizzling clock speeds—has been memory. With DOS, it has been memory beyond 640K. And that's what this book is all about.

2 How memory works

As recently as when the first edition of this book was printed, there really were no practical limits to how much memory you could add to existing systems—any existing system. There were—and are, of course—some finite limits, but they were almost entirely in a gee-whiz land of make believe.

Today that gee-whiz land is here. Most of us have not yet reached the final limits of our systems. And some of us, in one way or another, have used more memory than we actually have—no matter how much that is, thanks to something called virtual memory or a variety of less sophisticated swap-to-disk techniques.

Today, more than ever, it's crucial to understand the limits of your systems. And for that you need to understand the way computers access memory—not all the gory details, mind you, but some basic facts of life (see FIG. 2-1).

By now I'm sure that almost everyone who has been around computers has at least heard memory discussed in terms of addresses. Every piece of memory—each byte of RAM installed—has some specific address given to it. It has to. Otherwise the CPU would have no way of knowing where it parked some bit of information when it needed it again.

It's sort of like a post office with rows and rows of boxes, all containing the same junk mail, most likely, but each one belonging to a different renter. Other than junk mail, each renter can get only at things addressed

2-1
The granddaddy of them all, the 4-bit Intel 4004, was the world's first true microprocessor. Its use was limited to simple calculating machines.

specifically to his box number. Both a post office and a computer have a *lot* of addresses. So how does a computer handle them?

Let's start with a simple analogy: say a post office has only two boxes—numbered 0 and 1—and some sort of automated sorting machine. For such a system, only two tracks would be needed, each carrying mail to one of these two boxes. And to switch between these tracks, only a single switching device would be required. Operated electrically, if the switch wasn't turned on, the mail would be sent to box 0; turn it on and the switch would send it to box 1 (see FIG. 2-2).

This is a *binary* system—a system that has only two states. And that's exactly how it's handled by computer (CPU) chips. Some of those funny pins that stick out of a computer chip—and in some cases a lot of them—are address pins (or contacts); each is capable to pointing in either of two directions, depending on whether it's on or off.

Starting with a single address pin, the number of discrete addresses a CPU can deal with is limited to two. Two pins, then, could deal with four specific addresses—in other words, doubling the address capability. The interesting thing about these address pins is that every additional address pin you add doubles it again. So you go from 2 to 4 to 8 to 16 and so forth. So by the time

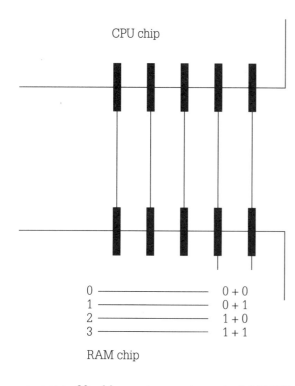

CPU chip

RAM chip

2-2
Address pins have only two states: on or off. Each address represents the combined states of all the address pins. The two pins on the right control four addresses. A third pin would increase the number of available addresses to eight, a fourth to 16, and so on.

0 ———————	0 + 0
1 ———————	0 + 1
2 ———————	1 + 0
3 ———————	1 + 1

you get to 20 address pins, you're up to 1,048,576 discrete addresses, as shown in TABLE 2-1. Rounded off to keep things simple, that's one megabyte (1044 kilobytes of 1024 bytes per kilobyte).

An 8088 computer's centipede-like chip has only 20 address pins (the rest are there for other reasons). And now you know where DOS's one-megabyte limit comes from: from the simple fact that it's all the address space an 8088 could ever deal with. Ever!

This table of the powers of 2 shows the relationship between address pins on processor chip and the mathematically possible range of addresses. I've deliberately taken it well beyond the 20 pins of the 8088 to show how rapidly the numbers escalate through the 80286, until you reach the 4-gigabyte potential of the 80386. Note, however, how these numbers also coincide with other numbers commonly encountered in computer systems: 32, 64, 128, 512, 256, and 1024, for instance. Not only just addresses but virtually everything you do with a computer has its roots in this table.

Reading down the table, you can see at a glance just how much address space an 80286 can handle with its 24 address pins and, farther down, how many pins an 80386 must have for four gigabytes. These numbers are immutable, the finite limits of the hardware. It doesn't mean that you have memory at all those addresses—it's memory only if you have RAM installed

2-1
Powers of 2

Address pins	Possible addresses
1	2
2	4
3	8
4	16
5	32
6	64
7	128
8	256
9	512
10	1024
11	2048
12	4096
13	8192
14	16,384
15	32,768
16	65,536
17	131,072
18	262,144
19	524,288
20	1,048,576
21	2,097,152
22	4,194,304
23	8,388,608
24	16,777,216
25	33,554,432
26	67,108,864
27	134,217,728
28	268,435,456
29	536,870,912
30	1,073,741,824
31	2,147,483,648
32	4,294,967,296

there—or even that the motherboard allows it (for example, IBM's original AT could handle only 12 megabytes although the CPU was good for 16).

Once you get beyond 1,048,576 bytes, the numbers are completely meaningless to DOS—they don't exist, and neither does any RAM you have there. The introduction of the 80286, then, should have brought with it a new and better operating system. But it didn't. We did get DOS 3.0, which was a whole lot better than the 2.1 we had been working with, but it was still DOS and, as such, still limited to just one megabyte.

It was only later—and not until the world had figured out the 80286 chip was a dud—that there was something else to even look at. And even that, OS/2, was hardly worth the effort. Most of those who even tried it shook their heads and went right back to DOS. Back to DOS and back to living with one megabyte of address space.

The PC was conceived before there was a DOS, at a time when the idea of a desktop machine *ever* needing as much as one whole megabyte of memory seemed utterly ridiculous.

A shrunken megabyte

It was in this climate that some crucial—and once made, irrevocable— decisions were made as to what to do with all that address space. Of course it was all pretty academic at that point—sort of like the play money in a Monopoly game—but somebody had to do it. So, as shown in FIG. 2-3, a whopping 384K of the address space was generously reserved for system use, both immediate and future.

In the 384K, someone intelligently put the system ROM (complete with a diskless BASIC kernel) clear at the outside edge of the available megabyte of memory: the topmost 64K segment (F000h to FFFFh). Then they did something that was pretty stupid; they put the video clear down at the bottom of the system's 384K area (starting at A000h), leaving a vast (nearly 300K) wasteland in the middle. So the better part of 300K was cut off forever from the *huge* 640K they'd left for us poor peons.

We were cut off from the better part of an additional 300K because DOS and applications written for DOS can run only in contiguous blocks of memory. This is crucial because it will come back to haunt you. So the better you understand the problem, the easier it is to deal with. Given that, then, let's take a moment here to look at this a little closer (see FIG. 2-4).

Assume for just a moment that there's no video—or if there is, it doesn't take up any address space. Never mind any "reserved" signs—with just the top 64K used by system ROM, you would have 960K of contiguous, usable DOS address space available. In fact you do have, even with an ordinary 8088. You don't have 960K of memory, but generally you have an unbroken 960K of address space below the system ROM (except with PS/2s, which have a 128K ROM). All of this could be used by memory (RAM). Except for the fact the video is there.

Video—which, by convention rather than in actual fact, begins at A000h— not only uses at least part of that 960K, but also splits the remaining addresses into two separate blocks. And, whether you realize it or not, programs can be run in either of those blocks. Both of them, in fact. And

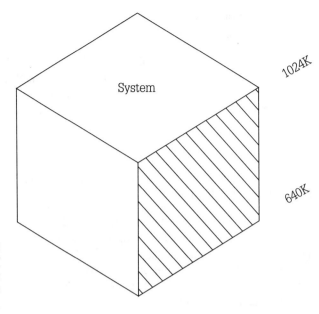

2-3

Suddenly free of the earlier 64K system limitation, PC designers grabbed 384K of the 1Mb address space for system use.

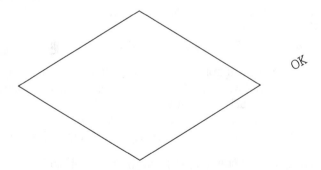

given a little time-slicing support (something we'll look at a little later), you could even multitask them. What you can't do is span across the chunk the video chews out to use both pieces for the same program (ignoring programs using expanded memory for the moment).

By convention, you normally run programs—at least primary applications (plus the operating-system kernel) in the block below the video (0000h–9FFFh). There's nothing sacred about that area other than the fact it's always the biggest single piece of address space there is. Also, it's always there, whereas the smaller block above the video is often fragmented into even smaller pieces by the installation of such hardware goodies as network

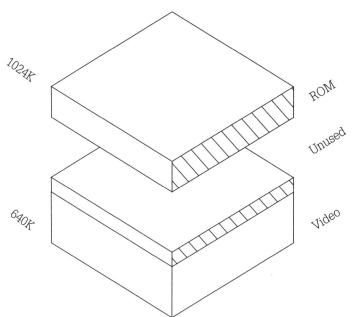

1024K

640K

ROM

Unused

Video

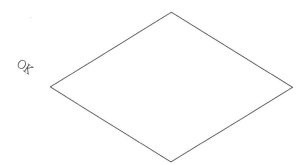

0K

2-4
Of the original 384K set aside for system use, only the top 64K and bottom 128K were actually assigned for specific usage. Of the latter 128K, many monitors needed no more than 32K at the top, leaving as much as 96K wasted (in addition to the 192K in the middle). There is still much unused space above 640K.

cards and fancy videos (and each piece is at least theoretically capable of running some lesser piece of software).

Stick something in the middle of that block above 640K and suddenly, instead of one block, you have two—or three or four—up there. The blocks keep getting smaller, but, up to a point at least, each one is still capable of loading or running something. And it goes almost without saying that *anything* you can load or run up there will free up at least some of what would otherwise be used below 640K for bigger things.

A little perspective In fairness, before I throw too many rocks, I need to put the PC in perspective—or at least in the perspective of its day and its creators. Mainframes were computers; little desktop guys were only toys—but there was a market for computer toys. There were a bunch of them already on the market; none really did that much, but they were selling. And those sales meant dollars to some greedy Big Blue eyes.

So it was just a toy, nothing more—which is why the PC didn't even have a floppy drive at first. Just a keyboard and a green screen, built-in BASIC, and typically a (then) rather generous 32K of RAM. It also had a cassette tape-recorder interface if anyone did anything worth saving—which wasn't really all that likely.

But the PC did have one thing going for it, one thing no one else had ever given their computer toys: a name. This one was an IBM, which meant the company wouldn't just fade away and disappear. And more, it had something that came to be called *open architecture*, which, given a name like IBM, left a very attractive door wide open for a lot of little guys with big ideas.

So a whole new industry was born. The need was there—the need for simple, inexpensive computers that could do real work. What the world was waiting for was just the right computer, and IBM—the name—was all it took to get the ball rolling. The rest, as they say, is history. The point, however, is that none of this was really planned. It all just sort of happened: an idea whose time had come, feeding on itself and swept along by raw enthusiasm.

Microsoft & Windows At this time, Microsoft (barely more than a one-man operation that Bill Gates started while he was still in school) was marketing a BASIC program language that was seemingly the best around. So Microsoft originally got involved with IBM because of BASIC.

Since the PC really was intended as a diskless toy, it followed that whatever "software" it required had to be built in. To be saleable at all, it had to include, in addition to just elemental I/O (input/output) functions, keyboard and video to let you see what you were typing and software to play with. BASIC was a logical choice, and it could be burned into a ROM chip right along with I/O functions.

Therefore, Microsoft was at the right place and time when, to almost everybody's shock and amazement, people started putting floppy drives in PCs—which were more costly then than 100Mb hard drives are today. Suddenly there was an urgent need for I/O functions that the PC didn't have in ROM—something called a disk operating system.

Bill Gates didn't have an operating system, but he knew someone who did: a little, now long-forgotten outfit called Seattle Computer Products. They were marketing something called QDOS, which, according to the story, stood for

Quick and Dirty Operating System. It was actually pretty much a clone of Digital's 8086/8099 version of CPM called CP/M-86. In fact, the command structure as well as enough function calls and other internal features were similar enough to raise serious questions about the origins of the code—more than enough to make a lot of lawyers very wealthy, were it to happen today. A lot of things were different then, however.

Anyway, to make a long story short, Gates bought the rights to QDOS from Seattle Computer Products, and Microsoft was in the operating system business.

As you should have guessed—if you didn't already know—Microsoft's newly acquired DOS was not the only contender for the PC market. Digital's CP/M-86, an offshoot of their original CPM, was used by several other crude computers of the day. With its track record, it should have been the more logical choice.

For a while, IBM—still looking down its corporate nose at the exploding PC market—sold both the Microsoft DOS and CP/M-86. CPM was significantly more expensive, however, and DOS, as it was finally marketed, was actually somewhat better despite its questionable origins. Ultimately, the combination of these factors soon pushed Digital aside. (Digital Research never really went away, but ultimately carved out a niche for itself, not only for CP/M-86, but also for a proprietary line of business-oriented software. It wasn't to be seen again in the DOS arena, however, until the introduction of its own DOS—DR DOS. In its first release, DR DOS 5.0 arrived on the scene, with Microsoft and IBM still in version 4.x.

Fortuitous shortsightednes

As chaotic as these humble beginnings appear—and as shortsighted in forever cutting us off from what otherwise might well be usable address space—the very act of limiting conventional memory to only 640K was surely the salvation of DOS in the long haul.

Think about it: if, a year or so into the PC, programmers had known there was going to be something like 896K rather than 640K to work with, they would have used it. And once used it would have been pretty much gone. As it was, they confined themselves to just 640K as long as they could, but when they outgrew that the wasted address space above 640K allowed them room to hold data for code running below 640K—and a scheme, in fact, where they could swap a lot of data in and out.

Without being sure that there would be a 64K block of address space available above 640K as an access point—it doesn't matter exactly where as long as it's there—there would be no such thing as the expanded memory. Expanded memory was the first glimpse beyond 640K, ultimately allowing as much as an additional 32 megabytes. As this technology evolved, ways were found to make 640K or more of it available at any given time, and we had multitasking.

Most of the rest of that fragmented space above 640K had to await the power of the 80386 computer chip. The ALL Computer Company (Toronto, Canada) ultimately developed an adapter called the ALL ChargeCard that provided the necessary additional hardware support to 80286 machines to allow mapping RAM to unused address space above 640K as effectively as with 386 machines. The 386 was already successful by that time, however, making this more a "catch up" than ground-breaking technology. And by that time extended memory had come of age, as well. But DOS still ruled the world, and everything beyond one megabyte—anything that couldn't be made to at least *appear* at addresses below one megabyte—did not exist. At least in DOS.

The evolution of the so-called "DOS extender" muddied the waters by making it possible to run DOS-based applications well beyond the megabyte that DOS rules, and in the process blurred the distinction between what is and isn't DOS—at least in the minds of many DOS users.

There are some things in DOS that cannot—repeat *cannot*—change to keep pace with technology. And that old one-megabyte bugaboo is one of them. Therefore, as long you use DOS, in order to have anything more than just one megabyte, you've got to somehow:

❏ Fool DOS (and whatever software running under DOS) into thinking you're still working within that one megabyte (which is what expanded memory manages to do).
❏ While balancing with one foot still rooted down in DOS (below one megabyte), launch yourself off into a world completely outside of DOS, a world that's governed by a set of rules completely alien to DOS. This is a DOS extender, which is what extended memory is all about.

Is it time to move on to another operating system then? For many users—even of the die-hard DOS school—the answer is yes, given the powerful multitasking support OS/2 2x has for DOS and Windows applications plus its own. However, just plain DOS, for all its shortcomings, still outsells everything else out there—all the others put together, and you'd be surprised how many would rather fight than switch.

Still the standard   Regardless of your position, one of the most important facts of life today is that, despite the many shortcomings of DOS, given more than a decade of absolute, unquestioned domination of the PC world, it has become such a force—by sheer weight of the size of the installed user base and the billions of dollars invested in DOS software—that much of the measure of success for any operating system offered as a DOS replacement will be in terms of DOS compatibility.

You have only to look at OS/2, whose beginnings are matched only by Windows in terms of the fumbling and stumbling on the way to market. From the first, OS/2 was, unquestionably, a far better operating system than DOS. Programmers loved it—as did a number of corporate users, particularly those who did most of their own programming in-house. Unfortunately, support for DOS applications software was poor, limited to one DOS session running in a compatibility window that soon earned the nickname "penalty box," and a lot of good DOS software wouldn't even run there. So OS/2 1x just never made it.

Certainly much of the sudden popularity of OS/2 2x—popularity that caught even IBM off-guard and, for a time, left them scrambling to try to meet demand—is attributable to the seamless preemptive multitasking support that OS/2 now has for both DOS and Windows applications. And, oh yes, for a whole new generation of emerging OS/2-specific applications as well. But at least initially its real appeal has been and continues to be the relatively painless, cost-effective upgrade path it offers and the ability to take DOS and Windows applications software with you.

This doesn't mean that OS/2 or any DOS-supporting operating system such as Microsoft's NT will necessarily—or even has to—automatically embrace the old DOS software—particularly as the DOS environment so many of us work in has become so complicated with expanded and extended memory, the HMA, and upper memory. But the capability to recreate the DOS environment needed to not only run applications but run them in the way we're used to running them must be there.

I cannot stress the compatibility factor too strongly. And because of that, OS/2 2x offers two levels of DOS support, both of which, using slightly different mechanisms, provide not only extended and expanded memory as required, but upper memory and high memory areas as well. But just as it's generally necessary to configure and reconfigure when you install a different memory manager for DOS, a little fine-tuning can make a world of difference in OS/2-DOS.

As far as DOS support in Windows NT is concerned, at this writing it's still a little early in the game to judge. The indications are, however, that as in DOS Windows, providing support for nonWindows applications isn't that high on Microsoft's list of priorities. I'll examine NT's DOS support in greater detail in the Windows section later in this book.

In any event, for all the wondrous things new 32-bit operating systems offer, DOS—just plain vanilla DOS—is still *the* standard. If not by acclamation, then by sheer weight of the size of the installed user base. And it will most probably be the standard for a long time yet to come.

As if any further proof were needed, even UNIX now increasingly boasts DOS compatibility, allowing DOS and UNIX sessions to be run concurrently on 80386 and higher systems using a merge add-on feature. X Windows offers yet another way to bring the two together. Due to slight differences in file formats between these two operating systems, they cannot share files directly (although they can easily be converted back and forth if need be). Another limitation lies in the fact that Unix cannot (through SVR4) share system resources such as floppy drives with DOS when running concurrent sessions. Still, though strange bedfellows they might be, DOS and UNIX are an item these days.

The pundits have been writing epitaphs for DOS for years. Yet as new DOSs come along—with interesting and surprisingly different offerings from Microsoft and IBM—and new tricks and techniques keep being added to make things possible it wasn't supposed to do, you can be sure DOS is going to be around long after something else grabs center stage. Like it or not, that really is a fact of life.

3 The Zen of DOS

Let us meditate. Let us contemplate the true meaning of DOS in this earthly plane.

True, it isn't common to wax philosophic about operating systems. But until now it has never really been a philosophic issue. DOS has always been DOS. You could complain about it—as many have—but, like the weather, it was just something that was there, and, from a practical point of view, there was really nothing anyone could do about it. Now all that has changed. This time around, it's a philosophical issue. Microsoft made it so the day they threw the gauntlet down and IBM accepted the challenge.

It's more than that, though, for unlike times past there are real choices—exciting choices from which to pick. This time around there are real performance issues. And this time the real war is between the DOSs and the DOS pretenders rather than being a question of what third-party fix makes life with DOS most bearable.

This time around, at least from the point of view of memory use and management, the changes are dramatic, with the role of third-party developers significantly—and probably forever—altered. This time, in fact, most of the DOS choices bring with them better memory management than all but the very best third-party add-ons—and, in at least two cases now, third-party add-ons aren't even options!

However, better does not automatically mean "best" by any means. Not on an individual basis—and particularly not in view of the different memory-management philosophies.

The true meaning of DOS

Before tackling the philosophical, however, you need to really understand just what DOS is.

In the last chapter, you saw how DOS came to be. It was a fix, a work-around, allowing the use of (originally) just floppy drives with IBM's diskless toy. It was never intended as a serious operating system, rather more an I/O patch that included a few basic utilities—and most of them used only in the context of the new I/O functions it performed. Just look at the list:

CHKDSK.COM	DISKCOPY.COM
COMMAND.COM *	EDLIN.COM
COPY	FORMAT.COM
DIR	REM
ERASE	RENAME
COMP.COM	MODE.COM
DATE.COM	SYS.COM
DEBUG.COM	TIME.COM
DISKCOMP.COM	TYPE

That's eighteen out of the total of 21 commands DOS 1.0 included (COMMAND.COM really isn't a command per se) that were for use, if not strictly with disks, primarily for that purpose. Of the remaining three, two—BASIC.COM and BASICA.COM—were extensions of the built-in ROM BASIC. That left only LINK.EXE (an Assembly-language programming tool, really of little use without disk storage for programs when you stop to think about it). I repeat: DOS was originally intended only as a fix, a work-around.

DOS 1.1 added one more Assembly-language programming utility, but otherwise made just three of the original external commands (DATE, REN, and TIME) internal to COMMAND.COM and added DEL as an alternative to ERASE. In DOS 2x there was another 17 disk-oriented commands, which constituted nearly half of the new functions—with seven of the other half being batch file commands and, without disk storage, of little use.

As PC programming became more sophisticated and demanding, DOS's role expanded to provide new or better I/O services for software, while basic disk and other hardware services—services not envisioned in the original PC design—were added to the system ROM of new machines.

Here too, I must quickly point out that DOS cannot provide any services not inherent by virtue of the way the CPU chip itself is designed—nor any other operating system for that matter. An operating system can provide only the key to features that are already there.

In some cases, an operating system (or other software) can exploit certain existing features in ways that weren't envisioned by the chip's designers. The ability of some memory managers to map at least some RAM to addresses above 640K on 80286 and 8088 chips is a classic example of that—but, by the same token, the differences between the extent that this can be applied to 8088, 80286, 386, and higher chips clearly demonstrates that software alone can't add power to the CPU. It can only, at best, make do with what's already there. (This is not entirely a function of DOS—the memory used is generally drawn from whatever pool of nonDOS memory the memory manager commands, and ultimately provides as if it was actually located under one megabyte.)

What an operating system does—or can do—is provide a uniform and readily accessible interface to existing CPU chip features for programmers. It can't do anything those individual programmers themselves couldn't achieve on their own and in their own (possibly better) ways.

Once codified in this manner, it makes the use of these features not only easier but safer than having a bunch of loose canons taking potshots at the CPU—as was the case with early DOS extenders and part of the reason the implementation of extended memory was slow even after the introduction of the 80386.

However, the nature of DOS being what it is, it's severely limited in just what services it can provide. Multitasking, for instance, is a prime example of a service ordinary DOS itself could never provide effectively, while more sophisticated operating systems like OS/2 and Windows NT take it right in stride—that and many things that DOS can never do. Yes, Novell's DOS 7 does multitasking, but only on an 80386 or higher system, and then by playing protected-mode games on virtual machines—all outside the realm of ordinary DOS.

What recent DOS releases do provide in lieu of true multitasking is task switching via the DOSSHELL. *Task switching*, however, only swaps to disk, putting operations for all but the foreground operation on hold, while true *multitasking* allows continued concurrent processing of any or all background operations. DOS doesn't inhibit multitasking in any way, but its ability use only 640K in which to run two or more programs concurrently, including itself, severely limits the possibility.

Traditionally, then, a lot of what's in DOS—DOS as you've always known it—has been essentially a carryover of largely supplanted hardware services to maintain backward compatibility with older machines. And another major part has been—and is—devoted to providing interfacing for a bunch of new devices, such as 3½-inch floppy drivers when they first came along, then higher densities (most recently the 2.88Mb floppies) until everybody's ROM provides for them.

Beyond just I/O
There are really two sides to DOS. The one side, the side that's always been there going back to DOS 1.0, is the working side. This side is invisible not only by virtue of the fact that the files are hidden, but even more because you can't work with it directly. You can deal with it only through:

❑ A command interpreter such as COMMAND.COM.
❑ Applications or utility software that typically bypasses the user interface— the command interpreter—to deal directly with the underlying DOS.

The other side of DOS is the utilities that come with it. Along the line, DOS has added an arsenal of utilities to make life easier—though many of them are disk-related. These are what give DOS its personality, or, historically, lack thereof. Because they're utilities, however, there isn't anything sacred about this side of DOS—in fact, a number of third-party developers have made a comfortable living writing friendlier and more powerful replacements for almost all the bundled DOS utilities, ranging in complexity from little one-shot add-ons to such power packages as XTREE for file management and 4DOS (an alternated command interpreter).

What muddies the water here is the fact that for some strange reason Microsoft has always chosen to make its DOS utilities not only proprietary but version-specific. It's rare, for instance, that you can run a DOS utility from one version with any other version, the most notable exception being SETVER, which allows you to use MIRROR.COM from DOS 5 under DOS 6 by fooling it into thinking it's still in DOS 5.

Try to run an MS-DOS utility with DR DOS, for instance, and you're out of luck. On the other hand I've had no trouble running any of several DR DOS utilities, such as XDEL.EXE, under Microsoft or IBM releases. (DR DOS's XDEL.EXE allows the total, nonreversible elimination of file data rather than just an alteration of the FAT entry, which still allows sensitive data to be recovered. There are also several third-party utilities available that accomplish the same thing when security is a concern.)

But there's really nothing all that unique about most of the utilities that come with DOS—anybody's DOS. Unfortunately, this fact is not well understood, with too many users—intimidated by the fact that most Microsoft or Microsoft-based utilities will run only in conjunction with their specific DOS version—blindly assuming that anything that looks and walks like a duck must be. Which is bunk.

The fact is that any command utility in your DOS directory, be it proprietary, version-specific, or whatever—anything that looks like a DOS command but has a .COM or .EXE file extension attached—is really nothing but a utility. In a default MS-DOS 6 installation (assuming the SETUP program finds Windows installed on your hard disk), this amounts to something over 8 megabytes: 8 megabytes of just utilities, most of which have little or nothing to do specifically with MS-DOS 6, or even DOS in general. But then IBM's new DOS 6 is hardly a lightweight either, with the total package weighing in at about the same size in total.

The actual DOS has become such a small part of the package that it's lost on many users. And to make it even less apparent, it's *hidden*. The real DOS is in just two files that don't even show up in ordinary directory listings. You have to look for them specifically, by issuing the command DIR /ah at the prompt. You'll see something like the following:

```
Volume in drive C is AST MS-DOS
Volume Serial Number is 1A56-646A
Directory of C:\

IO       SYS     40038 12-06-92    6:00a
MSDOS    SYS     37480 12-06-92    6:00a
         2 file(s)      75518 bytes
```

With DOS 6, you'll also have some other hidden files if you installed the new DoubleSpace data compression utility (or the alternate disk compressor in PC DOS 6.1). And with IBM's PC DOS, the names are different: IBMIO.COM and IBMDOS.COM. But these two files are the very heart and soul of DOS: the true DOS, at least as we've always known it. If the basic mechanisms aren't provided for in these two files (often called the kernel), then DOS—at least the version we're looking at—can't do it. To be totally correct, only MSDOS.SY or IBM DOS's equivalent IBMDIS.COM constitute the kernel, but IO.SYS (IBMIO.COM) is often linked with it for purposes of discussion.

This still leaves the door wide open for third-party programmers if they can find some chip design (hardware) features overlooked by DOS—which happens a whole lot more than you might suspect. This, in fact, is one of the reasons that new DOS versions often conflict with older application software. These conflicts often (although not always) arise when DOS adds new functions that overlap third-party developments but go about things in a different way.

So what about it? COMMAND.COM isn't really down-and-dirty DOS, not the real DOS. It, too, is a utility and nothing more. It's in a special class, functioning as something called a *command interpreter*, and DOS can't function without a command interpreter. It really isn't all that fussy, though.

Commands need to be interpreted for DOS. DOS doesn't understand such things as COPY or DELETE; it understands only function calls—and those are in hexadecimal form. The command interpreter's first job is to try to translate English (or whatever language) commands into function calls. If it doesn't understand (if the command doesn't match something in its internal command repertoire), then it must go out and search the path for a .COM, .EXE, or .BAT file with the name it's looking for.

Will the real DOS please stand up?

So what about COMMAND.COM?

The role of the command interpreter, then, is crucial. But there's nothing sacred about COMMAND.COM. In fact, if you delete it DOS will hang and tell you "Bad or missing command interpreter"—no name mentioned. (Unlike earlier releases, in IBM or MS-DOS 6 you're given an opportunity to tell DOS where it, hopefully, can find a valid command interpreter rather than just leaving you hanging.)

DOS, in fact, could care less what you use for an interface, as long as you have *something* it can live with. And, as anyone who has ever used 4DOS will probably tell you, COMMAND.COM isn't even a good choice, given the many additional commands as well as powerful enhancements for mundane commands 4DOS offers. (4DOS—and now a companion product, 4OS2—are shareware from J. P. Software. They're available on CompuServe as well as various bulletin boards.) COMMAND.COM just happens to be the one that comes with DOS and is, therefore, the default. And this isn't throwing rocks at DOS either. OS/2 2x's default command interpreter (CMD.EXE) is just as bad.

So when we talk about DOS—the real DOS—what we're really talking about is something on the order of 100K (even including a command interpreter), with a good part of the just under 75K that constitutes the kernel largely devoted to I/O rather than being a true operating system. By way of comparison, the bare OS/2 2.0 system kernel is nearly 10 times the size of the DOS kernel (715,744 bytes) with the minimum code required to boot up under OS/2 well over 1 megabyte—and that *not* including either multitasking or DOS/Windows support, which, by themselves, account for an additional 5+ megabytes.

Viewed in that light, then, Windows is far more of an operating system than DOS—as it now claims to be—although as long as Windows is a child process of DOS (until NT) it seems to be stretching a point. If, on the other hand, you consider Windows to be an operating system, then possibly DOS really isn't.

Given all of this, perhaps it's time to redefine what does or does not constitute an operating system. Certainly, within the context of this book, we need to reevaluate and redefine just what DOS is and what it isn't. In other words, the true meaning of DOS.

Down to the nitty gritty   Stripped of all those megabytes of utilities that take up hard-disk space, stripped down to just the portion that creates the "DOS environment," the basic frame on which software developers must hang their hats when writing DOS applications, we're talking something pretty small indeed.

Given that, it's not hard to see how other operating systems can devote at least a portion of their vast resources to the creation, re-creation, or, at very least, emulation of an environment that's friendly to DOS applications—an environment that (hopefully) DOS programs won't see as being anything different from the plain vanilla DOS environment they were written for.

In practice, this isn't as easily done as said, but, as both OS/2 and Windows NT demonstrate, it can be done. It can even be done complete with emulations of all the beyond 640K embellishments we're used to like extended and expanded memory and, at least in OS/2, UMBs and an HMA as well.

The bottom line, then, is that the DOS environment is no longer exclusive to conventional, real-mode DOS—Microsoft or any other. It's almost as generic as the gasoline we run our cars on: you might have preferences—by force of habit mostly—but any gas you find will get you home.

Unlike gas, however, the concept of a truly generic DOS environment is actually quite new—too new for many users to grasp the significance. Originally, the DOS you bought for IBM machines was somewhat different from the DOS made for clones, and the less said about the DOS box that the first OS/2 (1x) provided, the better.

Today, there are some major philosophical differences behind the different DOSs and DOS pretenders out there. DOS has now, in fact, reached a point beyond which it seems unlikely that the underlying kernel—that well-under 100K of code that's the real DOS—will undergo much further real, significant development. DOS 5, in fact, might mark the high-water point for all practical purposes.

It behooves us, then, to look not so much for a "better" DOS today, but for a DOS that—based on the philosophy of the developer—best suits our own individual preferences, work habits, anticipated future needs, and hardware platform.

You need only look to Microsoft's new MS-DOS 6 to see a DOS that's more a marketing tool than a leap in DOS technology beyond what MS-DOS 5 offered. True, there are a number of new utilities with this release, including for the first time an optimizer that facilitates the use of upper memory (and as such of particular interest within the context of this book). But we're talking utilities, not DOS down where the sun don't shine.

The catch in Windows

Before you even get MS-DOS 6 installed, the SETUP program is busily determining if you have Windows on your system—any Windows, including OS/2's WIN-OS2. If so, SETUP by default installs three of the more significant new utilities (there's that word again) in such a way that they're accessible only—repeat *only*—from Windows!

And I'm not talking a small change here, either; this is two or three megabytes of new DOS utilities that, in a default installation, cannot even be accessed from the DOS prompt.

If you don't go the default route, you *do* have other options. But even doing a custom installation—as opposed to the express installation SETUP recommends—you don't even see these options displayed unless you specifically reject the default.

The problem is that, based on past experience, the majority of users who upgrade to 6 will accept the defaults rather than somehow screwing up their new DOS installation and possibly their entire hard disk in the bargain. Users—even those of us used to dealing with the consequences—do tend to be a lot more cautious when fooling around with the operating system than with application software, so this one is a "gotcha."

And it goes without saying that Microsoft doesn't want anybody using OS/2: not OS/2 as OS/2, certainly not OS/2 as DOS or, God forbid, OS/2 instead of Windows. Consider the following warnings, captured from a prerelease version of MS-DOS 6:

```
OS/2 Files Detected

Drive C contains both DOS and OS/2 files

Although you can install MS-DOS, these OS/2 files use
considerable disk space. For more information, see
'Getting Started.'

If you continue Setup without removing your OS/2 files,
OS/2 might be disabled.

Continue Setup after reading 'Getting Started.'
```

Whether as a means of discouraging DOS users from moving to OS/2 or simply a fortuitous coincidence, Microsoft began development of a new, proprietary disk compressor called DoubleSpace. DoubleSpace is not OS/2 compatible and, once installed on a hard disk, cannot easily be uninstalled (which programs such as Stacker can) short of reformatting. More about this issue in a later chapter.

Stacker, on the other hand, has developed a fully-compatible OS/2 version of their DOS disk-compression package. Assuming a disk is formatted for the FAT file system, you can use it with either operating system by simply loading the appropriate device driver when the system boots.

The PC DOS 6.1 alternative

IBM needs DOS—IBM perhaps more than almost anyone else. And, as an integral part of their marketing strategy, they need a DOS that offers the best possible performance, whether on an 8088 or on any higher platform in the 8086 family. And not just for IBM machines.

Hardware-dependent differences that once distinguished DOS for IBM machines and MS-DOS—which were mostly as a result of IBM DOS's reliance on the ROM BASIC kernel as opposed to the freestanding GWBASIC that Microsoft supplied with MS-DOS—are long gone, making IBM's new

DOS as much at home on any decent clone as any IBM machine. In fact, BASIC, which was at one time so important, is completely gone from IBM's new DOS release, with QBASIC-dependent MS-DOS utilities such as EDIT.COM replaced by new, freestanding IBM equivalents. And this is only the beginning of what's different. (A freestanding BASIC (essentially the BASIC that IBM included with their DOS 5*x*) is available on request for IBM DOS 6 purchasers.)

Outwardly, it's really surprising just how different the IBM and Microsoft DOS 6s are, considering both started building from the same foundation code (kernel)—which is still available to IBM as a result of licensing agreements that predate the split between them. Here again, the differences you see aren't down in the hidden layer that's the heart and soul of DOS, but rather in the utilities.

In terms of DOS utilities, IBM's PC DOS 6.1 contains a mix that, while including some from Microsoft, also features:

❏ Utilities developed internally by IBM (including several in the area of memory management that are unique).
❏ Utilities based on technology licensed from third-party sources (including one of special interest in the area of memory management as well as disk compression, where maintaining compatibility with the disk compression available for OS/2 2*x* is of vital importance).

Unlike Microsoft, IBM *must* have a DOS that offers all the features found in MS-DOS—including file compression—but always with an eye to maintaining compatibility with OS/2 2*x*. (The initial PC DOS 6.1 release in June of 1993 did not include the disk-compression feature. It was planned for release in the fall of 1993, at which time it was to be made available at no charge to those who had purchased PC DOS 6.1.)

Novell DOS 7.0

A DOS unlike any other major DOS to date, this is a DOS that, by preference, runs on machines that support the protected mode—which means 80286 and higher systems—although, being a 16-bit system, it will still run on 8088s as well. It's a DOS that reflects Novell's networking superiority by offering true peer-to-peer networking support similar to their NetWare Lite as part of the package. It also incorporates true multitasking (32-bit systems only) reminiscent of the single-user multitasking capabilities of Digital Research's DR Multiuser DOS 5.0 (which was a strictly protected-mode DOS environment).

The Digital Research DOS (DR DOS) that preceded it was interesting because of a number of features that were unique at the time it was introduced (opposite MS-DOS 5), including multiple and on-the-fly startup configurations and superior memory management (as discussed in the second edition of this book). It also demonstrated how perfectly—and seemingly easily—the DOS environment could be cloned.

This old DR DOS, which came as part of the package when Novell bought Digital Research, was actually a far better DOS than many users realized. However, it had far less impact on the market than it seemingly had on both Microsoft and IBM, with MS-DOS 5 adding features seen first in DR DOS 5, and variants of other features that were added by DR DOS 6 showing up in IBM's DOS 6.1 and MS-DOS 6.0.

DOS, of course, had been cloned in varying degrees—and with varying degrees of success—before Digital Research, but mostly by special multiuser systems such as PC MOS.

In the aftermath of Novell's acquisition, DR DOS just faded quietly away. But now Novell is striking back. In fact, Novell just made the game more interesting with their new DOS 7.

DOS in OS/2 2x   Even a greater surprise than the marked differences between IBM and MS-DOS in version 6 is the really remarkable DOS support in OS/2 2x— remarkable both looking back to really poor support in 1x and compared to what we've seen so far in Microsoft's new NT system.

Both the DOS and Windows support in OS/2 2x—the only aspects relevant to this book—are noteworthy. Not only is the multitasking seamless, but because it's an integral part of the OS/2 operating system itself rather than a DOS add-on, it adds no overhead to DOS (as compared with DESQview or DOS/Windows, which sometimes requires some fancy juggling to come up with big enough DOS application windows).

In addition to providing what DOS applications see as expanded or extended memory, UMBs, and an HMA, OS/2 adds a few tricks of its own to squeezing out more memory to run DOS applications, including one in particular—one we'll look at later—that ordinary DOS with ordinary multitasking cannot do.

OS/2 2x, in fact, provides two separate DOS-support mechanisms. The first one is an emulation of the DOS environment at the DOS 5 level. Supporting multiple concurrent DOS (and Windows) sessions intermixed with other sessions under OS/2, this is the most important mechanism of the two, and most applications you've been running under DOS can "migrate" to this emulated environment without a hitch and without requiring any special attention.

Applications you run under ordinary DOS can run just as easily under OS/2's DOS emulation—or both, thanks to a dual-boot option that allows you to switch back and forth, making either operating system the default at will.

There are, however, some DOS applications that don't run properly under OS/2 (though in fairness, some of the same ones don't run properly in DESQview either). For these, OS/2 2x allows you to run a single real-DOS session—pick your own DOS version—concurrently with emulated DOS, Windows, and OS/2 sessions.

OS/2's ability to handle even multiple concurrent Windows sessions in a mix of DOS and OS/2 is really something. All in all, OS/2 now enough to make a believer out of all but the most dyed-in-the-wool DOS or Windows users. To do it right you need a bunch of RAM, but then the same is true of any multitasking environment. Including Windows.

DOS sessions running under Windows are a whole lot better under 3.1 than under 3.0—in the enhanced mode anyway. In standard mode, Windows won't multitask DOS applications, no matter how much RAM you've got available.

DOS under Windows & NT

In the enhanced mode, given enough RAM so it isn't swapping off to disk all the time (which is really no more a factor with Windows than with any multitasker) DOS performance is generally pretty good—especially when using one of the latest third-party memory managers that provide up to 736K of "conventional" memory in DOS windows rather than HIMEM.SYS.

Even without a better memory manager, DOS performance in Windows is generally better with the new DOS 6s, thanks to the addition of optimizers for upper memory. Prior to DOS 6—and ignoring DR DOS, which in version 6 didn't offer an optimizer—the only way to get top-drawer DOS performance under Windows was with third-party memory managers because the amount of RAM available to DOS applications under Windows is directly related to the amount of real-mode conventional RAM your system has available before loading Windows (as opposed to OS/2).

Windows NT is another story—one as of this writing I haven't seen enough of to allow for more than superficial observations. Yes, Windows NT has support for DOS—and even limited (character-based only) support for OS/2. (NT was still in beta with a general release not scheduled until several months after this book went to press.)

To date, the NT DOS support I've seen has been quite disappointing, however, with a number of DOS applications that wouldn't run. And even when they did, performance was quite poor, typically taking as much as 10 seconds or more to write or update the screen—a lot of fun when you're trying to work on something and the display is that far behind your keyboard input.

In fairness, it's quite probable that a good part of this sluggish behavior was due to a lack of adequate system RAM—16 megabytes of RAM was all I had available on that machine (it takes 14 megabytes—minimum—just to load the bare NT operating system) and the fact that I was running only on a 33-MHz 386. It seems strange having to apologize for running with *only* 16 megabytes of RAM—almost a thousand times what it used to take to get a PC up and running.

Choices, choices Aside from whether you're ready to even think in terms of such vast amounts of RAM or not, never have there been so many choices. This time around, I think it's imperative that we all take a new a different look at DOS and at what DOS really is (or should be)—especially with this current crop.

Until now it has always been an assumption that each new operating system release was automatically more powerful and therefore better in some way that made it worth the effort to install and, if need be, reconfigure the system for. Until now there's always been a reason for a better DOS, a DOS that could do things the old DOS couldn't—not so much the new utilities and frills but down-and-dirty DOS itself, the part that lives down in those hidden system files.

I think most of you reading this book will agree that DOS—DOS per se—has pretty much run its course. DOS is not on the endangered list by any means; it has too large a following. Microsoft would have us believe otherwise, but there are too many millions of copies being used worldwide for that—by users have no need now or will likely have in the foreseeable future for the likes of Windows, OS/2, UNIX, NT, or whatever.

Still, I think it's equally clear that few—if any—really powerful new 640K DOS-only applications will appear: nothing to compare with Lotus, dBASE, or any of the old standbys so many of us started with. There are a number of good reasons, not the least of which is the fact that so few programmers today write the kind of tight, assembly-language code they had to write when there was no world beyond 640K.

Today the real action is in extended memory, where DOS plays no real role except for providing I/O services—and some of today's more advanced DOS extenders are even taking over some of those duties in order to bypass bottlenecks imposed by DOS's 16-bit (maximum) services. So for the vast hordes, happy and content to stay with what they've got, there's little need for any "better" DOS. And for almost anyone who works beyond 640K today—particularly with 386 and higher systems—the role of DOS itself is actually diminishing.

So it's in light of that diminishing role I think we need to take a critical look at DOS today—what it is and what its legitimate role should be, particularly since Microsoft has seemingly put MS-DOS 6 out on the street more to promote Windows than to serve any real need within the established and still prospering DOS community.

Let us contemplate, then, the true meaning of DOS. And then, enlightened (hopefully), go forth and do that for which it was intended, following whichever path best leads us where we want to go.

4 DOS extenders & the world beyond 1Mb

As we all know too well, DOS is a 1-megabyte system, effectively reduced to 640K of contiguous memory for applications plus some scraps of address space. The nominal upper limit of DOS, however, (ignoring the high-memory area for the moment) is 1024K. Any RAM at any address space beyond 1024K is outside of DOS. Any RAM that, in any context whatsoever, is or even seems to be at addresses outside the 1-megabyte DOS limit is outside of DOS. And once out of DOS, it doesn't matter how far. Out is out. Period.

There is a reason for belaboring this point: in the DOS world, RAM or even just plain address space either falls within the 1024K block that DOS can deal with or it doesn't. And if it doesn't, DOS can't deal with it. At least not directly. Beyond 1024K, DOS can't see a thing. Not on an 8088 machine that's physically limited to dealing with a maximum of 1024K of discrete addresses or on a Pentium-based machine that can physically address gigabytes.

For DOS or DOS-based software to look beyond 1024K requires some sort of add-on mini operating system that, while 100% compatible with DOS (a "perfect superset" of DOS as it's often called) sets down a set of rules applicable to address space outside of DOS. In other words, it becomes a kind of "DOS extender." What few users understand about these DOS extenders, however, is that we've been using them for a long time—since the first time anyone went out of DOS while still in DOS in fact.

Even the relatively simple task of providing an interface between DOS and extended memory—without which there could be no place for DOS extenders to perform—itself requires an extension of the rules of DOS.

Enter the DOS extender The promise of a true 16-bit operating system for the ill-starred 286 remained still unfulfilled when the 80386 burst on the scene with a protected mode that really worked and, even more, with full 32-bit processing power. Much of the incentive, therefore, faded for a 16-bit OS/2. There was a lot of talk of something else: a 32-bit OS/2 perhaps. But operating systems aren't born overnight—and even if they were, a 32-bit operating system would be of no use to the hundreds of thousands of 16-bit 80286s being used.

It was in this vacuum that several software developers began to look at work-arounds, some way to work in extended memory *from* DOS—essentially to use DOS as a launch pad while doing the actual processing out in extended memory. The logic was impeccable because it didn't need a whole new operating system, just a superset for DOS: a 16-bit instruction set that could run on 16- or 32-bit machines and/or a super 32-bit set for 80386 and higher systems. And it was something that could be done within a reasonable time frame and with far less in the way of capital and human resources than a full-blown operating system (see FIG. 4-1).

Other than developers whose interest was limited just to managing memory beyond one megabyte, those active in the development of what came to be known as *DOS extenders* generally fell into one of two categories:

❑ Those who had applications with specific needs that couldn't be adequately met by DOS plus EMS expanded memory.
❑ Those who saw the need for some sort of common modular interface that could be packaged and sold for use in the new or existing applications of other developers.

Oracle, for instance, went its own way, writing its own proprietary DOS extender. The company succeeded in developing a DOS extender that met its need, but its success was really the exception rather than the rule. DOS extenders are a complicated business. There's much that must be done beyond just merely interfacing with a bunch of memory out somewhere in the great beyond.

The greater task at hand A DOS extender is actually a special runtime environment—essentially a mini operating system—that loads on top of DOS, picking up where DOS leaves off. While the way extenders operate is entirely different than memory managers (DOS extenders, for instance, are generally not installable devices, but merely part of a program loadable from the DOS prompt), they're in their own way parallel because each provides important services lacking in the underlying operating system.

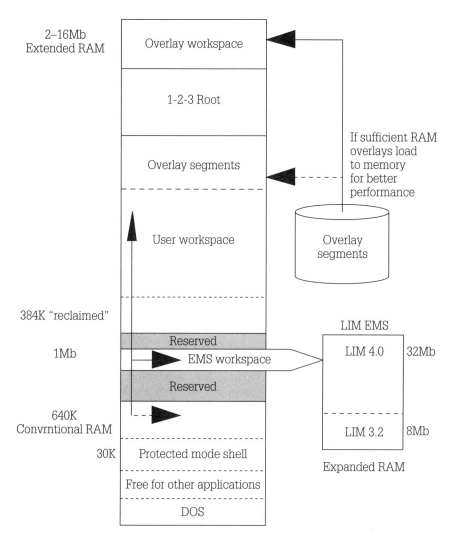

4-1
In one of earliest uses of DOS extender technology, Lotus used a mix of expanded and extended memory—even just the 384K that was often wasted on machines that came with 1 Mb installed. Modern DOS extenders rarely use expanded memory at all, but such kluges helped to bridge the gap at a time when extended memory was fairly rare and precious.

In addition, a DOS extender must provide a way to interface with DOS. This, in fact, is one of the most crucial functions of a DOS extender—even more so with extenders written for the 80286 and having to cope with the difficulties of getting that chip back into real mode. This, and when multitasking is involved, provide a common interface. There's a lot that must be done.

When DOS services are needed, in some cases the DOS extender will handle DOS calls itself. For others—file I/O for instance—it will switch the processor back to 8086 real mode and let DOS do the work. Mechanisms vary according to the task at hand, but a look at at least one DOS call might give some insight into what goes on behind the scenes (because a protected-mode program can't access DOS directly). An INT 21h call made from protected mode is handled something like this:

1. The INT 21h software interrupt call is intercepted.
2. Any extended-memory data buffers are moved into conventional memory.
3. The processor is switched to real mode.
4. The interrupt call to DOS is reissued.
5. The processor is switched back into protected mode.
6. Any returned data buffers are moved to extended memory if necessary.

While specific features vary between the various extenders on the market, most can call real-mode routines up from protected mode and vice versa. And some can write directly to the screen to save the time that would be wasted going through the BIOS. Support for virtual-memory demand-paging varies from good to nonexistent.

A modular solution

The most significant work in this area was done by a small handful of independent developers such as Phar Lap, Rational Systems, and AI Architects (later known as Ergo Computers), each of which developed off-the-shelf 32-bit runtime environments that, for the most part, supported standard DOS calls.

Several 16-bit DOS extenders were developed as well, with some developers—among them Lotus—opting to hedge their bets and go the 16-bit route, trading off the greater processing power of the 386 to (hopefully) appeal to the larger market of 16-bit machines. Much of this, I should point out, was at a time when the 80386 and 32-bit processing were relatively new and represented only a small part of the installed user base.

Even then, the clear superiority of 32-bit processing made it the platform of choice for most developers. And although 16-bit DOS extenders are still being sold (at this writing, Borland was bundling Phar Lap's 16-bit extender with their C++ compiler), it was the 80386 with its far superior protected and virtual 8086 modes that was the real key to the success of DOS extenders as we know them today.

Today developers can buy DOS extenders basically "off the shelf." They contain libraries of custom modules along with special linkers and debuggers that make the venture to the outer limits relatively painless, whether developing new software or enhancing an existing product. And they support most of the most commonly used higher-level languages: C and C++ of course, but also Visual C, Fortran, etc.

DOS extenders are sophisticated to a point of supporting virtual memory as well as the real thing. This typically requires an add-on to the basic extender module, but it means that—within limits—developers need not even concern themselves with how few users really have sufficient RAM to run their applications in real memory. Obviously, an application that requires a minimum of, say, 4 megabytes of code in RAM at any given time could never run in 2, no matter how clever the virtualization. It's surprising, though, how readily most applications can be broken into smaller pieces to run, albeit at far less than peak efficiency, on RAM-starved systems.

This ready availability of generic DOS-extender modules, more than any other single fact, is probably the main reason for the rapid emergence of DOS-extended software—this combined with the fact that so much of the software existing at the time was unable to run at peak efficiency due to the constraints of EMS expanded memory.

DOS extenders took care of this problem, in ways that would allow existing applications to be ported to a modified environment faster and more economically than might be possible with some all-new operating system. Many programmers claimed, in fact, that it was much simpler and faster than trying to get a product up and running under OS/2 (1x). Eliminating EMS management code and recompiling was often all that was required to gain the added speed and performance of running in extended memory using the full 16- or 32-bit processing capabilities of the system—typically two to three times faster on a 32-bit system than an 80286, and much faster there than on an 8086/8088.

Even more important, a lot of application software—including programing languages—that had never migrated to DOS because of segment and size limitations could suddenly be ported to DOS to run in this new DOS-extended environment. It was an idea whose time had come. (DOS, catering to the architecture of the 8088 and 80286, which harks back to the 8080 and an age when 64K was the maximum total memory that a chip could address, assumes a memory broken into 64K segments, no matter how large that memory is.)

But just as there had been hardware problems that held back common usage with the 80286, there were a number of problems to be overcome before the DOS extender truly came of age. Not the least of these sprung from the fact that so many different independent developers were mixing in this new arena, usually in secret. Secrecy is, of course, important in the creation of any new product, but with developers pretty much going off in their own direction and doing their own thing, there was often chaos when DOS-extended software based on different DOS-extender philosophies came head to head.

One of the most common of these was that that no matter how much extended memory you had, you couldn't run more than one application at a time there because the second would most likely overwrite the first, corrupting its data. You couldn't, for instance, use extended memory both for a RAM disk—like VDISK—and disk caching or print spooling simultaneously.

"But wait," you say, "isn't that what the protected mode was designed to prevent?" Exactly. But without some help from the operating system—or, lacking that, from some sort of supplemental software that picks up where the operating system leaves off—you really don't have protected mode, only the capability. And you don't even have a truly protected mode unless everyone trying to run up there in extended memory at least follows the same set of rules about what constitutes protection and to what degree. Everybody need not use the same exact extender, but whichever ones are used must all comply, at some point, with some "standard."

And indeed there are now standards, but they didn't come easily and not without generating more than the usual amount of ill will.

VCPI: a little order out of chaos
The problem ultimately wasn't even so much between the various DOS extenders that emerged so much as between applications using DOS extenders to run in protected mode and control programs such as DESQview—problems that included microprocessor switching, hardware interrupt processing, and sharing of extended memory.

The abbreviation VCPI comes from *virtual control program interface*, the *virtual* referring not to the kind of program—let's face it, you can have virtual memory, but a virtual program?—but rather to a control program for virtual machines, that intriguing third mode of operation. The conflict specifically is/was between programs running in protected mode alongside programs using the virtual 8086 mode of the 386—such as DESQview 386, which creates a separate virtual 8086 machine with its own megabyte (plus expanded memory) for every application loaded into it—or at least for every window.

Without some sort of interface that resolves these issues satisfactorily, a control program (such as DESQview) must be turned off in order for the user to run a protected-mode application. It's that simple—or complicated, depending on your point of view.

Borland's Paradox 386, wrapped around Phar Lap's 386 DOS extender, for instance, originally could not run under DESQview. Quarterdeck (DESQview), however, was one of the prime movers in an effort to bring the two conflicting environments under some mutually acceptable set of rules. Aside from Quarterdeck, other initial sponsors of what came to be known as VCPI were Phar Lap Software Inc., A.I Architects Inc., Quadram, Inc., Qualitas Inc., and Rational Systems Inc. (and aren't we glad they didn't try to make an acronym, like LIM, from that one: QOSPLASIAIQIAIQIRSI).

The VCPI developed a set of guidelines that, when followed by control programs, allowed them to coexist without conflict in extended memory—"control program" referring particularly to programs such as DESQview. (Quarterdeck Office Systems, developer of DESQview, played a major role in the development of the VCPI. They are, however, now involved in the development of the DPMI.) This, while of crucial importance, addressed only the 386 (and higher) platform level, which is where most of the interest—and activity—continues to be.

Although the VCPI primarily addressed conflicts between memory managers and programs running in extended memory, it was a major step. For the first time there was at least a set of reasoned guidelines founded on the combined experience of the companies that had a hand in drafting it. And what it said was that any program adhering to the VCPI standards could coexist with any other running program, which meant multitasking on the same (physical) machine but in virtual 8086 mode. And in the "happy endings" department, with a standard and a few adjustments here and there to make accommodation for each other's needs, with the VCPI Paradox 386 ran nicely under DESQview.

Still, having a standard and having everybody accept it as a standard are two different things. For reasons that aren't entirely clear, Microsoft chose not to. And having chosen not even to be party to the drafting of the VCPI specification, it found Windows left out in the cold and incompatible with any software that supported the VCPI specification. The problems weren't unforeseen, but extended memory is serious business.

A window has two sides, however, and which side is in and which is out depends on where you're standing. Whichever side is which, Microsoft clearly did have a problem with VCPI—several problems, in fact, because there was more at stake than Windows. There were other issues raised by the VCPI of concern to others as well.

DPMI: a light in the window

With prerelease work on its (then) all-new Windows 3.0 already at a very advanced state, Microsoft summoned other industry leaders and persuaded them to join in a Microsoft-sponsored interface specification, the DPMI (DOS protected-mode interface).

Obviously, Windows compatibility was of paramount importance to Microsoft. High on the agenda, however, was yet another important feature of the 80386 architecture that was overlooked by the VCPI: the 80386 provides for multiple levels or rings of protection that can be managed on a need-to-know basis, analogous to the war room at the Pentagon. (The protection scheme incorporated into the 80286 was predicated on the same four levels of privilege, so this feature wasn't unique to 386 and higher chips.) Only those with specific clearance could get past the first level of security, with increasingly higher security clearances required as you get closer to the center, and only a privileged few having full access.

In the 80386, this inner sanctum is called Ring 0. If you can get to Ring 0, you have full access to everything the chip possesses. This is the operating-system level; obviously, the operating system itself, whether DOS or UNIX or whatever, has to have free access to Ring 0 because any less would limit its effectiveness by making certain features off limits.

Under the VCPI, access to this inner circle was not limited exclusively to the operating system, however. To a large degree, the VCPI bypassed the protection levels of the outer rings, allowing any application access—even applications written by developers who weren't properly qualified. A poorly written program—or just one that encounters a problem—with access to Ring 0 can bring down the whole house of cards—a polite way of saying "crash the system."

Now consider all the virtual machines you can create using the virtual 8086 mode of the chip—multiple machines for multitasking and increasingly for multiuser systems—where a system crash could be extremely costly, potentially taking down the design department, bookkeeping, and inventory in one fell swoop.

Microsoft and others argued that *only* the operating system—and in multitasking and multitasking environments only the host operating machine—should be allowed Ring 0 access. Virtual machines and applications should have lesser access, no more than absolutely necessary in fact. By properly limiting access, a problem application couldn't crash the entire system. It could, at worst, bring down the virtual machine it was running on. If someone in the warehouse screwed up, then the computer for the inventory might go down, but everybody else could keep right on working as if nothing happened—because, as far as they're concerned, nothing had.

While in practice—and speaking from considerable experience with VCPI (DESQview) multitasking—the number of problems are relatively few, they do occur. And when they do, they sometimes—but not always—bring down the system with the loss of any unsaved data. The issue is of much greater importance as you move beyond simple multitasking to multiuser systems of increasing complexity.

There are other issues as well. The DPMI specification is far-reaching, even including features that can bridge the gap between DOS and UNIX and OS/2 to a point where applications in the future might not be classified on the basis of operating system but simply on the basis of the hardware platform they require. That is for the future, though.

A double standard   At that point—and for some period of time—we had a double standard, with most of those most active in the writing of the VCPI specification still supporting it. One of the major players in the game, for example, continued to field questions about the DPMI as being more a UNIX issue than of DOS importance. Certainly the differences between the two standards are of such a nature that those who had embraced the VCPI scheme couldn't just slip a different module in their code and switch to DPMI support instead.

DOS-extender technology by then, however, was rather quickly able to produce a new generation of extenders that could "read" the system, determine whether VCPI or DPMI support was required, and do it, automatically and invisible to the user. The user didn't even have to know there was a difference, and for a time the world beyond one megabyte marched to the beat of different drummers.

Interestingly, while these two schools of thought weren't compatible, they also weren't mutually exclusive. At least two of the most powerful memory managers, QEMM386 from Quarterdeck and 386max from Qualitas, had eagerly embraced the VCPI specification. Both, however, fully supported Windows 3.0, which supported the DPMI instead—and not only did they support Windows 3.0 but both significantly enhanced its memory utilization.

On closer inspection, this seeming duality wasn't necessarily inconsistent with the fact that the VCPI and DPMI are, themselves, incompatible. Ring 0 protection under DPMI is reserved only for the operating system but is addressable directly by VCPI software, so memory management would certainly seem to be on par with DOS for having a justifiable right to full direct access privileges when dealing with the CPU. Windows 3*x*, however, runs *on top* of the DOS environment, granting only the lesser privileges allowed under the DPMI to Windows and to applications running under it.

Ultimately there were DPMI issues that were best served by DPMI-supporting memory managers. And ultimately both QEMM386 and 386max fell into line. At this point the VCPI has largely been succeeded by the DPMI. The VCPI hasn't gone away, however, and is still supported by the latest DOS-extender versions.

While the DPMI ultimately resolved a number of issues, it also left a number of loopholes—which any good standard should do so as not to stifle further development. And Novell has now gone beyond the basic DPMI specification, writing their own DPMS (DOS protected-mode services) specification. Unlike the VCPI/DPMI controversy, this isn't a third standard, but rather an enhancement of the DPMI scheme geared primarily for smaller programs (TSRs, device drivers, etc.) for which a full implementation of the DPMI would be too cumbersome.

Into these muddy waters

DPMS is a DOS version-independent, Windows-compatible API that provides specific protected-mode support for device drivers and TSRs. Implemented in Novell DOS 7, this API allows DOS device drivers and TSRs to reside in extended memory on 286 and higher systems, substantially reducing the overhead they would otherwise impose on conventional or upper memory. Typical of the kind of high overhead that can benefit from this new specification are several new utilities Novell has included in its DOS 7—applications including disk caching and compression drivers, peer-to-peer networking, and CD-ROM extensions.

Since it isn't version dependent (meaning that compliant applications should run under any DOS) and is Windows compatible, this specification should appeal to a large number of developers, and a DPMS SDK (software developer's kit) is available from Novell (through the Professional Developers Program for $195).

There will no doubt be other standards and extensions of existing standards as our needs become increasingly complex and unforeseen issues emerge. The important thing to keep in mind at this point is where the DOS extender fits into the scheme of things and the role that extenders of some form will continue to play as long as there is DOS.

It's also important to understand that most of what I'm dealing with in this book then is not so much DOS itself—real DOS, emulated DOS, or any other kind of DOS—but rather extensions that go far beyond the basic set of rules DOS goes by, taking us to places DOS was never supposed to go.

In fact, much of what we do within our little 1024K cocoon wouldn't be possible without the use of DOS extenders. We map memory to unused address space between 640K and 1024K—legitimate DOS address space—but where does the memory we draw on come from? Generally, somewhere out beyond 1024K—which means we have to use a DOS extender just to get it.

Once we move on to another operating system, past DOS and into OS/2 or NT or some other operating system, this whole business of protocol on top of protocol goes away. There are no OS/2 extenders or NT extenders because the operating systems themselves are designed to deal with a flat memory model and virtually limitless amounts of RAM or other address space, thereby automatically bringing it all to heel under a single, unified set of rules. But as long as we use DOS, any time we want to poke even a pinky past 1024K we'd better have a DOS extender standing in for us or it just isn't going to happen.

5 Basic hardware considerations

Traditionally, the progress of desktop computer technology has been measured primarily in terms of processing power and clock speed, issues revolving around the computer (CPU) chip and largely divorced from other hardware considerations. Other things—particularly how much memory the motherboard would hold—just sort of fell in behind the CPU.

Early on, most motherboards didn't support much memory—even second-generation IBM PCs supported only 256K on the motherboard. At the time our needs were simple, however, and that was more than enough for most purposes. And by the time it wasn't, there were plenty of expansion cards available to take us to 640K and, when the need arose, beyond. In fact, a whole new industry evolved to fill the need (see FIG. 5-1).

Memory needs kept increasing, but basically no faster than the need for more powerful CPUs. So to a point—until quite recently—when buying a new machine, you could pretty well assume the motherboard would hold all the RAM you'd likely ever need—which then quietly pretty well killed the expansion-card business, to say nothing of most of the little companies that specialized in RAM expansion cards. AST was one of the few exceptions, and that was only because it got completely out of manufacturing expansion cards and into building whole computers.

History has a funny way of repeating itself, however, and suddenly the demand for more RAM—and more and more—has outstripped the rate at which most motherboards have kept pace. And so we've come full circle.

5-1
Early motherboards used individual RAM chips, typically supporting no more than 1 megabyte of memory, often even less. Chips gave way to SIMMs that could pack as much as 16 megabytes of RAM on a single small plug-in module, but already designers are looking for a new module design that will support still larger blocks of memory.

Still, even given the limitations of current machines, few of us to date have fully utilized the hardware we have. So let's look at what we have and how much farther we can go before thinking about a new machine.

It's about memory   For the purposes of this book, a computer can be broken down into just two component groupings:

The microprocessor   The business end of the machine.

Volatile (temporary) memory   The only place code and data can be actively accessed and manipulated, without which there would be nowhere to deal with memory—conventional, extended and expanded.

This, admittedly, is an overly simplistic way of viewing a highly complex subject. But for all that's involved in a computer, these two elements are all you should be concerned with here—and the microprocessor only because it governs which set of rules memory can run under and how you can or must address it. Since the chip you use, then, establishes the rules, let's start with that.

While today there are a number of CPU chips to pick from, there are really only three levels at which the basic technology changes from the point of view of memory—four if you count the new 64-bit Intel Pentium as separate:

❑ The 8088, capable of managing a total of one megabyte of address space.
❑ The 16-bit 80286, which contains more processing power and faster clock speeds, and is capable of managing 16 megabytes of address space and protected-mode operations.

❑ A succession of 32-bit chips with still higher clock speeds and still greater processing power, and (typically) capable of managing as much as 4 gigabytes of memory—*four thousand* times the address space an 8088 is capable of handling. Also the unique property of these chips—and common to all of them—are functions that facilitate memory mapping and allow them to emulate multiple 8086 processors (virtual 8086 mode).

❑ A 64-bit chip, the Intel Pentium, that for now raises more questions than it answers. For the foreseeable future—and within the context of this book—it's really just a faster 32-bit chip, however.

Once the 4-gigabyte level was reached, which was so astronomical at a time when 40 megabytes was still a big hard disk, no one really gave much thought to the steady increase in memory usage and demands. Some vendors started increasing the amount of RAM installed at the factory to two or four megabytes, more the latter because, with the coming of the 1Mb SIMM, the old 256Ks just didn't make much sense and standard SIMMs can be installed only in groups of four. They weren't really giving you anything. In fact, four megabytes of RAM wasn't really even a selling point, particularly with Microsoft claiming two megabytes was enough to run Windows 3*x* in enhanced mode.

The big selling point was always faster clock speeds and more powerful CPUs. You needed more processing power and a faster clock for Windows. And sure enough, Windows performance on an otherwise good 386 with maybe 4 megabytes of RAM was pretty dismal: video performance that was sluggish and performance that was just generally slow. Video accelerator cards helped by freeing the CPU of much of the tremendous overhead imposed by bit-mapped graphics; the video was cleaner and free to devote itself to other things, so Windows wasn't quite so slow. But still slow enough to make the faster, generally hotter 486s look increasingly attractive. And as if to make the point, many of them came with Windows already installed on the hard disk.

The big sell

What few users realized was that for less than the typically $300 (and more often higher) price of a video accelerator card, you could add another set of 1Mb RAM chips (four at roughly $50.00 each) and Windows performance would generally improve at least as much and often more. Or, in a worst-case scenario, you could replace any 1Mb or smaller SIMMS with four new 4Mb SIMMs—typically about $650 for a set of four today, which still isn't out of the ballpark compared to the price of high-end video cards.

Other than for Windows, OS/2, or the (now) seemingly astronomical amount of RAM required by NT (as of this writing, NT required almost 16 megabytes just to load the bare operating-system kernel), the benefits of adding more RAM than whatever you probably have now are oftentimes more subtle. But they're there. It's sort of like quitting smoking: you don't just wake up one morning and say "Wow, do I feel better now." Rather, you're just aware of little things that seem a whole lot easier.

The most important thing at this point is simply to get past the mindset that says CPUs and clocks are all-important in this business. Taken by themselves, they're virtually meaningless. It's memory that matters: how much you have and how you use it.

Give me a 386 with plenty of memory—lots of memory—and most days I'll run rings around the majority of 486s out there, running undernourished on the two or four megs someone stuck in at the factory. It's that important.

Having said that, a good, fast 486 with plenty of memory—16, maybe 32 megabytes of RAM—will obviously blow the socks off any 386. And Intel's latest little darling, given a decent complement of memory, will do the same to a 486. At least according to the benchmarks—and even without the memory if benchmarks are your game.

Performance—real performance—is measured not in benchmarks, however, but in how long it takes to do a real-world job: how many times your system has to do a disk read or write, create the illusion of memory that you don't really have (virtual memory), or effectively cache your hard disk's I/O. There are a lot of little things that, used effectively together, can often make older, "slower" boxes really sizzle.

Let's start at the bottom, the beginning of computer technology today, and build from there.

The ubiquitous 8088   Historically, the roots of the PC and the dynasty it founded can be traced back to 1972 and the 8008, introduced by Intel as the first commercially available 8-bit microprocessor. To understand this "bit" business and what it means, however, you really need to go back one generation further to the earlier Intel 4004, which, as the name implies, was a 4-bit chip.

The significance of four bits is that four in a binary system (meaning counting by twos) is the minimum number capable of representing the numbers 0 through 9. Since one bit can count to two (0 and 1), two bits can then count only to two twice (four), and three bits only to eight. You have to have that fourth bit to make the system capable of counting all the way to 16 (2^4=16) to reach a count of ten.

As long as all you want to do is work with simple numbers, then four bits is fine. The 4004 was therefore used in simple calculating machines. It could add, subtract, multiply, and divide and was a veritable wonder of technology compared to the myriad of springs and gears and cams and cogs of contemporary mechanical office machines.

Until someone got the bright idea of representing letters, too. Not just the six that got dragged into the act to fill out the hexadecimal count to 16 (012345679ABCDEF), but the whole alphabet—and other things too. Hence the quest for an 8-bit chip—it really doesn't make much sense in binary systems to do anything except in multiples of two (and more often in fours).

Eight bits means a possible 256 combinations. That's more than enough for ten numerals, a full alphabet in both upper- and lowercase, plus some of the more common foreign-language variants and punctuation. And a lot of special symbols: things like operands and the Greek letters used in calculus and complex mathematical formulas. (16- and 32-bit machines deal with the same 8-bit characters, but they can do it faster.)

So Intel developed the 8008, which was really little more than a 4004 that could address more bits, and shortly afterward the 8080 chip, which, in its day, represented a quantum leap.

These developments really only opened up a whole new can of worms, however. As long as you had only four bits to play with and stuck to simple addition, subtraction, multiplication, and division, no real programming was required. Everything was done in real time and there was no disk storage. Life was simple in a 4-bit world.

Not so in the vast, new, untamed 8-bit frontier. Like the hulking mainframes of the day, some sort of programming was required. Except there was a problem. There was no suitable programming language in existence—and even if there had been "programs" in existence, there was no easy way to store or load them.

One group of engineers split off and, deciding that the 8080 was not the way to go, fathered another chip, the Z80. Also an 8-bit chip with 16 address pins to address a whopping 64K of memory, the Z80 is of special significance because its proponents developed the first rudimentary operating system for a microprocessor chip. Patterned roughly after mainframe systems, it evolved into what came to be known as CP/M (control program for microcomputers).

Meantime, Intel kept refining and polishing its 8080—still largely an orphan—and spinning off new variants in search of market share. They tried a somewhat similar but different 16-bit version called the 8086, which evolved still further to become the 8088. Though a chip with 16-bit potential, it found its niche in 8-bit systems, which were cheaper to produce and close enough in design to the earlier 8008 and Z80 to enable programs written for these systems to be converted easily to run on it. (While a somewhat faster chip than the 8088 in that it allows generally faster clock speeds, the 8086 was not an immediate success. It found use in the Compaq Deskpro and the AT&T 6300, but, tied to an 8-bit bus in both of these, it never achieved its full potential. It has more recently appeared in the PS/2 model 30 and is used in a number of clones.)

While the exact chronology of what was going on behind closed doors is hazy, somewhere in this timespan IBM was working on what would become the first PC (IBM personal computer)—which quickly evolved into something far beyond the wildest dreams (or nightmares) of its creators. Intel kept designing new and better chips around which three new generations of machines have been built. But the more things change the more things stay the same, and we still have 64K segments rooted in a 1Mb operating system that's no longer even mentioned in the same breath as the PC and its faster, fleeter offspring.

Still, despite its limitations—even alongside the 80286 and especially the 32-bit chips that have followed—the 8088 remains a dependable workhorse and is still being sold in great numbers today. And with proper configuration and LIM EMS 4.0 expanded memory, it can support up to 32 megabytes of EMS memory (which is the maximum any 8086-family chip supports). It can even achieve full multitasking using windowing environments like Quarterdeck's trend-setting DESQview.

There has also been some success with mapping LIM 4.0 EMS memory—and lately even EMS 3.2 memory (only with IBM's PC DOS 6.1)—to unused address space above 640K. The amount of recoverable upper-memory address space isn't impressive compared to that on 32-bit machines, but with IBM's new DOS 6.1 UMB drivers it can run as high as 60 megabytes (8088 with Hercules card). On 8088 and 80286 systems, the use of upper-memory addresses generally precludes the use of traditional expanded memory since the address block that serves as the page frame is generally mapped.

But any gain is worth the effort, and the ongoing development of this technology—most notably by IBM—would clearly seem to indicate that we'll still be seeing DOS-running 8088 machines on dealer's shelves for quite some time to come.

Initially, the 8088 even supported Windows, but unable to use EMS expanded memory (unlike DESQview 8088 multitasking), performance was marginal at best and, beginning with release 3.1, Windows no longer supported real-mode (640K) operations.

One of the most significant limitations of the 8088 for many applications is that it's essentially an 8-bit chip. Some call it 16 and it is—but it really isn't. The chip contains two 8-bit processors that, running side by side, effectively amounts to 16-bit processing. But by design the chip is limited to only 8-bit data communication with the outside world and, accordingly, the standard open-architecture bus of the PC and its various clones and spinoffs is an 8-bit bus. Given an 8-bit architecture, then, the operating system and any software that's truly compatible with it must be scaled to run in and through an 8-bit world.

The 8086 differed significantly from the 8088 in that it could transfer 16 bits and therefore operate more effectively given access to a 16-bit bus. Internally both chips can actually manipulate 16-bit data, so they're not directly interchangeable. This, by the way, is essentially the difference between the 386SX and DX chips, where only the DX chip is capable of 32-bit communication (supports a 32-bit bus), although both are 32-bit processors.

Still, even in office environments that often require the best that technology has to offer in order to meet more sophisticated needs, a lot of old PCs are still doing yoeman service.

Let's face it; it makes about as much sense to buy a 386 or 486 just to keep track of the family budget or write the occasional school term paper as it does to buy a high-performance sports car only to drive to the corner market occasionally for a loaf of bread.

However, with the price of 386 and even 486 machines becoming more and more attractive—and the likelihood of wanting or needing something better in the not too distant future—for all but the most basic entry-level needs, you should probably set your sights a little higher.

The 80286

From its introduction the 80286 has been somewhat of an orphan, caught somewhere between the 8088 it was supposed to replace and a promise it somehow never quite fulfilled. It brought something euphemistically called *extended memory*, along with such esoteric terms as *real* and *protected mode*. But after the initial hype had died away, about all we really had it seemed was a faster PC with a different kind of RAM disk.

The 80286 could address more memory than the 8088 was capable of handling—up to 16 megabytes—which was, interestingly, the same limit that for many years applied to IBM's (then) multimillion-dollar mainframes. (While the 80286 chip is capable of addressing 16 megabytes of actual memory, specific computers using that chip might have substantially lower limits imposed by other design factors. The IBM AT, for instance, had an official limit of 3 megabytes except for extended and/or virtual memory.) And it made provision for something called *protected mode*, which was supposed to assure data protection and integrity—an issue that's crucial when dealing with more memory, particularly when running two or more processes concurrently.

The idea of something like a protected mode—and several other features supported by the 80286—actually dates back to the mid '60s and came out of a joint project sponsored by Bell Labs, MIT, and General Electric. Unfortunately, although this work and its implications were well known, DOS had been written on the basis of some shortsighted assumptions that made no allowance for a protected mode or any possibility of life beyond one megabyte.

Therefore, as long as DOS was the only viable operating system available there was a major problem. Or so it seemed, because while some software developers ventured cautiously into the ungoverned area of extended memory, it proved to be a risky business fraught until rather recently with all sorts of dangers. The result was only limited usage and a lot of bad press based largely on common misconceptions—misconceptions based in part on irreparable flaws in the design of the 80286, but in hindsight more on a lack of understanding by programmers and, worse, a lack of any real consensus on how extended memory should be used.

The software problems would have to await the development of DOS extenders, which, at least, obeyed a common set of rules. That day eventually arrived. The design flaws in the chip itself, combined with needs that never were addressed just wouldn't go away, however, leaving the brief heyday of the 80286 as one of the most enigmatic to date; its greatest contribution was not only the lessons learned from its shortcomings but also other weaknesses it pointed to in our technology.

You can't go home again   I'm sure the 80286 wasn't why that phrase was coined. But it could have been. Basically, the problem with the 80286 chip—aside from the lack of an operating system or even an accepted add-on interface to protected mode until recently—is that while the chip will transition easily from real mode (DOS) to protected mode (by definition, beyond DOS), there's no easy way to bring it back.

And that's a serious problem because while a program can *run* all day in protected mode given sufficient data to calculate, extrapolate, interpolate, and otherwise chew on, even the most sophisticated DOS extender-based application software has to come back to the real world for disk access, file management, and other DOS services. DOS, keep in mind, ends at one megabyte (FFFFh) and any time you go past that limit you must go out of DOS—at least until you need DOS services again. There's one exception that I'll discuss in a later chapter. That exception, defined by Microsoft in EMS 2.0 allows DOS to use the one additional 64K that lies almost entirely above 1024K.

Going either out of DOS or coming back into real mode from protected with the 80286 (or any higher chip in the 8086 group), there's yet another peculiar device that must be dealt with. It's something called the A20 gate and, unless turned off, it wraps calls to addresses above 1024K back around to the bottom of the address range rather than allowing them to pass through into the extended memory range.

Apparently, at one time a lot of programmers used the rather sloppy trick of throwing in addresses above 1024K when they really just wanted to wrap back around within DOS—a carryover from a still earlier programming era, it seems. So unless specifically turned off by command, that's what the A20 gate does. Programs calling for addresses beyond 1024K, then, must turn this gate off before even being allowed access to extended memory and, when re-entering real mode, turn it on again.

So much for what it does—or what it's supposed to do. In the 80286 it simply didn't work, at least reliably or in the manner it was documented. As a result, crashes were more common than successful returns.

To get around the problem, one trick programmers used to return to real mode was to take advantage of an undocumented feature of the 80286 chip, discovered early on by hackers. Commonly referred to as the LOADALL function, it was likely built into the 80286 to serve some internal testing or quality-control need at the factory. And, in fact, it does provide a relatively easy and direct means of returning from protected mode.

The problem with this technique, however, is that Intel not only never documented it, but it never provided any assurance that the feature would always be there in later revisions of the chip. So there was a definite element of risk involved for any programmer who chose to ignore the danger signs.

The more common and more accepted solution—and one that requires only well-documented features of the 80286 chip—is something called a "triple fault." While a full technical explanation is beyond the scope of this book, the curious might find a thumbnail sketch amusing if nothing else. It goes something like this:

Using the triple fault technique, when a program running in protected mode needs to return to real mode it does something utterly outrageous: loading a register with a value that can be interpreted only as an error. Having detected the "error," the system goes looking for instructions as to how to deal with it. At that point, it finds another value indicating a second error at that level (also put there by the program), which then sends the chip to its third and final level of error protection, where it finds still a third invalid value. And everyone knows three strikes and you're out.

So after the third fault, the 80286 gets ready to reboot—which, of course, would not only clear the faults but also jettison whatever you were working on. But on checking its various registers, the chip discovers a pattern of data bits indicating that the system wasn't just turned on after all. So it doesn't reboot. Not completely, anyway. It just resets certain registers and puts you back in DOS. The same thing can, in effect, be noted very occasionally with other chips during a cold boot, and somewhat more often during a warm boot. The processor chip will detect some bit pattern that indicates the system is really alive, and only reset rather than rebooting, leaving you in limbo somewhere. In those cases, a reboot must be forced, typically by shutting down the power to force a total restart.

Convoluted and weird? You bet. But dependable enough it seems—and anyway, OS/2 was coming and the problem would just go away, right? In fact, at this point DOS was supposed to do its "old soldier" thing and simply fade away.

OS/2—a new operating system that would match the 16-bit capabilities of the 80286. Hence the origins of OS/2, originally a 16-bit operating system no longer limited to DOS's one megabyte of segmented address space. OS/2 would have only one mode, protected mode.

It was the ultimate solution, at a time when the installed user base was still seemingly small enough to deal with such a massive change. And OS/2 would supposedly run DOS applications too, making the transition relatively painless—or so we were told. Unfortunately, it just never happened. OS/2 as first released by Microsoft was a colossal flop.

A far more complex operating system than DOS, it was released before it was really ready. Overall performance was poor and the "DOS box"—which was supposed to let you bring DOS applications with you—was abysmal, soon earning the nickname "penalty box." And as if all of this wasn't enough, the 32-bit 80386 was on the scene by then, leaving little reason to continue working on a 16-bit system (although Microsoft continued to dabble with OS/2 until IBM took it over from them, redeveloping it as the powerful 32-bit system currently available).

Even beyond the lack of a 16-bit protected-mode operating system, the 80286 has a number of serious shortcomings—shortcomings made all the more apparent in the glare of the spotlight on the 32-bit chips that followed. Unlike the 386 (and higher), the 80286 doesn't have address registers that can be easily remapped to allow tucking bits and bigger chunks of usable RAM into unused and otherwise unoccupied address spaces between 640K and DOS's 1Mb limit. Nor does it have the virtual-machine multitasking capability inherent in the 32-bit chips. Some even go so far as to call the 286 a "brain-dead chip" for all the things it can't do.

There is, however, a large installed user base of 286 machines out there, and there's some quite good 16-bit DOS-extended software—software that will run on anything from 286s up. And in addition to the 16 megabytes of linear memory (1 Mb for DOS plus up to 15 megabytes of DOS extended memory), the 286, like all the other members of the 8086 family, can handle up to 32 megabytes of EMS 4.0 expanded memory. Between the two you can run Windows 3x (standard mode only), multitask with DESQview, or run any software not exclusively for 32-bit systems. And interestingly, for certain applications 286s tend to outperform the 386SX.

And people are still buying them, although perhaps even more than with the 8088s, the rationale is hard to justify with entry-level 32-bit 386s at or very near the price of 286s.

If any single event marked the coming-of-age of desktop computing, it was the advent of the 80386—the first of the group of 32-bit processors in the 8086 family. There have now been a flock of them, originals from Intel as well as a bunch of clones. And Intel hurrying to try to stay ahead. Clock speeds have gone from fast to super fast, and then doubled. Each generation has added significantly more raw processing power, with the 486DX incorporating the equivalent of a math coprocessor.

The 32-bit revolution

Each generation has boasted something new and different to justify it, but there are some major threads of commonality that run through all of them—beyond the fact that they can run full 32-bit software. It's what they share that is within the purview of this book: how these chips deal with memory—particularly in protected mode—and games they all can play with it (like emulating several 8086 processors concurrently).

Therefore, throughout most of this book whenever 32-bit chips are part of the discussion, it will basically be a generic 32-bit chip because, from a user point of view, the same memory-management technology with pretty much the same results applies to all.

After the 286 fiasco, Intel made sure they'd done it right when they introduced the 80386. Not just a fix—the 286 chip really is unfixable, it seems—this was a whole new chip. It was and is compatible with anything that runs on any member of 8086 dynasty. And it promised higher clock speeds than were seen with 286s. The real news, however, was in features never seen before, features that initially attracted little attention because they were so new and different.

Unfortunately, many users simply looked on the early 386 machines as faster ATs—and indeed, with only software written for the 80286 to work with initially, that's all they were. It would take the advent of a whole new generation of software to unleash the power of these chips, but as so often is the case, the software came available before most users understood what they were missing—there are even many today who don't, unfortunately.

With the introduction of the Intel Pentium in 1993, another generation of microprocessors was born, but a generation in many ways ahead of its time. It's a 64-bit chip loosed on a world that has no 64-bit operating system—nor any even being developed seemingly. Nor is there any 64-bit application software—which, lacking a 64-bit operating system, would require some sort of extension of a 32-bit operating system much as we use DOS extenders today.

64 going on 32

The Pentium is clearly a sizzler when it comes to running 32-bit software, but in terms of DOS usage it offers nothing new. And whether the world really needs a chip like this in quantities sufficient to justify its existence is problematical. There will surely be enough sold to justify it in the marketplace, but there's often little correlation between sales and actual need. Other than a relative handful of high-end users who will truly benefit, its introduction now, so far ahead of its time, would seem more a matter of Intel being forced to keep one jump ahead of the clone makers in what seems to be more and more a losing battle, judging from how fast the 486 was successfully cloned.

The 64-bit data path of the Pentium also raises a number of questions regarding the other hardware needed to support it. For instance, using the standard SIMM technology in place today, it appears that RAM installations/upgrades would probably have to be in groups of eight SIMMs at a time, just as 32-bit systems require upgrades in increments of four (for reasons discussed later in this book). Based on current cost estimates for 16Mb SIMMS, that would be something like $5,000 a crack just for RAM. Granted, that's 128 megabytes at a time and, using 4Mb SIMMs, the cost would probably drop to something around $1,250—a much more manageable figure. But 4×8 is only 32 megabytes of RAM—the minimum for running Windows NT—putting 4Mb SIMMs for a Pentium in about the same category as 256K SIMMs today.

Of course, the whole SIMM standard has come into question with the need for 16Mb SIMMs—a need that was already apparent before the Pentium. And there are solutions, ways to upgrade one module at a time using different module configurations. But that means coming up with another new "standard." And there are other hardware issues as well.

This isn't to say the Pentium is frivolous, however. Windows NT with its 16Mb (approximate) operating-system kernel can clearly use all the help it can get to keep with DOS Windows on a decent 32-bit system. OS/2 2.x will benefit—as will any multitasker. And other applications will also benefit.

As far as this book is concerned, the Pentium behaves essentially like any of the 32-bit chips that have preceded it, and for DOS use will have the same memory-management requirements. So read "32 bits" to mean "being used as or behaving like 32 bits," and everything I say about 32-bit technology should suffice to cover Pentiums—and probably whatever comes next.

Memory to go Another of the features unique to the 32-bit family of chips allows memory to be mapped to any block of addresses, no matter where it is. And while this might not sound like much, it was in fact a revolution and probably a whole new lease on life for DOS. For the first time usable RAM could be assigned— or "mapped," as it's called—to unused blocks of DOS address space up in the system area above 640K. It could be assigned into little unused nooks and crannies up above the video area and worked in around such things as network cards, hard disk ROM, the page frame for expanded memory, and system ROM.

This isn't generally RAM you can use directly to run bigger applications—although it can be in some circumstances, particularly when running only character-based application software. In that case, the video graphics area can often be mapped. In the case of the A000h to AFFFh block (or to B7FFh in some cases), this memory is contiguous to DOS's conventional memory and can therefore be used as such, totalling sometimes as high as 736K.

Use of this otherwise unused address space is complicated by the fact that it's usually fragmented: 8K here, 32K there, 64 or 96K somewhere else. But with mapping—and proper management of memory that's mapped—it can be used to relocate device drivers and TSRs that otherwise would be using precious memory below 640K—little TSRs in little cubby holes and bigger ones wherever they fit. And every one that's moved makes that much memory available below 640K—sometimes up to as much as 200K or more.

One of the most important—and exotic—features of the 32-bit breed was the addition of a third mode of operation: virtual 8086 mode. With this, a single microprocessor chip could act like several 8086s, each behaving like a separate machine and, just like separate machines, running different applications—even different operating systems—concurrently. This was really an extension of the protected mode, which, even in the first of the 32-bit chips, Intel had finally gotten right. But it was more than just an extension of protected mode. It was something totally unique and something many users even now don't appreciate (though many use this feature daily without even knowing it). See FIG. 5-2.

The reality of virtual machines

With virtual machines, as these emulations of multiple CPU chips came to be known, multitasking took on a whole new dimension. We'd had a taste of multitasking even with 8088s and 286s, thanks to EMS 4.0 expanded memory (and AST's earlier EEMS scheme on which the EMS 4.0 specification was founded), but it was nothing like the multitasking the virtual 8086 mode afforded. This multitasking was not only faster but safer, thanks to the fact that it was all in protected mode (which I'll discuss in more detail in a later chapter).

In addition to conventional DOS memory (640K), virtual machines running DOS can have extended and expanded memory as well—even a high-memory area (HMA) and upper-memory blocks, basically anything a real machine can have. And the use of virtual machines is not, by any means, limited to DOS. Any operating system that can run on a 32-bit 8086-family machine can run on one of these virtual machines. Within the DOS world, DESQview and Windows are perhaps the best-known applications of virtual machines. And outside of DOS, OS/2 2x and Windows NT use them.

In fact, with full-fledged virtual machines the separation is so complete that even if you totally crash a virtual machine, whatever other virtual machines you're running at the moment will never know it. With rare exception—

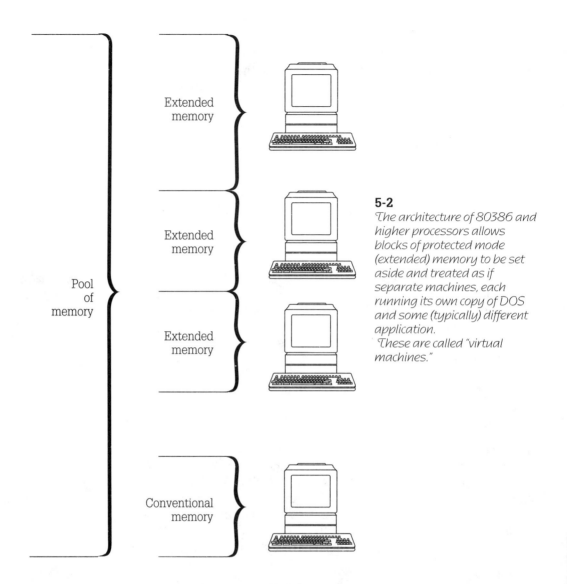

Pool
of
memory

Extended
memory

Extended
memory

Extended
memory

Conventional
memory

5-2
*The architecture of 80386 and
higher processors allows
blocks of protected mode
(extended) memory to be set
aside and treated as if
separate machines, each
running its own copy of DOS
and some (typically) different
application.
These are called "virtual
machines."*

generally the fault of the program that controls this little one-man band—
they keep right on running unaffected. And you can simply reboot crashed
virtual machines independently of all other processes you're running, much
the same as if you indeed had a bunch of physical machines piled on your
desk and one of them had crashed and been rebooted.

Hurry up & wait

Of course, this still doesn't get around the fact that in real or virtual mode
alike you only have one processor that has to divide its time between how
many different applications you want to run concurrently. Mathematically
that means that two should run at only half the effective speed of one, four a
quarter speed, and so forth. In practice, using increasingly sophisticated

techniques to determine which (assuming there are several) process or virtual machine(s) are really active and which are idle, waiting for user input tends to reduce any effective loss of speed significantly. As a practical matter, it often isn't even noticeable.

In fact, overall clock speed is probably one of the most deceptive measures of computer performance there is today. With clock speeds going higher and higher, other factors are becoming increasingly crucial. Take the bus, for instance: 12 MHz is a fast bus—faster than some cards can even operate.

One of the most severely limiting factors is the kind of RAM—not just the rated speed of the chips (which at best is no match for today's clock speeds), but the physical nature of the chips/SIMMs themselves. Most machines today use something called *DRAM* (dynamic RAM).

The DRAM used today is generally faster than the old, slow stuff that used to be on 4.77-MHz 8088s. But not actually that much faster: three times, maybe, with 60-nanosecond SIMMs the fastest generally available. And this increase in the same time period that's seen clock speeds increase by a factor of ten or more. By resorting to various design tricks like interleaving banks of DRAM chips, manufacturers can mask how slow the chips really are—up to a point. But beyond that point . . . wait states.

Wait states, as the name implies, are pauses inserted by the system— basically wasted clock cycles—to allow RAM the extra time it needs. In truth, no matter how high clock speeds go, RAM can be driven only at some finite speed, beyond which things begin to fall apart. Which means that when you have to slow the system down and wait for it, you're not getting the performance you thought you paid for.

Unfortunately, to overcome this obstacle—at least for now—and genuinely increase the speed of the overall system, we have to get away from the use of DRAM and use a faster media. And there *is* a faster RAM technology available: SRAM. *SRAM* (static RAM) chips have refresh rates that are typically as short as 25 nanoseconds. It should be possible to run a machine at about 50 Mhz with zero wait states using SRAM, but SRAM is considerably more expensive and few manufacturers have yet to show much enthusiasm. CompuAdd was one of the first who actually did, offering an SRAM daughterboard as an option for one of its high-end tower machines. However, the SRAM it supported was basically just enough to cover the needs of the DOS area.

One day we'll overcome all of this. Perhaps a whole new RAM technology will come along to fill the gap—but even if it does, there will be other bottlenecks. We've come a long way, though, and 32-bit chips have set the pace. Their processing power is only now really beginning to be used in ways that demonstrate its true potential.

Along with the chips themselves, there have been parallel evolutions of both software and auxiliary hardware, like video and other coprocessors, with RISCs (reduced instruction set chips) already beginning to appear on premium motherboards. Perhaps these are harbingers of the parallel and distributed processing that's coming—maybe not as fast as we were led to expect, but coming nonetheless.

These things are surely coming, but it seems certain that DOS will still go on and on—DOS for the 8088 and for all the members of the growing 8086 family. And as long as there is DOS, the issues I examine in this book will remain.

The virtual machine

It might seem that we're getting ahead of ourselves, jumping into something as esoteric as the virtual machine at this point. It's necessary, however, because that's what's going to be used more and more on 32-bit machines.

Windows, in case you didn't know, runs exclusively on virtual machines (enhanced mode only). DESQview runs on virtual machines on 32-bit systems. One of the more powerful third-party memory managers creates a virtual machine. And even one of the new DOSs, Novell's DOS 7, is intended more for virtual machines than for real mode.

And you see already that there's a problem because, while virtual machines can exist only in the protected mode, protected mode is not in itself a virtual environment. So it's crucial that we come grips with virtual machines and their relationship with the protected mode up front so they'll make sense when I discuss them later on.

The dictionary defines the word *vir-tu-al* as an adjective, existing or resulting in essence or effect though not in actual fact. (Middle English virtuall, effective. Medieval Latin virtualis, Latin virtus, excellence.)

**The good
& not so good**

As you can see, while the actual definition of *virtual* is something other than real, the word itself is linked to excellence, which really has nothing to do with virtual. I'll be using the word in more than just one context in this book as well:

Virtual machine   Certainly one of the most important facets of our technology today.

Virtual memory   No less virtual than virtual machines and anything but excellent. A necessary evil at best—and something to be avoided as much as possible.

There are two important points to keep in mind as we explore the unreal world of virtuality. First, no matter how lifelike it can to be—as in the case of virtual machines—it's an illusion. Secondly, you can't automatically infer excellence simply because of the word *virtual*.

In the context of virtual machines, *virtual* is good. Unfortunately, it isn't so good in the case of virtual memory, which you'll see for yourself a little later on.

The incredible machines that aren't   Certainly one of the most unique features of the 386, 486, and now the Pentium—and surely anything else that comes down the pike at this point—is the ability to support not only real-mode machines, the kind most users are familiar with, but also almost any number of virtual machines, all running concurrently. Such virtual machines can be used for multitasking by a single user on a single physical machine or by several different users at remote locations—or a combination of the two. Multitasking is possible in real mode, as demonstrated by DESQview's ability to do full multitasking even on an 8088, provided LIM 4.0 EMS memory (or equivalent) is available and that the machine can be configured to allow bank switching at all addresses (typically) above 256K. It's a more cumbersome process than working with virtual machines as supported by 386 and higher chips, however.

Calling them "virtual machines" isn't just advertising hype or a matter of semantics, either. What we're dealing with here is radically different from the kind of multitasking many users started with—many with the old 8088 back when EEMS memory from AST was something new and any kind of multitasking—real multitasking—was a gee-whiz wonder. This is something very different. And yet the transition from mere bank switching—swapping blocks of RAM (EEMS and later LIM 4.0 EMS expanded memory) in and out of real-mode addresses to this new, completely different mode of operation went largely unnoticed.

The introduction of the virtual machine went unnoticed by most users because, superficially, there was nothing to notice. The press talked about it, but many of the writers who wrote about it had little idea what it was themselves. And not without some reason. To Quarterdeck fans, for example, DESQview had the exact same look and feel on 80386s as on 8088s. It generally ran a whole lot faster, but then 386s had a reputation for having faster clocks and just being faster anyway. So hardly anybody noticed they weren't working on a real machine. There really wasn't any reason to. See FIG. 6-1.

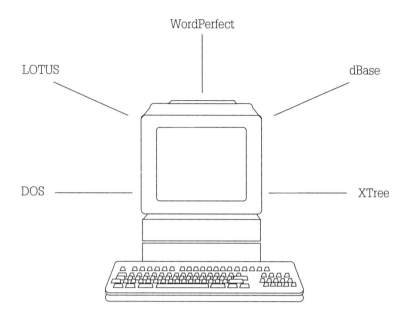

LOTUS

WordPerfect

dBase

DOS

XTree

6-1
Since DESQview, the first practical multitasker, had been able to run entirely in real mode using EEMS or EMS 4.0 expanded memory, the advent of the virtual machine went unnoticed by many users. Today most multitaskers—including DESQview—run applications on virtual machines however.

And if you didn't enter the world of virtual machines with DESQview, then how about Windows 3x in the enhanced mode? There's more to enhanced mode than just running 32-bit code. There are virtual machines in there as well. And OS/2 2.0 . . . There's no getting around it. Sooner or later, you're going to be running on a bunch of virtual machines, no matter how real that box looks on your desk. So you might as well get used to the idea. And learn at least a little bit about the nature of the beast.

The skinny on virtual

Virtual machines are exotic both in concept and in execution, and for that reason they're probably the least understood of all the features of 80386 and higher machines. The ability to concurrently emulate multiple 8086 machines is essentially just an extension of protected-mode operation. That, however, is overly simplistic because it ignores some added design features that are found only in 80386 and higher processors—an 80286, for example, supports protected-mode operations (sort of), but lacks the special qualities required for virtual-mode operations.

Virtual machines are created by putting the CPU into virtual mode—more correctly called virtual 8086 mode because that in fact is what the CPU is emulating when it runs in virtual mode: one or more 8086 processors, each endowed with—and suffering the same limitations as—that venerable ancestor.

The illusion of being not one but multiple processors is so complete, in fact, that when the virtualizing capabilities of these higher-order chips are fully utilized, they can even support the concurrent use of different operating systems. This is where it gets really spooky, but it's true.

A 386 machine, for example, might boot up in real mode under DOS but play host to virtual machines, one or more running UNIX tasks while still others running under a different DOS. And OS/2 2.0, in addition to the DOS emulation it provides—again, thanks to virtual machines—allows you to boot an MS-, PC- or DR DOS session (on yet another virtual machine) from a floppy in drive A:.

And it's no illusion; you actually have to boot a virtual machine the same as you would boot a real machine. At least to some extent—depending, among other things, on the degree to which hardware virtualization is implemented.

Virtual machines are not all equal

With more familiar multitaskers like DESQview and Windows, virtual machines are quite invisible to the user. However, neither of these does a complete job of virtualization. With either, for instance, all the virtual machines share a common DOS environment, inheriting the path, comspec, custom prompt, and such things from the "parent" process—typically Windows or DESQview.

In fact, it goes beyond the basic parent/child process relationship. As implemented in these multitaskers, although the master, or parent, environment (at least the portion most commonly referred to as being *the* environment) is never altered by any changes made to child environments, such things as substituted drive designations, when started from one child process, become immediately available in any other child processes running at the time.

And, of course, with both of these more familiar multitaskers, all of the virtual machines they spawn share a common set of device drivers. This often means that a device driver—a scanner driver, for example—that's used only in conjunction with one particular process (one virtual machine) is going to occupy the same block of memory they all share, even if other processes might be able to use it to better advantage. I don't say this to knock either Windows or DESQview, particularly since, with the advent of Stealth (Quarterdeck) and other high-tech management schemes, there's more upper memory available today than ever—more than most of us can even use. This does, however, set the stage for yet another feature of full virtualization.

Once you effectively separate the virtual machine completely from the host device, a number of interesting things begin to happen. With each virtual machine operating under its own copy of whatever operating system in its very own block of seemingly ordinary RAM, it follows that any device drivers loaded into that virtual machine will serve only that virtual machine. And this means that only that virtual machine will have to give up memory to load it. The same applies to TSRs in general.

Taking that logic one step farther, it follows that if more than one process requires the use of the same device driver or TSR, then that same driver or TSR must be loaded by every virtual machine that needs it. But this isn't always possible. In fact, multiple virtual machines are able to share such real resources as hard and floppy drives and parallel or serial ports only if special provisions are built into the system.

Here, again, is a level of virtualization quite different from that found in DESQview or Windows, where drivers reside in memory that, along with the operating system itself, is common to all processes—which makes it a problem most users haven't (yet) encountered. It *is* a problem, though, and one that's particularly apparent when it comes to running nonstandard block devices, like nonstandard mass-storage devices and disk-compression schemes.

Certainly one of the most significant and visible characteristics of virtual machines is the stoic, almost noble way they die. Just as they lead separate lives, often totally oblivious to the existence of their sibling processes, unless the control program (the multitasker itself) fails—which is remarkably rare—they die quietly and all alone. So if, for instance, a word-processing session crashes on one virtual machine, a spreadsheet session running on another virtual machine and database on yet another will be totally unaffected.

Where one goes, the rest don't necessarily follow

Typically, the crashed session—the crashed virtual machine—can be restored by simply rebooting that one machine. And in many cases, depending on the control program in use, the old three-key combination (Ctrl–Alt–Del) is all it takes to get that session up and running again, while all the other virtual machines keep right on as if nothing had happened. This is a particularly important consideration in multiuser, multitasking environments such as VM386, a system we'll look at in some depth in a later chapter.

This is a very touchy area, though, and not all multitaskers treat warm boots the same way. *Do not* try the three-key combination if an application crashes when you're running Windows in enhanced mode—or OS/2 2.0. They'll reboot you all the way. (There was talk at one time of having Windows 3.1 treat this differently, but I've found it to be a killer.) The three-key boot when you're running DESQview on a 32-bit machine will kill whatever virtual machine happens to be running in the foreground—crashed or otherwise—but doesn't reboot the session that was running. And as long as you're running under DESQview, you can't reboot the host machine/control program that way even if you want to. VM386 and DR Multiuser DOS (if configured to do so) automatically reboot the foreground session. And NT won't even let you log on and load until you Ctrl–Alt–Del when prompted—even from a cold start. So as you can see from just this sampling, there is no fixed rule.

The boot cycle   As with so many things connected with the use of virtual machines, there are vast differences in the way they boot—or appear to boot—under different multitaskers. With DESQview, Windows, and several other multitaskers, you don't have the sense of actually booting a machine—which, again, is why so many users are oblivious to the fact that they're really running in a different realm. If you look to one like VM386 that completely virtualizes the hardware—which I'll explain in greater depth in a later chapter—it becomes quite obvious, however.

Booting and rebooting sessions under VM386 requires individual CONFIG.SYS and AUTOEXEC.BAT files for each virtual machine (not required for virtual machines running under OS/2 2.0). And if it would take, say, 30 seconds to boot up your real-mode machine to start the day, if you want to run three virtual machines you've got to start by booting up a real machine and then three more machines. That's a couple of minutes anyway—not including loading your application software on each one. For that reason, it's significantly slower getting up and running with a bunch of fully virtualized machines than, say, DESQview or probably even Windows in this respect.

Most virtual machines are created to run one specific application. It is in this respect that you can start to see some of the real benefits of full virtualization. With every virtual machine running with its own completely independent copy of DOS (or whatever operating system it was booted with) and started with its own unique set of startup files, each one can be optimized for the specific job it is intended to perform with its own unique set of device drivers and TSRs, HMA utilization, and so forth.

In fact, as implemented in both VM386 and OS/2 2.0, you can customize *individual* DOS sessions (windows) that don't require full VGA graphics support to use up to 736K of contiguous conventional memory, while concurrently providing other DOS sessions with everything your VGA or SVGA can give. This is something that can't be done with Windows (since it runs only in full graphics mode) or even DESQview—although DESQview does allow you to infringe on video memory if *none* of your applications require graphics support.

While on the subject of IBM's OS/2 and virtual DOS machines, OS/2 release 2.0, in addition to providing its own more-or-less generic DOS, also allows you to boot DOS sessions of either the Microsoft or Digital Research/Novell variety from a floppy in drive A:. VM386 also allows individual machines to boot under operating systems other than the DOS under which the control program runs. Virtual machines: the virtualer they get, the realer they behave . . . .

You must remember, though, that no matter how real the virtual machine might seem, you still have only one CPU that must be shared among however many different "machines" you're running, as in any multitasking situation.

As implemented in VM386, once you're booted up and running your virtual machines, they'll typically run a little slower than real machines and actual operations—just enough that you might notice, but not enough to really slow you down. There's more involved than simply the degree of virtualization this particular multitasker employs, however. In this case, the developer has chosen to trade off a little something in performance for greater protection.

The important thing to keep in mind is that if a program can be run on any real 8086-family machine, it can be run on a properly configured virtual machine. This doesn't automatically mean that just any old virtual machine spun off by just any old control program can necessarily do it; it simply means it can be done. There are a few notable exceptions—including, even within DOS itself, FORMAT and CHKDSK with the /F switch. But again, depending on manner and the degree to which virtualization is implemented, this isn't always the case, with DESQview providing a notable exception to the exception, taking both of these in stride.

If it will run on any 8086 machine . . .

And programs that require extended or expanded memory? Regardless of whether you're talking about full or partial virtualization, each virtual machine can have its own, the difference being that, since virtual machines run only in protected mode, their memory, once allocated during the bootup process for that session, is the exclusive property of that machine. This despite the fact that up until that point it was and would remain part of a common pool. But when you terminate a virtual machine (short of shutting off the host machine), that memory is released.

There's one important issue regarding memory management. Programs like VM386, OS/2, NT, and to a large extent Windows in the enhanced mode— programs that create and manage virtual machines—do their own memory management. They won't even work in the presence of another memory manager like QEMM or DOS 5's HIMEM.SYS. Whatever DOS you use must boot up pretty bare—typically FILES and BUFFERS are the only items in the CONFIG.SYS you'd use to boot your host machine. The CONFIG.SYS and AUTOEXEC.BAT you use to boot up individual virtual machines look more like what you would expect.

Theoretically, the ability of an 80386 (or any higher) chip to create virtual machines is almost unlimited. The entire 4-gigabyte address range is available for remapping. As a practical matter, however, it isn't as unlimited as it might seem at first glance.

No matter how clever the illusion is, you just come back to time slicing because there are no virtual clocks—just one.

No virtual clock

With memory as cheap as it is these days, it's the clock that then becomes the ultimate limiting factor in the equation. Ultimately, the use of parallel processors might largely get around even that limitation, but fortunately developers have devised some clever work-arounds to squeeze the most out of that finite resource. These generally involve sensing periods of inactivity on some virtual machines and devoting more than just the allocated share to CPU-intensive tasks on other virtual machines. The underlying technology goes back to previrtual-machine multitasking, but it, too, has matured significantly.

In a single-user multitasking situation, you can usually stretch your precious time slices, using them only where they'll do the most good by simply freezing any background operations that don't have to keep on processing. Fully half the applications I use in a normal day fall in that category.

On a multiuser system, however, things are different. What appears as background activity from the perspective of someone working at the box that houses both the host as well as his or her virtual machine(s) consists of the foreground tasks for other users on the system. Therefore, foreground and background activity are equally important, depending on your point of view. And you want to keep all those other users working, not just sitting there, because the moment they have to sit and wait their turn a multiuser system is no longer viable.

So the virtual machine in its varying and diverse guises, for all the unique benefits it confers on us, brings with it its own set of problems. One thing is sure, however. I've only barely scratched the surface in the world—the very *real* world—of the virtual machine.

Part two
Memory beyond 640K

7 Extended memory & the protected mode

Extended memory is far and away the most important kind of memory there is today—what's called extended memory in DOS, that is. The same memory for other operating systems such as Windows NT or OS/2 is just plain old ordinary memory, but given DOS's one-megabyte limit, anything outside of that requires a different treatment—and therefore a different name.

This is the memory where Windows 3x runs—where all DOS extended software runs by definition. It's where virtual machines are born and live their lives. It's a place where you can work that knows no limit like the 640K barrier in DOS. There are limits, but so far . . .

Theoretically, you can access the gigabytes of memory with any of several Intel chips and their clones. The realities, in general, fall short of that—far short of that. But call it what you like, extended memory for DOS or just plain RAM in protected mode for something else is the good stuff: continuous linear memory. It's not only bigger and better, but far faster than the expanded memory that first let us escape the confines of 640K—particularly on 32-bit systems. (The 16-bit 80286, while supporting up to 32 megabytes of EMS 4.0 expanded memory, as do any of the other members of the 8086 family, is physically limited by design to only 16 megabytes of extended memory.) To the CPU, extended memory looks like an unbroken string of RAM with addresses that starts at 1024K and keeps going right on up until your CPU runs out of address pins or you run out of money—more likely the latter.

Promised with the introduction of the 80286, a promise that chip could never quite fulfill, extended memory was a long time coming. With the rapid acceptance of the 80386 and all the other 32-bit chips that followed, it quickly became the most dynamic area there is, not only for today but for tomorrow—or for as long as we have DOS. And not just for the 32-bit platform, either. Using new DOS-extender technology, many software developers have taken a new look at the 80286.

Where is it? In the DOS world, after skipping over the 384K of address space set aside for system use between 640K and 1024K, extended memory starts precisely where DOS leaves off. Ignoring for the moment the high-memory area (HMA), which we'll look at in the next chapter, extended memory begins with the very next byte above one megabyte, assuming there's RAM to fill that slot. FFFFh is where DOS ends, so 10000h, 10001h, 10002h, and so on, right up as far as you care to go (or care to buy SIMMs for), is linear, consecutively-addressed extended memory. See FIG 7-1.

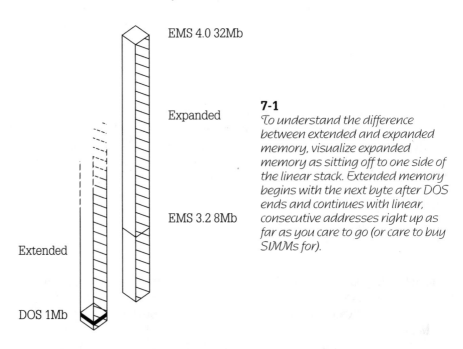

EMS 4.0 32Mb

Expanded

EMS 3.2 8Mb

Extended

DOS 1Mb

7-1
To understand the difference between extended and expanded memory, visualize expanded memory as sitting off to one side of the linear stack. Extended memory begins with the next byte after DOS ends and continues with linear, consecutive addresses right up as far as you care to go (or care to buy SIMMs for).

Extended memory, of course, assumes at least an 80286 or higher because, as explained in an earlier chapter, an 8088 is physically incapable of dealing with any discrete address beyond 1024K. Therefore, the beyond-640K options for an 8088 exclude any possible use of extended memory. And extended memory is where the power is.

To visualize just what extended memory is, try to imagine DOS as a 16-story building: ten floors of living space on the bottom, another six above that for machinery, and an elevator that goes another thousand stories right straight up, a direct, linear continuation. Fix this image in your mind because when we get to expanded memory a little later I'll be comparing it to a lazy Susan on the table. And once you get both the lazy Susan and the sky-scraping elevator fixed firmly in your mind, you should never say extended when you mean expanded—or vice versa—again. And boy, will that impress your colleagues.

Having told you what it is and where it is, that's really all there is to say about extended memory. Extended memory is dull. And it's easy; even the crudest memory manager will suffice to interface with it. And it does just about anything. It even does Windows—in fact, that's one of its specialties. In an upcoming chapter, I'll be devoting pages and pages to just one little 384K area in DOS, the area above 640K. But here—with something you could spend a fortune on and gigabytes of address space to work with—there's really nothing to say. Except that you need more; it doesn't matter how much you've got, you need more. And tomorrow you're going to need still more.

This, of course, assumes that when you wake up some morning and you're maybe gigabytes into this thing that you're still using DOS. If not, it will be just plain old memory for Windows NT, OS/2, or who-knows-what, and you won't even need a memory manager to interface with it.

One of the most exciting and important things about extended memory, at least within the context of this book, is how many things you can do with it— beyond just running huge applications, multitasking, disk caching, etc. You can also use it to create (or emulate) EMS expanded memory. You can nibble off the bottom 64K and, with a little legerdemain, present it to DOS as an extra little bonus called the high-memory area. You can even take bits and pieces of it and map them to DOS-addressable space above 640K. And all these are just fringe benefits.

More than just "more memory"

There's more to this than just more memory, more than simply plugging in more chips, SIMMs, or whatever other kind of module suits your system. Even moving on to other operating systems, where extended memory to DOS is just plain memory, there's nothing plain about it. Whether you're talking gigabytes or just the 384K left over out of the 1Mb factory-installed memory in hundreds of thousands of machines (left over not because the manufacturer was generous but simply because there's never really been a way to stop at just 640K since they stopped using 64K chips), it's very special memory. It's protected memory.

Protected mode

More people say more and know less about *protected mode* than almost anything, except perhaps the weather. What it is in concept is really rather simple. Beginning with the 80286, Intel's designers tried to implement a scheme that would protect virtual addresses—in DOS terms, linear addresses beyond 1 megabyte—so that multiple operations could be run there concurrently, the integrity of each and their attendant data protected from the others.

The most significant difference between running in real mode and protected is that, in protected mode, segment registers contain selectors rather than actual physical addresses. This is crucial, and it's important to grasp the difference.

Selectors are a lot like substitution tables; a call directed to any specific segment or address is intercepted and rerouted via a selector to the place that code or data is actually located—something it knows because it put it there in the first place. It's sort of like having an appointment with the President. First the Secret Service has to look you over, and then maybe they'll tell you where he is.

These selectors provide an extra level of indirection when accessing memory. Instead of being the base address of the segment in memory, a selector is merely an offset into a table of *descriptors*.

Each descriptor contains the base address and length of the segment as well as additional information required to implement the memory-protection features of protected mode. This means that the values loaded into the segment registers don't correspond directly to physical addresses.

For an application to access a particular physical address (like screen memory), it must first load the base address of that area of memory into a descriptor and load the selector that corresponds to that descriptor into a segment register. Two tables of descriptors are available to each process. One table is called the *local descriptor table* (LDT), and the other is called the *global descriptor table* (GDT). The GDT is shared by all processes in the system, but each process has its own LDT. The GDT normally maps system-wide data structures and the LDT maps process-specific data structures.

This, of course, requires a chip with an architecture that, unlike the 8086 and 8088, has the internal capability of doing this. Overall, though, it's a relatively simple, logical process—and you have to have something like it going on to prevent utter chaos outside the relatively well-ordered but narrow realm of DOS.

Except it didn't work. Not with the 80286—at least not well. In hindsight, it appears that someone dropped the ball rather badly when the 286 chip was designed, and to this day you hear cries of "foul" and see fingers pointed in various directions. But the bottom line, whatever the underlying cause, is that with an 80286 you cannot slip easily back and forth between real mode and protected mode without crashing the system—or walking a very fine line on the brink of doom. This is attributed by some experts to a conflict between

DOS's own internal access needs and the internal addresses needed for the instructions necessary to shift the 80286 in and out of the protected mode. (In real mode, the 80286 or higher chip behaves just like the original 8086 with the original 640K/1Mb limitation.)

A number of important design differences in the 80386 (and all later chips) changed all of that. Protected mode is now a practical reality. The possibilities are hard to even comprehend, like complex applications as big as 2 gigabytes. Huge. In fact, it appears that some implementations of OS/2 might use this ability to allow real-mode PC/MS-DOS applications to run concurrently (multitasking) with protected-mode operations running under OS/2 or some other protected-mode operating system.

When the 386 was introduced, however, there were still obstacles to overcome before extended memory could come into its own. Like any frontier area, there were disputes, even about how it should be accessed.

In the absence of a standard—a consensus even—for how extended memory should be accessed during the first three or four years after the introduction of the AT, software developers were left pretty much to do their own thing. It was a lawless place. There were no good guys and no bad guys, just a few guys scratching out a living up there. Or trying to.

Bottom's up

RAM disk, print spoolers, disk-caching schemes; there was little more at first. Soon, though, other people started looking at it. AutoCAD—one of the first— and several others started stuffing data up there, but there was still no law and order. Try to put two tasks, two sets of data, or two anythings up there . . . there were few survivors.

During this time, two quite different philosophies evolved. IBM's VDISK, beginning with DOS 3.0, was capable of using either conventional or extended memory, starting at the bottom of the pile and eating its way toward the top. Then there was another school of thought that said extended memory should be accessed from the top down. And there were a number of logical arguments to back it up, not the least of which being that it's less complicated and easier to see who else is running up there and how much space they're occupying when you start at the top (providing everybody else is also working from the top down—which they weren't).

Of course, everyone knows what happens if you try to burn a candle at both ends; you end up with a mess, drips all over everything. Well, it got messy in extended memory real fast. If you tried to run more than one program at a time, someone's data usually wound up dripping all over someone else's data and you ended up with corrupted files and all kinds of nastiness.

The situation was further complicated by several noncooperating applications that arbitrarily assumed that any extended memory present when they were running was their exclusive property. They then went into protected mode and simply started writing directly to it without even bothering to check for other users.

It's no wonder that extended memory got such bad press in the beginning—made even worse by the grotesque gyrations required to bring an 80286 back down to earth from protected mode once you got up there.

Finally, in 1988, Microsoft released the extended memory specification (XMS), which defined a standard for extended memory comparable to the role played by the LIM EMS standard for expanded memory.

XMS defines what is now the industry-standard interface for allowing programs to access and use extended memory on machines with 80286 and higher processors, but it goes much farther than that. Primarily, it defines a set of rules governing:

❏ Extended memory use at addresses as high as you've got bucks to buy the chips for.
❏ The high-memory area between 1024K and 1088K (the extra 64K of DOS), addressable memory available to 386 and higher machines.

The XMS also defines a hardware-independent mechanism for controlling the A20 gate that must be opened every time control passes back and forth between real and protected modes—as when a program running in extended memory must return to real mode for keyboard input or any disk I/O.

Quarterdeck had done much of the pioneering work in both the UMB and HMA areas, but although much of their work was seemingly incorporated in the new specification, they weren't a party to its being drafted. In any case, given a formal standard the world could live with and the evolution of the DOS extender, the doors to memory—more memory that you could possibly imagine—weren't just opened, they were blown away.

With all that memory to work with—or at least the potential of having all that memory to work with—it didn't take long to find creative ways to use it: bigger applications, better multitasking, and graphical applications such as AutoCAD and Windows. And then of course, with all that memory to work with, we got brand-new operating systems, too. Like OS/2 from IBM, and the even bigger NT from Microsoft.

When enough is not enough Probably the biggest issue we're confronted with today, in regard to extended memory, is where we're going to put all the the SIMMs (or other memory modules) we're supposedly going to need.

Supposedly, we're all going to need something like 32 megabytes of RAM and probably more not too far down the line. In fact, you'll need close to 16Mb now if you want to run Windows NT, which, at this writing, won't run successfully in less than 12 megabytes of RAM.

Even if you don't believe the predictions, historically our need for RAM has increased tenfold, on average, every four years since the PC was first introduced, which would go something like this:

1983	64K
1987	640K
1991	6400K
1995	64,000K

By 1991, 6Mb was about right for Windows in enhanced mode or to get the most out of DESQview. And halfway to the next step, 1995, we already have a Windows NT that won't run on much less than one quarter of that projected figure.

My main concern here—one I explain in more detail in chapter 5—is where you're going to put it when you have to have it. Of the three 32-bit machines in my office at this moment:

❑ One will take only 4 megabytes (already at capacity).
❑ One will take up to 16 megabytes (currently at 7 megs)
❑ One will take up to 32 megabytes (currently at 16 megs)

What that basically says is that two of the three are already obsolete, with the third one dangerously close to being so, based solely on their inability to be upgraded with sufficient RAM.

Almost from the beginning, most memory expansion boards offered a choice of either extended or expanded memory (or a mix of options that also generally included backfilling any empty address space below 640K). In fact, extended memory was available long before many of us had any way of using it.

Unfortunately, unlike the good old days when you could just plug in one or more RAM expansion cards and keep going, there are technical problems that make that option highly questionable. OS/2 2.x, for instance, doesn't take readily to RAM on expansion cards, due, apparently, to timing problems caused by the fact that expansion-card RAM runs at a much lower bus speed than motherboard RAM.

This almost seems to be an issue no one is giving serious thought to. You hardly ever see it mentioned in the computer press, and even the ads for new computers—the ones that splash their claims of having the fastest, hottest CPU chips across the pages of computer magazines in livid color. They rarely mention how much RAM the motherboard can hold. Maybe in the fine print, but never in the big banner headlines.

At this writing, motherboards that support more than 32 megabytes of RAM represent only a small fraction of those on the market, whether you're talking simply motherboards or fully assembled, off-the-shelf machines. And that says to me that either (or both) of the following are true:

❑ More than 95% of all machines in use today and a majority of those currently being manufactured are already borderline obsolete before they're even sold.

❑ Those who prophesy a mass exodus from DOS to something that takes 32 megabytes of RAM to buy into, even at the entry level, are in for a rude surprise when it doesn't happen—if only for lack of a massive installed user base that can support it.

Further complicating this situation is the fact that not all motherboards even support the larger SIMMs in use today. Many—particularly those that date to the 256K-SIMM era—will not support 4Mb SIMMs, limiting their expansion capability to 1 megabyte per SIMM socket, or only ¼ the total RAM that the same number of SIMM sockets would accommodate on most more recent boards.

Even on new machines, there is a practical limit to the number of SIMM sockets of any capacity that a motherboard will hold, short of going to higher-capacity memory modules, designing to accept a stack of daughterboards with extra socketing, or going from today's smaller boards back to bigger ones that occupy more desk space. There are clearly a number of practical considerations that must be dealt with here.

I'll look at these issues later on in other contexts. It's ironic, though, that now, several years into a generation of 32-bit processors and with the first of the 64-bit CPUs—that have the capability of handling as much as 4 gigabytes of RAM—we should find ourselves concerned with how to deal with even $\frac{1}{100}$ of that power with the hardware we have—and, for the most part, will likely be using for several years to come.

In the meantime, there's enough extended memory—or at least the socketing for enough—to run *most* of the software *most* of us are going to want to run. At least for now. As long as we keep using DOS.

8 DOS's "extra" 64K: the HMA

For a long time everybody thought DOS was strictly a one-megabyte operating system. But there's an extra 64K just above the 1Mb limit that DOS can use on 80286 and higher systems. And intriguingly, beginning with version 5.0, DOS can even load most of itself up there.

Called the *high-memory area* (HMA), this unique memory resource can be used in combination with ordinary extended memory, expanded memory, or both. Extending up as high as 1088K (11FFFh), it can be used in combination with EMS memory mapped to unused DOS address space between 640K and 1024K—and *extending* is the operative word because it's closely related to, actually created from, extended memory. But it's also quite different. See FIG. 8-1.

True, DOS can deal with only one megabyte of address space—1024 kilobytes—which is why this high-memory area is really a separate issue. It's there, though, and with a little sleight of hand you can use legitimate addresses right at its outer limit, allowing DOS to get its hook into an extra 64K block of usable DOS memory. This, of course, assumes that:

❏ There's some extra RAM available to use.
❏ That the CPU has address pins enough to deal more than 1024K of discrete addresses.

This, of course, immediately rules out the 8088 because, with only 20 address pins, an 8088 can't handle anything beyond 1024K—the same reason 8088s

8-1
The High Memory Area really belongs to extended memory, but with a little clever manipulation, the first 64K—the 64K that is contiguous to DOS—can be accessed by DOS on 80286 and higher systems.

Extended memory

64K {

HMA

← 1088K
← 1024K (1Mb)

DOS

will never be able to use extended memory, which is the memory area from which the RAM for this extra 64K segment must be drawn. Even one more address pin (and a bunch of other internal goodies an 8088 doesn't have) would allow access to this high-memory area—one more would in fact exactly double the address range if you'll recall the way it works with address pins. The first chip that meets this criteria, however, is the 80286—with not one but four more address pins.

But there's a lot more to it than just having CPUs that have the capability of reaching higher addresses because DOS really is a one-megabyte system, which is why it was a couple of years after we had the 80286 and at least some access to extended memory before anybody even found it. And, having found it, figured out a way to use it.

If you'll recall from the previous chapter, there are two ways to access extended memory: from the bottom (VDISK fashion) or from the top. At the risk of being repetitious, there's a point at which one byte is the top of DOS (FFFFh) and the very next byte—consecutive to it—is the bottom of extended memory (10000h).

With a little sleight of hand

In OS/2 or other operating systems compatible with the 8086 clan (except one-megabyte DOS look-alikes), this point would be no more noteworthy than when the odometer of your new car rolls over from 99.9 to record its first 100 miles, but to DOS it's a big deal because, in going from FFFFh to 10000h, you also add another digit. DOS wasn't written to accommodate another digit. There are ways to work around the problem, obviously, but it takes some doing.

You must look to one of the things that's peculiar—and anachronistic—about DOS: it works in terms of 64K segments, not nice, whole-program chunks. 64K segments are the biggest chunks DOS can swallow; come to the end of one segment and you have to start another, a process that follows a set of formal protocols. This is of concern more to programmers than to users—and not even so much to programmers because these details are normally all worked out when code is compiled. Segments are a very important part of the way DOS is structured, however, and, though crude and anachronistic, segmentation is the key to this extra 64K segment. Only one, though—and then only because, as rigid as this segmented structure is, somebody found a loophole.

We normally tend to think of these 64K segments as starting at addresses that are multiples of 64K, but in truth they don't have to. Like most things, DOS is full of loopholes—which is really what keeps it going. So, in actuality, all the one-megabyte limit *really* means is that you can't have a 64K code segment that doesn't start inside of 1 megabyte. Once started, the rest can sort of slop over the top if need be—almost an entire segment, in fact.

Suppose, then, you were to start a 64K segment at FFFEh, only 16 bytes short of DOS's one-megabyte limit, as shown in FIG. 8-2. Would DOS be able to deal with it? The answer, interestingly, is *yes*. Just as long as the starting address of the segment is a legitimate DOS address.

Now, as most users know, the top 64K in DOS on most machines (F000h–FFFFh) is set aside for system ROM and is off-limits. However, in an earlier chapter, I explained that at least certain parts of this region were either unused or expendable (or relocatable to some other block of addresses), and could therefore be mapped with RAM. As it turns out, a

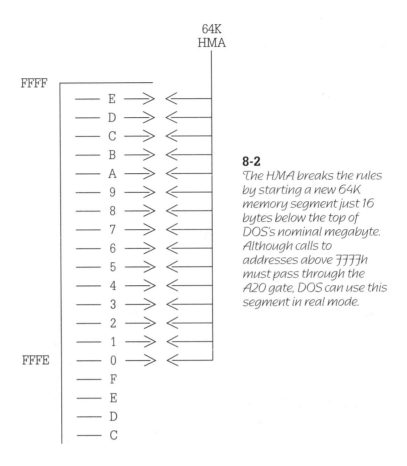

8-2
The HMA breaks the rules by starting a new 64K memory segment just 16 bytes below the top of DOS's nominal megabyte. Although calls to addresses above FFFFh must pass through the A20 gate, DOS can use this segment in real mode.

small piece right at the top of the F block isn't crucial and can be mapped and written over to provide the jumping-off place for another segment.

Of course, to access any of the data in a segment lying even partially beyond the 1Mb barrier requires not only a CPU chip that can read from and/or write to addresses beyond one megabyte, but also a set of special instructions—a superset that both is both compatible with DOS and goes beyond the 1Mb limit. The key, though, is that you've got to start this extra segment from *within* 1 megabyte.

And that, in fact, is exactly what Quarterdeck did as far back as 1986 when they were anxiously looking for someplace—anyplace—to load and run DESQview without stealing gobs of precious memory from user applications. They reasoned that if a CPU chip had more than 20 address pins (1024K) and memory with contiguous addresses beyond 1024K, it should be possible to start a 64K code segment near the top of DOS's 1Mb limit: just enough inside for DOS to get a toehold but with the rest of it—all but about 16 bytes— beyond the "limit." And they were right.

Needless to say, they jumped at it. In fact, by April of the following year (1987) they were actually shipping a special proprietary device driver for running DESQview on 286 machines called QEXT.SYS that performed this bit of "magic."

Still, it does take some doing because, if you'll recall, the 80286 and 80386 (and higher) CPU chips have something called an A20 gate to screen out dummy calls beyond 1 meg and wrap them back around to zero—as was commonly done by many programmers at one time. Every legitimate call to an address above 1 megabyte first has to open the A20 and then close the door on the way out—quietly. No crashes please.

While really quite simple, even in its original form the QEXT driver was highly effective; it made itself look like a 64K VDISK so that the memory area was reserved and other programs wouldn't use it. QEXT also kept an eye on other extended-memory functions so that if a program (like VDISK, which can coexist with QEXT) did some work with extended memory, then the A20 line wouldn't get turned off. QEXT would be active doing these things only while DESQview was running.

This, by the way, is all done without leaving real mode. Once the A20 gate is open, it's really just a matter of being able to work with addresses beyond one megabyte—addresses that require more bits than ordinary DOS software is geared to.

For a time Quarterdeck, while making no secret of it, was sole owner of this high-memory area. But not for long. A freebie like this was just too good for a lot of people to pass up. Microsoft put their oar in the water, announcing they had found an extra 64K of memory to work with when Windows 2 came out in 1988. And subsequent to that, the existence of the high-memory area was codified in the extended memory specification (XMS) released by Microsoft. Along with this, Microsoft released a rudimentary device driver very similar to DESQview's QEXT.SYS—called HIMEM.SYS, which is described as an *extended memory manager* (or an XMM).

The HMA can, of course, be used in other ways. It won't go to waste because, if we forget about it and don't otherwise exclude it from extended memory, it *is* extended memory. What sets the block apart as a unique memory resource is that you can use it for DOS without leaving DOS because, properly accessed, it belongs to DOS.

Even as first released, QEXT.SYS could load a big chunk of DESQview's code beyond 1024K. It set up a 64K code segment starting just 16 bytes inside DOS's 1Mb outer limit. That gave them almost a full 64K of extended memory, for a total of just 16 bytes shy of 1088K. With further refinement, Quarterdeck now can load over 63K of actual DESQview code up there and run with it. And to this date no one has done it better or used the HMA more effectively than Quarterdeck does with DESQview.

All that glitters . . . As a practical matter, Microsoft added nothing that wasn't already known (and, in fact, already in use) when they released the XMS specification. And DOS itself didn't formally embrace the HMA prior to the release of version 5.0. But Microsoft's acknowledgment formalized the legitimacy of the area between 1024K and 1088K as a unique memory resource. With that, a number of other software developers have released products that can reach beyond DOS's nominal limits to include a few more precious kilobytes of memory accessible directly from DOS. And the race was on, but all that glitters . . .

While the high-memory area is closely akin to IBM's VDISK in some respects, it's also quite different. In one very crucial way in particular: VDISK, like any RAM (or other virtual) disk, can hold any number of different programs or files simultaneously at any given time, up to the total of the available RAM. You can keep cramming them in until you get a DOS disk-full error message.

You can't do that with the high-memory area, however, at least not casually. Recently a way has been found to work around this problem—IBM, in fact, has implemented it in PC DOS 6, and we'll come back to that a little later in this chapter. However, to most of the world (including Microsoft, apparently) the HMA is still a one-shot deal, and for the moment I'm going to treat it as such because it's much easier to understand on those terms.

The reason we've traditionally been able to load only one program into the HMA—even if that program used only 1K and wasted the other 63K of the segment—is really quite simple: There's only one legitimate DOS starting address below 1024K (FFFFh). Following normal DOS rules, any other program loaded after that program would have to start at an address above that program (assuming it was small enough to fit in the space remaining). But that, even ignoring a couple of other DOS rules for the moment, would give that second program a starting address beyond the 1Mb DOS boundary, and you can't do that.

So as the HMA is *usually* used today, it's limited to dealing with a program (or segment) of anything up to but not exceeding 64K. This, then, becomes a replay of the problem we looked at earlier with regard to loading TSRs and device drivers into upper memory, except this time you can chose only one, and any space left over simply goes to waste.

Ideally, then, you'd want to find a program (or segment of a program) that uses right up to the 64K limit—not one byte more or less. That, of course, is highly unlikely. It's important, though, if you're going to use the high-memory area most effectively, that we load the biggest under-64K program (or divisible portion of a program) to waste as little of it as possible. And this is where *you* come in, because:

❑ As more and more software developers set greedy eyes on the HMA, several seem committed to the credo that their use of it is by some divine right more important than anyone else's, no matter how much—or how little—of it their software actually uses.

❑ Unlike upper memory, where optimizing programs can arbitrate and determine the best option for you, you're on your own here in a game akin to liar's poker.

What makes this game frustrating is the fact that the program that squeezes the biggest chunk of itself into the HMA might not actually free the most conventional memory for you. A lot depends on just what's happening in upper memory as well. Especially when dealing with larger programs—something like DESQview, for instance—and one of the slicker memory managers like QEMM386 or Helix's new Netroom 3.

The important thing to keep in mind here—as in everything else you do for the sake of DOS—is that the bottom line is conventional memory. It doesn't matter how clever you are. All that matters is how much conventional memory you manage to squeeze out. Try letting one program that wants the HMA have it and then check to see how much conventional memory you have. Then try another if you have more than one.

Ultimately, the test of how effectively your software utilizes the HMA—or any memory resource other than conventional memory—is how much space you have left over to run your applications. And beginning with version 4.01, DOS has provided a handy, easy-to-use utility called MEM.EXE to tell you just that and more, where the amount of conventional memory remaining is spelled right out.

Digging for it

Actually, the information has been available from DOS for quite a while. CHKDSK, among other things, reports the total conventional RAM on the system and how much of it is free, as shown below:

```
655328 total bytes memory
554128 bytes free
```

MEM, however, is much faster. And, when used with the optional /DEBUG switch, it provides a good deal of additional information, though more than the average user really wants or needs to know in most cases. (The /PROGRAM, or /P, switch is not supported in this latest release, but other switches have been added to give other information.)

Of course, this information is of little value unless you know how much free memory you had available before you started fiddling with the HMA. So if the HMA is enabled, you need to start off by disabling it and checking first to see how much usable free memory is available in order to gauge precisely how well any software you load up there can use it.

From that point it's just a matter of trial and error. To do it right, you have to deal with DOS about as raw and unadorned as you can make it—the easiest

way is probably from a bootable floppy with nothing in the CONFIG.SYS or
AUTOEXEC.BAT except the specific software you want to test. You can't do
this from within DESQview or Windows because a windowing environment
might mask the actual numbers, as shown here:

```
203776 bytes total conventional memory
203776 bytes available to MS-DOS
123168 largest executable program size

3047424 bytes total EMS memory
 327680 bytes free EMS memory

3407872 bytes total contiguous extended memory
      0 bytes available contiguous extended memory
 212992 bytes available XMS memory
        High Memory Area in use
```

This is an exaggerated example, but it demonstrates that the size reported
might have little to do with the actual amount of memory available.

Once you've determined which of your programs makes the best use of your
HMA, there are several possible strategies you can use to put the one you
want up there. Most programs that can use the HMA give you a yes/no
option when you install them. MS- and PC DOS (5.0 or later) will use the
HMA themselves only if you put a DOS=HIGH line in your CONFIG.SYS—
which can be the same line that specifies mapped memory if you're using
HIMEM.SYS and EMM386.EXE:

```
DOS=HIGH,UMB
```

PC DOS 6.1 and MS-DOS 6 also provide another mechanism for controlling
access to the HMA. If the HMA isn't used for the DOS kernel, you can specify
some minimum size that will prevent any program smaller than the size you
set from loading in the HMA. This size is specified in the CONFIG.SYS on the
HIMEM.SYS command line, as shown in the following:

```
DEVICE=HIMEM.SYS /hmamin=nn
```

Where *nn* is the size in kilobytes. This is probably the least effective method,
though, because, unless you know specifically what use your software could
make of the high-memory area, you don't know whether to set /hmamin= to
5 or 50K. You don't even need the /hmamin= if you take more direct means of
controlling HMA access.

Bending the rules
As mentioned earlier in this chapter, the HMA is nominally a one-shot deal.
Most books will tell you that, in fact, but there are ways to get around it.
Don't expect it to be as easy to play around with as UMBs any time soon,
though. Loading code belonging to more than one program into the HMA
requires two things:

❑ That the programs be specifically aware of each other.

❑ That they be written according to a special API developed specifically for this situation.

DOS itself is probably one of the best candidates for this treatment. Able to load something like 47K of the kernel of IBM and MS-DOS 5 into the HMA, and a pretty good piece in DOS 6, the DOS kernel by itself still doesn't fully utilize anywhere *near* the full 64K available. So using functions that aren't well known but that have been documented, IBM's PC DOS 6 has begun using some of the typical 17K left over by the kernel. Initially, they rewrote only SETVER, but there are other likely candidates, as well.

Digging a little further, I found that Digital Research's DR DOS 6 had already quietly done some pioneering work up in the HMA. And the new DOS 7 from Novell has managed even greater utilization of the HMA. In fact, in one documented case I know of, Novell's DOS 7 has used all but 700 bytes, wasting less than 1K of the 64K HMA. In that case, in addition to the kernel, DOS 7 loaded the resident code for COMMAND (COMMAND.COM), SHARE, and KEYB, as well as buffers. And they told me that NSFUNC could load there too (but not with only 700 bytes available).

This isn't that big of a deal—a few kilobytes at most—and, as with UMBs or any other memory, the size during the initialization (loading) phase cannot exceed the space available. But every little bit helps, and this is just one more indication of the extra effort both IBM and Novell have put into their latest DOS releases.

Regardless of whose DOS you're using or what version, the name of the game is to try to find whatever combination gives you the most *usable* conventional memory in which to run your applications after DOS and everything else is loaded. In the HMA, the game rules are a little different but the object is the same: whoever winds up with the most bytes wins.

9 Mapping memory to wasted address space above 640K

The 80386 brought with it more than just the power to use extended memory *as* extended memory. It had the (then) unique ability to allow memory to be mapped to any unused DOS-addressable address above 640K—even to the extent of mapping over areas that might contain system data that for one reason or another wasn't needed. This opened up a whole new area to DOS above 640K, often as much as 200K or more that DOS could use for loading TSRs, device drivers, etc. This, in turn, freed the space they otherwise would have occupied down in conventional memory for use by applications.

Technology moves in mysterious ways, often in fits and starts. And nowhere is that more evident than in this area. After an initial spurt, triggered by the popularization of the 80386, the technology pretty much leveled off to use this area, which was dominated by a couple of third-party developers. Now, suddenly, there has been a new spate of activity with a number of other players coming into the game—most notably the DOS boys themselves (albeit with licensed technology). And suddenly some new technology has now emerged as well, making this probably the most exciting—and dynamic—area in DOS-related technology today.

There are a number of problems inherent in trying to work with DOS-accessible address space above 640K. For one thing, it's usually fragmented, and as such difficult to use effectively. The problem is further complicated by the fact that many TSRs and device drivers that would *logically* seem like ideal candidates to load in blocks of memory above 640K behave rather badly when you try, often refusing to load at all.

Still, it takes little imagination to see the import of being able to migrate TSRs, device drivers, and such to above 640K if you can overcome the obstacles. On a typical system, after loading DOS—just DOS, no TSRs, drivers, or other extras—you'll most likely have something on the order of 600K left. Decrease that by, say, 200K of device drivers and TSRs (not an unrealistic number), and you've got maybe something like 400K left to run your DOS applications. Now, if you could relocate all 200K of extras *above* 640K, you would actually be increasing the amount of conventional memory available to DOS applications by a whopping 50%!

Ridiculous? Not by a long shot. In fact, even going back several years to a time when such performance was much harder to achieve than it is today, I often had more than 200K of address space above 640K in use—and that without even trampling on the EMS page frame. The often badly fragmented bits and pieces of unused DOS address space above 640K are, in fact, some of the most valuable real estate your system possesses: byte for byte, a hundred, possibly thousand times more valuable than even extended memory. It's so valuable because, unlike extended or expanded memory, there's only so much space available.

And yet, as important as this upper-memory area is in DOS, it's probably one of the most underutilized resources there is, in part because many users still don't fully understand how different using UMBs (memory mapped to upper-memory blocks) can be. And probably also because, until quite recently (prior to the release of MS- and PC DOS 6 and Novel DOS 7), there was really no practical way to use this area except by using one of the better third-party memory managers, most notably Quarterdeck's QEMM386 and Qualitas's 386max (and BlueMAX for PS/2).

Let me clarify a point here. Beginning with DOS 5x, both MS-DOS and PC DOS provided the basic tools not only for mapping memory to unused address space above 640K, but for relocating TSRs and device drivers there as well. In fact, in the 2nd edition of this book I demonstrated that (at that time) I could pretty much duplicate results obtained with either QEMM386 or 386max using DOS's HIMEM.SYS and EMM386.EXE (and their equivalent in DR DOS 6.0). However, as I also pointed out, the tools DOS provided were extremely crude and of little use to anyone except the occasional power user.

With the release of these new DOSs and the sudden (in my opinion) emergence of Netroom (Helix Software) as one of the most powerful memory managers to date, plus a couple other third-party memory managers that would have been dynamite a year or so earlier, the situation has changed— not only rapidly but drastically. Now it's a game almost anyone can play, and so easily. Where previously only QEMM386 and 386max/BlueMAX (and a couple of lesser memory managers) provided a means of automating the process of memory mapping and figuring out how best to use whatever memory they mapped, now almost everyone has optimizing programs that can do it automatically. Even DOS, beginning with this latest round of new releases.

Some of the software technology for memory mapping has even trickled down to 286s and, to some extent, even to 8088s. (We'll look at some of these issues later in this chapter.) For the most part, however, mapped memory is the domain of 386 and higher systems. The rules don't change on lesser systems, but the numbers do.

386 and higher systems more readily support the use of mapped memory and the technology is more readily available from more sources, so I'll concentrate on those systems. Later in this chapter, though, I'll look at the options available for and the feasibility of mapping memory to upper address space on 80286 and 8088 systems as well.

The mechanics

As originally implemented, the ability to map memory was (typically) a function of EMS 4.0 memory managers such as earlier versions of Quarterdeck's QEMM386. Because of this and the fact that strictly XMS (extended memory) drivers such as HIMEM.SYS don't support memory mapping (except with the aid of an 4.0 EMS emulator such as EMM386.EXE), there's a common misconception that the memory used for mapping can be drawn only from expanded memory. This is not so.

RAM is RAM, and the memory for mapping can be drawn from any pool of managed memory, provided the memory manager itself is endowed with the necessary capabilities. In fact, the trend, increasingly, is to throw all memory beyond 640K into a common pool at system startup, drawing as needed from that pool and then manipulating, mapping, or otherwise managing whatever memory is drawn to present it to the system in whatever form is required.

The bottom line is that there's nothing that says you have to start with extended or expanded memory. All that's required is memory of some sort outside of DOS's one megabyte and a means to manage it in such a way that at least a portion of it can be mapped to unused address space.

The concept of memory mapping has been around for quite a while, but yet few users understand just what it is or how it works. It's relatively easy to understand the concept of specific bits of memory having specific addresses when RAM is plugged into the motherboard—essentially hard-wired to address pins on the CPU. Figure 2-2 back in chapter 2 shows the relationship between between specific address pins and specific addresses in low (conventional) memory—in this case, I've shown expanded memory being used, but as mentioned above it can be—and today more often is—extended or "pooled" memory.

Somewhere, typically just above 640K, there's a block of addresses used for video, so these address pins, rather than going to user RAM, are normally reserved (they connect via the bus to the monitor card). As a general rule, you can't map memory to any of those addresses because they're in use—or at least there's an *assumption* that they are.

As most users probably know, however, in many cases they aren't. In almost any character-based color video mode, for instance, the first 64K of the video area (A000h to B000h) is in fact not used and can be mapped as additional conventional RAM (contiguous to 640K) by any of the better memory managers like QEMM386 or 386MAX.

But note that up near the top in FIG. 2-2 are some address pins that just dead-end. These are empty addresses that are like empty lots in a housing development. Empty lots have addresses, and so do unused address pins on CPUs. In either case you can send mail or messages; just don't expect anyone to pick them up.

Figure 9-1 shows two more elements: unassigned or free memory and a memory-management module. Assuming that the memory manager has already figured out which addresses are unused and available, it adopts those orphan address pins and acts something like a switchboard, intercepting any calls sent to those addresses and redirecting them to specific places somewhere in the pool of memory *it* owns.

A party of volunteers On 386 systems, memory mapping is like an electronic muster. The memory manager—the boss—looks the situation over and says something like "Okay number 4C000h (something up in the 4- to 5Mb range, for example), you and your group report for duty at B400h . . ." And for the remainder of that work session, 4C000h will answer every call the CPU makes to B400h, 4C001h will answer for B401h, and so forth.

The group you're dealing with here is typically 4096 bytes (4K), which is about the smallest block of unused (or reusable) addresses it's practical to work with.

DOS, through all of this, knows nothing about 4C000h and friends—it can't even count that high. Only the memory manager knows. It doesn't matter, though, as long as something *somewhere* picks up and answers all the mail to those addresses.

This mapping of memory to high DOS (UMB) addresses differs significantly from the manner other memory is managed, the difference being that once mapped those memory assignments generally remain fixed until the machine is powered down or rebooted. The physical memory addressed normally doesn't change, as it did through the page frame that came with LIM 3.2 EMS. In fact, when using expanded memory, these assignments don't

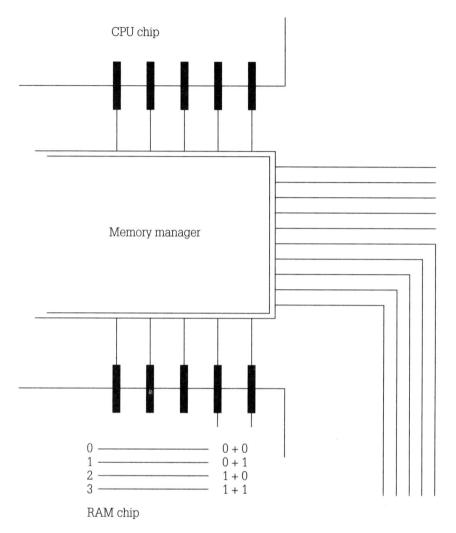

CPU chip

Memory manager

9-1
This illustration is similar to 9-1 except that the direct link between the CPU and RAM chip address pins has been broken and a memory manager inserted. The memory manager intercepts calls and reroutes them to different locations.

```
0 ─────────── 0 + 0
1 ─────────── 0 + 1
2 ─────────── 1 + 0
3 ─────────── 1 + 1
```

RAM chip

change even when bank-switching entire applications and their data in and out when multitasking. If they did—and if you bank-switched this upper memory as well—you'd have to reload any device drivers or TSRs you might need for each application running, neither a practical nor particularly workable solution. (Windows 3.0 does, in fact, support a feature that allows each window to have its own copy of customizing drivers, such as ANSI.SYS. Use of this feature is currently supported by both QEMM and 386MAX.)

Once those assignments are made (at the time the memory manager is installed from the CONFIG.SYS during bootup), they remain in effect until the system is rebooted. Unlike the memory used by applications—memory that can be returned to the pool when the application is terminated—mapped memory cannot be released back to the pool. It isn't and cannot be released even if you terminate, dump, or otherwise unload any TSRs or drivers you have loaded there. Once mapped, it remains mapped for the duration of the session.

However, this is the memory manager's and not the CPU's jurisdiction. The same actual physical bit of memory might well be repeatedly assigned to take calls to the same address. That is to say that the memory manager might well assign the same exact bytes to the same task (or map them to the same DOS addresses) consistently at boot time. But change any value on the CONFIG.SYS line that loads the memory-management device driver and the map determining who answers what will also change at the next reboot—and then perhaps continue to reboot that way until you make another change. This is unlike the old hard-wired way, where the pin x always connected to point y or to nothing at all.

Still, managing all those other addresses does require some very different management techniques. And HIMEM.SYS and its companion EMS emulator, EMM386.EXE, had the mapping capability in DOS 5x (as did DR DOS)—though few in their right mind would probably have bothered. There were two problems:

❑ The real key to using upper memory (even assuming you have enough to go around) was figuring out not only which TSRs/drivers could be loaded where, but what sequence must be observed.
❑ By default, the HIMEM.SYS/EMM386.EXE duo (and DR DOS equivalents) were overly timid, usually wasting as much mappable address space as they managed to use.

There is a lot more to this, however, than meets the eye. On both counts, in fact, which is why, prior to this latest round of DOS releases, some of the better third-party memory managers effectively had a monopoly on upper memory. One of the biggest problems—even bigger than the problem of fragmentation—still assuming proper programming that would allow device drivers and TSRs to run properly in upper memory, is the fact that upper memory is usually so badly fragmented.

Fragmentation   Complicating the task of relocating TSRs in upper memory is the fact that, unlike old familiar 640K, the memory mapped above 640K is often fragmented into bits and pieces. This is something you can see especially with some of the more powerful memory managers that are more aggressive in seeking out space that can be mapped. MS-DOS's HIMEM.SYS pretty much gives you just a single block of upper memory to work with, as shown in the following:

```
EMM386 successfully installed

    Available expanded memory . . . . . . . . 64 KB

    LIM/EMS version . . . . . . . . . . . . . 4.0
    Total expanded memory pages . . . . . . . 28
    Available expanded memory pages . . . . . 4
```

```
Total handles . . . . . . . . . . . . . .  64
Active handles  . . . . . . . . . . . . .  1
Page frame segment  . . . . . . . . . . .  E000 H

Total upper memory available  . . . . . .  75 KB
Largest Upper Memory Block available  . .  75 KB
Upper memory starting address . . . . . .  CD00 H
```

EMM386 Active

MS-DOS's EMM386.EXE also isn't very aggressive when it comes to finding mappable address space. Here, in fairly typical installation, only one 75K block has been found where in fact several mappable blocks exist.

On the same machine, any of the more aggressive memory managers would probably come up with at least three mappable areas, the others not generally as large, but probably big enough to be of some use in this game where every byte you relocate counts. There are, in fact, several usable blocks (minimum usable size is usually 4K) scattered around the high DOS area, including usually as much as 16K of ROM—often more—that can be mapped over if you know what you're doing.

So let's say you can pick up an additional 32K by mapping a piece of the video address space most VGAs don't use (B000h-B7FFh) and maybe another 16K in the ROM region by mapping over ROM BIOS functions that (typically) are used only at boot time. Add those to the 75K (32+16+75), and you get a total of 123K (not including an EMS page frame if you use extended memory).

There are typically some smaller bits and pieces tucked away up there that you could map as well, but keep in mind that, although this memory isn't contiguous to 640K (and therefore not part of conventional memory), no TSR or device driver can be loaded into memory that isn't in itself contiguous. That is to say you can't load part of one into a 32K piece and part someplace else. There are exceptions. DESQview, for example, owing to its size, is written to allow for bits and pieces to be broken off and scattered if need be.

If you look at memory fragmentation in the context of the overall picture, it's really pretty easy to see how we got into this whole mess to begin with. The creators of the original PC fragmented the megabyte they had to work with the day someone plopped the video at A000h, leaving us a 640K fragment to work with. Now we're working with the crumbs and the more you need the smaller you have to settle for. But the rules are still the same: you can load a program into contiguous memory unless the program itself specifically allows for fragmentation. DESQview, for instance, since 1985 has been written specifically to allow for the use of discontiguous areas to maximize the use of available resources.

To illustrate the point, I've taken a partial list of programs actually loaded successfully above 640K on a working system:

Program	Space
Squish	18.0
Superpck	20.0
Packrmd	2.7
Mode	0.5
Map	10.0

Here are 51.2K of assorted drivers and TSRs—clearly more than most of us could afford space for in conventional memory. Assume for the moment you have just 52K of recoverable address space in the high DOS area with RAM mapped to it.

Easy, right?—except let's say that high memory is fragmented. You've got one 20K block squeezed in between VGA graphics and text, and the other 32K up just underneath the 64K EMS page frame. While, to keep the example fairly obvious and simple, I've changed the sizes of the blocks, these particular locations correlate with high-memory blocks in an actual system. In the system the data was gathered from, the actual size of the lowest two blocks was actually 32K and 96K, respectively.

They *should* all fit, but let's see what happens. Three of the five files listed are device drivers loaded from CONFIG.SYS: PACKRAMD.SYS, MAP.SYS, and SQPLUS.SYS. PACKRAMD, a RAM disk driver, was already in use when the others were added to the system, so they were just tacked on to the end of the CONFIG.SYS. That means they're going to settle in before the system even looks to AUTOEXEC.BAT for whatever else you want to load up there, including that 20K piece of SUPERPCK.COM that has to be loaded somewhere for PCKRAMD to work.

Even at a glance, you can see if you let that 2.7K load first and pick its spot in the lower 20K block there won't be room for either of the 18–20K chunks. At least one of them *must* load into that 20K for everything to fit.

Okay, what about juggling things so the 18K loads first into the lower block? Still no good. MODE is the only other one you could fit, leaving 32.7 to try to squeeze into a 32K parking space. In fact, if you just let nature take its course, you probably wouldn't have space to fit that 20K piece up high at all. Period. So, as you can see from FIG. 9-2, even with HMA space to spare, you could easily wind up wasting 20K of conventional memory.

However, even bigger than the problem of fragmentation—still assuming proper programming that would allow device drivers and TSRs to run properly in upper memory—they rarely behave the way you might expect.

Bigger than life One of the biggest problems users encounter when trying to load TSRs and device drivers into UMBs is that there's no correlation between the size of the

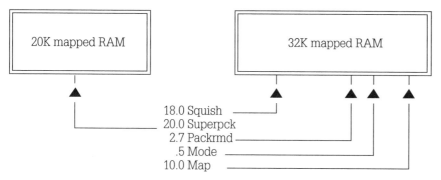

9-2
The loading order of blocks can affect how programs fit (or don't fit) into memory.

18.0 Squish
20.0 Superpck
2.7 Packrmd
.5 Mode
10.0 Map

original file—or even the amount of memory the program requires once it's loaded—and the size of the smallest block it can be loaded into. This fact in itself accounts for the reason that, prior to this latest round of new DOS releases, efficient utilization of upper memory was really possible only with third-party memory managers. Until recently, *only* third-party memory managers have had the capability of dealing with this problem.

For example, take a DOS utility like FASTOPEN, which, typically weighing in with a file size of something over 11K, is a real classic. Eleven kilobytes isn't that hard to come by usually, even as badly fragmented as upper memory tends to be. However, the fact is that in certain DOS releases FASTOPEN required as much as 68K of contiguous RAM to initialize, while in fact needing only a modest 3K to run—a discrepancy that borders on the obscene. Nor is this even an extreme example. In fact, as shown here for several actual drivers, this kind of behavior is more the rule than the exception:

Final size	Maximum size
44,960	44,960
2752	11,104
5040	62,784
1824	21,616

And it isn't predictable. The only way to determine exactly how much memory it's going to take to load any given TSR or driver anywhere in memory is to somehow trap the system at that crucial moment and measure just how much memory was required. This, of course, is something few of us have the means of doing, which, until now, has left us with only two alternatives:

❑ Blindly throw things at upper memory, seeing what sticks and what doesn't, and trying different combinations until you find one you can live with—which sometimes works if you have only one or two things to relocate to upper memory.
❑ Abandon whatever memory manager came with DOS in favor of one of the third-party memory managers that, though not necessarily more powerful,

at least have the ability to actually make the crucial measurements, analyze them, and work out a combination of upper and conventional memory usage and a loading sequence that best utilizes whatever resources are available.

And it wasn't even that the technology to do it was all that exotic. It was just that no one—Microsoft or IBM or Novell—even bothered. This was strictly power-user stuff.

Boot & reboot   None of the optimizing software that can analyze your upper-memory resources and the TSRs and drivers that you normally use is smart enough to simply look at a file and anticipate the space it's going to need—no more than you and I could. They all must initially reboot your system and measure and observe the way the various programs you've listed in your CONFIG.SYS and AUTOEXEC.BAT file behave when loading. They do have the advantage of being able to record the maximum amount of RAM each needs, particularly during that crucial initialization phase. But they have to do it to see it.

Given that raw data, they then do what computers do best; they run mathematical simulations of all of the possible combinations to see what fits, where the best offloads the greatest amount of overhead to upper memory. Depending on how badly the upper memory on your machine is fragmented and how many TSRs and drivers are in contention, the number of possibilities can range from only a handful into the millions (62.5 million on one of my machines). This is why truly efficient use of upper memory can be accomplished *only* by means of special optimizing software—software separate from the memory manager itself, software that once was found exclusively in third-party memory-management packages but now is offered in DOS as well.

Having done the analysis and examined all the mathematical probabilities, there are still two more steps to the process however. The first of these is to modify the CONFIG.SYS and AUTOEXEC.BAT entries so that when the system is rebooted programs will actually be loaded into upper memory. Typically, a line that started out as something like this:

```
DEVICE C:\DOS\WHATZIT.SYS
```

will end up as something like this:

```
DEVICE=C:\DOS\QEMM\LOADHI.SYS /R:2 C:\DOS\WHATZIT.SYS
```

Normally, this is the end of the process, but to be sure that what looked good mathematically really works in practice, optimizing programs usually leave themselves a back door, letting you have your original configuration back if everything doesn't work properly.

Note, though, that optimizing software works exclusively with upper memory. It doesn't have anything to do with the HMA—it doesn't even know there is such a thing. However, as you saw in the last chapter, the issues there are much less complex and more easily dealt with anyway.

Long before DOS even thought of giving us the tools to use whatever scraps of address space we had above 640K effectively, it became increasingly clear it wasn't going to be enough. Not only was there the problem of things often taking so much more space to set themselves up in, but there were more and more things clamoring for space up there. How to get it, though . . . Driven by this need, different third-party developers began exploring new techniques, not only for getting more but for using what there was to better advantage.

Puzzles with different pieces

In the "getting more" department, Quarterdeck and Qualitas got more aggressive, going after bits and pieces of the ROM space no one really needed once the system booted. Qualitas got real aggressive with the ROM—on PS/2s especially—shrinking the 128K ROM that IBM had used on them to something under 64K.

And there was some video address space—typically the 32K between B000h and B7FFh—that most often wasn't really being used by the video. A couple of developers even tried revectoring the video to get it out of the way, but most of those efforts proved unworkable in the real world.

Qualitas, then, figured out a way to "borrow" the 64K page frame while the system was initializing, giving them an extra 64K for rambunctious TSRs like FASTOPEN to thrash around in while they loaded, but returning the space for use as an EMS page frame once that was done (and before a page frame might be needed). This is what 386max's FlexFrame is all about.

Quarterdeck took a different tack, developing something called Stealth, which put the page frame almost right on top of the system ROM, leaving just a piece of it peeking out at the top. They watched for any calls to BIOS areas they'd mapped over and held them at bay until they could swap the page frame out of the way for them.

Most recently, Helix has come along with Netroom 3, which basically says "nuts" to all this, loads it own replacement BIOS up into extended memory to give the biggest block of contiguous usable upper memory yet on many if not most machines—and, as if that weren't enough, can create a virtual machine to hold even more stuff (networking).

I'll look at these various strategies in some depth in the next section of the book, where I examine the relative merits of each of the more successful memory managers. Clearly, though, we've come a long way, and there's much more to the story than just picking at the bits and scraps of address space wasted up there.

Not just for 386 & higher systems The 32-bit chips (and 64-bit Pentiums) descended from the 8086 have some unique design properties that facilitate memory mapping. This has led many users to believe that mapping is possible only on 32-bit systems. In point of fact, it's possible on lesser systems—even, in fact, on 8088s. On lower systems, however, special memory management is required and, even with that, the amount of address space that can be mapped is significantly less, typically no more than 64K.

There are exceptions, however. All Computers, Inc., a Toronto-based company, developed a device called the ChargeCard, which, installed on 80286 machines, adds external hardware support to the 80286 chip that is, in many ways, remarkably similar to that intrinsic in 32-bit chips (see more detailed discussion in chapter 5). The ChargeCard, it should be pointed out, is not an accelerator card in the usual sense since the original 80286 CPU chip is reused. In the case of most accelerator cards, the original CPU chip is actually replaced with (typically) a 32-bit chip and whatever additional support chips are required.

The ChargeCard has been highly successful. In some cases, software that won't run on ordinary 80286 machines will run on ChargeCard-equipped machines—one of which has been in service in my office now for several years.

Comparable devices have, at various times, been marketed for 8088 machines, but they've pretty much all fallen by the wayside at this juncture—as have most other vendors who, over the years, have marketed 80286 upgrade products that were functionally similar to the ChargeCard. They're still selling ChargeCards, though.

And as memory-management techniques have become more sophisticated, several of the more powerful third-party contenders have developed support for mapped memory on 8088 and 80286 machines that required no special added hardware.

Qualitas was one of the first with a product called Move'm, later (and currently) including that capability in their 386max packages. Quarterdeck quickly followed with QRAM. But typically these were hardware dependent, their use limited to machines designed around specific top-of-the-line auxiliary chip sets such as C&T's Neat chip set. Quadtel (now part of Phoenix) used their BIOS experience to support a number of other chip sets in a memory manager they called QMAPS.

Now IBM has gotten into the act as well, jumping in with both feet to offer upper-memory support even for 8088s, with a choice of four brand-new IBM-developed proprietary drivers, included in IBM's PC DOS 6.1—an area both Microsoft and, to an even greater extent, Novell have pretty much ignored.

There are some distinct limitations when it comes to mapping upper memory on 8088 and 80286 machines (with the exception of those equipped with All

ChargeCards or some other add-in hardware support device. Typically, upper-memory use is limited to no more than 64K—which usually amounts to a little less than 64K after loading the necessary driver.

Probably the most damning limitation to using upper memory on 8088s and 286s, however, is the fact that it normally requires most of the address block the EMS page frame requires when EMS memory is enabled. This, then, pretty much makes it an either/or situation, with the user having to choose either expanded memory—up to 32 megabytes—or upper memory. On a 286, any memory not used for mapping can be used as extended memory, of course, but on an 8088 it can be a tough call.

The whole purpose of this exercise, of course, is to increase the amount of conventional memory you have to run your application software. The first few chunks usually come pretty easily, but if you pursue the quest beyond those first few easy pieces you can run into a situation where the more you succeed in moving things high the less you have to show for it. Not less in the literal sense (hopefully) but in the sense that moving one or more additional TSRs up high might not give you even one more byte of memory.

It went where?

The same forces are at work whenever you relocate anything into upper memory—for instance, the 23K you move gives you only 16K of free conventional memory. A good deal probably, but where'd it go?

Numbers lie. Actually, it isn't the numbers that lie. It's that the rules in upper memory are different. Earlier, I mentioned that 4K was the smallest block size usable in upper memory for most purposes. If you have six contiguous 4K blocks, assuming no loading peculiarities, that will do it.

Down in conventional memory, you don't work with 4K blocks; 16K is a block size more commonly used there, but then when you're reduced to eating crumbs you have to lower standards. Programs can overlap those 16K boundaries and sometimes even share. So depending on where the break point falls, you might actually free only one 16K block with such a move. On the other hand, you might free two and wind up gaining 32K of usable space. In fact, in one extraordinary case I gained 32K of extra conventional memory by moving only 9K.

Even knowing this, it can get really frustrating trying to free up even one more block that you can use down low. Sometimes you can keep cramming more and more into upper memory without gaining even one more byte of usable conventional memory—I've been there. But then suddenly all kinds of neat stuff starts to happen—and at least in *this* game, unlike others, if you keep playing long enough and hard enough it *will* pay off. In any case, it's important to remember that it isn't what you load up high that counts. What matters is how big a chunk you've got down low to load your applications, and if you ever have to make a choice because you can't fit everything upstairs, go for the combination that leaves the most for you to use in conventional memory because that's what it's all about.

Stealing another 64K—maybe even 96K

Users working with only character-based applications can usually add an extra 64K, and up to as much as 96K, to conventional memory by using still one more trick some of the better memory managers have up their sleeves. And this is not limited just to 386s. You can do it with 286s, and even 8088s. And now with the most recent releases of QEMM, 386max and Netroom you can pass this benefit to text-based programs running under Windows as well—even though Windows itself has to have the video graphics area free.

The truth is that many—if not most—of us (other than Windows users) actually waste most of the address space normally reserved for video use. For character-based screens, we actually need only a few K, the remainder needed only when we venture off into some graphical environment.

It turns out that the little memory the video system needs even with EGA and VGA is somewhere in the B region, leaving at least the entire A000h-AFFFh 64K segment—contiguous to the legendary 640K—unused. And, if you'll recall from an earlier discussion, any block of free memory that's contiguous to the 640K of conventional memory can be added directly to it—it's only when you break the continuity that DOS has to put on the brakes. DOS can't normally use this space for anything but video graphics, but with mappable memory it's mainly just a matter of taking down the signs and letting DOS move in— right on up to B7FFh with an EGA or VGA, for a whopping 96K gain.

And this, let me repeat, is additional *conventional* memory for running more and bigger applications, bigger spreadsheets, more word-processing documents—all into RAM in one gulp. And you *still* have the HMA and every byte of memory you've mapped as upper-memory blocks above the video.

This, of course, is the same bonus memory I mentioned in an early chapter in conjunction with using CGA displays. In that context, a few vendors made it available to users, and others—most—didn't. Then with EGAs and VGAs, everyone pretty much forgot about it. If you treat your EGA/VGA like a CGA, the extra RAM is still there, though—but with the vastly better screen resolution you paid for when you bought the better monitors. Sort of like having your cake and eating it too.

Raw numbers don't always tell the story

A couple of interesting things happen when you map the video area with RAM, and the numbers often don't tell the real story. For one thing, if you map the standard VGA graphics area right on up as far as you dare go (A000h-B7FFh) as conventional memory, you're really not gaining 96K in total usable address space. Not if you were optimally configured before you started with B000h-B7FFh (not normally used by VGA graphics) mapped anyway. You might be adding 96K to conventional memory in this scenario, but at the cost of a 32K block of upper memory. That makes the net gain 64K.

The loss of 32K of upper memory likely means something you would otherwise have been able to load in upper memory suddenly gets bounced back down to conventional memory, but you can be sure the size of whatever gets kicked back down will total less than 32K, so you're bound to be ahead of the game no matter what. And the fact that you're now working with 736K of *contiguous* memory rather than 640K plus bits and pieces means that whatever gets moved down will likely load more efficiently. I have, in fact, on occasion been able to move programs that were occupying 128K or more of UMBs back down into a 736K block of conventional memory and *still* had more room left to run my applications than before I mapped the video region.

Again—and I keep coming back to it, but it's so important—there is really only one number that really matters here, and that's how much you have left to run your programs when you're done. If it takes a juggle like this to do it—and if you can get by with it—go for it.

There are, I've found, a very few character-based programs that seem to take exception to this incursion. And also the BIOS used by some computers makes assumptions about the use of the A000h to AFFFh area that make it impossible for most memory managers to map this region properly. Fortunately, most programs and BIOSs could care less, but it's something to file away in the back of your mind in case your display suddenly goes bonkers when you try to load something.

There *is* one catch, though. Once you map video graphics space as RAM, you can't change your mind in mid-session. With rare exception, once you map the video graphics space, you can't, for instance, start a Windows session at that point. Nor can you close a Windows session and then map the graphics address space with RAM. Whatever condition you establish at boot time can be changed only by rebooting the system, using the new multiple configurations or on-the-fly configuration capabilities to change it. 386max 7 is an exception to the extent that it allows the video space on DOS virtual machines running under Windows (enhanced mode) to be mapped when running character-based applications on the virtual machines. Overall, however, the rules still apply.

Clearly, though, there are many ways you can enhance the performance of your system with judicious use of upper memory. These are only a few. It's ironic, however, in this day of megabytes and gigabytes that an area no more than 384K at the very most should play so crucial a role.

10 Expanded memory: something for everyone

While much of its original luster has dulled, with most of the emphasis today moved to the arena of extended memory, expanded memory was the first glimpse any of us had of life beyond 640K. It remains—and will continue to remain—the only form of added memory available to *all* DOS users, regardless of the hardware platform they're working from, whether one of the original IBM PCs or the latest, hottest Pentium. (8088 and 80286 machines generally require the use of add-in EMS boards or some other supporting hardware.)

Today expanded memory has largely been eclipsed, with developers of larger applications generally opting for extended memory instead. But expanded memory will continue to play an important role as long as there is DOS, for three reasons:

❏ You can have expanded memory on any machine opening up a far larger potential market to software developers than is available for any hardware-specific products.
❏ Under the LIM 4.0 EMS specification, memory from the same memory pool can be used to backfill conventional memory address space (essential for true multitasking on 8088 machines).
❏ 4.0 EMS memory (3.2 EMS with PCDOS 6) can also, with proper management, be mapped to upper-memory blocks on 386 and higher machines, allowing that space to be used to load device drivers and TSRs to free the space they would otherwise occupy down low for use by applications.

These three functions, while all initially founded on the use of EMS memory, are conceptually created to fill different needs. (Memory-management techniques have evolved now to a point where it's no longer necessary to use EMS memory for mapping, though in practice it's still commonly done that way.) In this chapter, we'll look primarily at expanded memory as it was originally intended and is in fact still most commonly used by virtue of the fact that it's essentially independent of the hardware base, offering much the same advantage to the 8088 user as the proud owner of a Pentium.

To appreciate not only the origins of expanded memory but its continuing importance to a large part of the DOS community, however, we should start at the beginning.

In the beginning

Lotus was one of the prime movers behind the introduction of expanded memory to the DOS arena. They were responding to pressure from users unable to live and work with larger Lotus spreadsheets within the 640K memory model DOS allowed. The problem was not a lack of space to run their program code. The problem was insufficient space for storing data.

This point is crucial because it was the pivotal issue, from which the entire technology eventually evolved. The original issue was simply space to store data temporarily when not actually being used—whatever portion of a (then exclusively) Lotus spreadsheet wasn't currently being worked on. The thought of running programs in the background or any of the other functions we associate with EMS memory today never entered into it. It was initially intended as a cheap-and-dirty fix for an immediate problem. Nothing more.

The original expanded memory scheme, borrowing a bit of technology from mainframes—bank switching—was designed to allow users to access up to 8 megabytes. In practice, that proved overly optimistic. Few were able to achieve nearly as much that was actually usable—but then, at the time there were only a small handful who needed even half of that amount, so hardly anybody noticed. And with that Lotus, Intel, and Microsoft sat down and wrote a formal specification to define it.

Figure 1-3 back in chapter 1 shows expanded memory as it was originally configured, making small portions of as much as a possible 8 megabytes accessible through a 64K page frame on a revolving access basis managed by an expanded memory manager.

Like a lazy Susan

In chapter 7, I explained extended memory as being analogous to a hundred-story elevator in a 16-story building: right up through the roof. By contrast, expanded memory can probably be best compared to something like a lazy Susan on a dinner table. While the analogy is flawed in that no physical motion is involved, I think it's close enough to serve our purposes.

So imagine yourself at a table with a huge lazy Susan in the middle. The olives and cranberry sauce are in front of you, and the turkey is out of reach at the far side. You spin the lazy Susan and spear a piece of turkey with your fork. The olives and the cranberry sauce are still there on the lazy Susan even though they're currently out of reach. When you want them back, however, all you have to do is spin the lazy Susan until they're back in front of you.

Adding more expanded memory, then, is like building a bigger lazy Susan; the bigger it is, the more goodies you can pile on and bring spinning within arm's reach. With a little practice, even a blind man could find what he was looking for as long as everything was always in the same place on the merry-go-round.

Of course, given even the obvious loading options expanded memory opens up—multiple applications, not always the same set in the same sequence, and certainly not always with the same data files open—it really doesn't matter where things were stuffed during yesterday's work session. Or even where they are this minute as long as someone or some *thing*—some form of memory manager—knows where they are and can bring them back into some sort of a frame where DOS can see them.

This frame—sort of like having to reach through a croquet hoop to get at something on the lazy Susan—is called a *page frame*. In the case of expanded memory, the frame is simply a block of DOS-accessible addresses above 640K, which, in order to be accessed through DOS, must be below 1024K. The high-memory area (HMA) between 1024K and 1088K, discussed earlier in this book, does not violate this rule, but is a special case.

DOS, historically and for reasons that are no longer really valid or important here (they were not even valid at the time DOS was written and are in fact responsible for many of DOS's shortcomings), is generally broken into 64K segments: ten for us (0h through 9h) and six for the system (Ah through Fh). Not surprisingly, then, the block generally allocated as the page frame, as the window to expanded memory, is a 64K block.

As you can see from FIG. 10-1, there were blocks beginning at C000h D000h and E000h under the 3.2 specification. Referring to FIG. 10-2, note that the 64K block or frame is broken down still farther into something called *logical pages*, with each page containing 16K—four pages to the frame.

The page-frame base address doesn't have to be multiples of 64K, but rather can fall at multiples of 16K, using any 16K block of addresses above 640 not occupied by ROM or RAM. That actual physical block of memory the CPU "sees" at those addresses can, in fact, be anywhere in the up to 32 megabytes of actual installed and addressable RAM chips that expanded memory allows (now under 4.0 EMS).

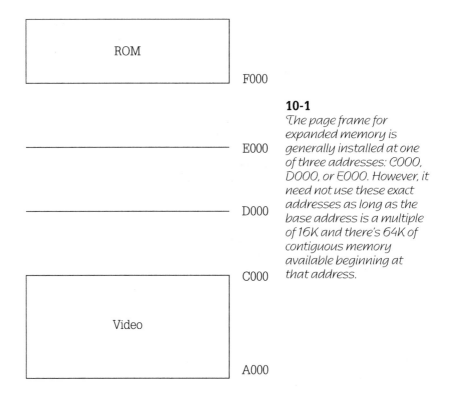

ROM

F000

E000

D000

C000

Video

A000

10-1
The page frame for expanded memory is generally installed at one of three addresses: C000, D000, or E000. However, it need not use these exact addresses as long as the base address is a multiple of 16K and there's 64K of contiguous memory available beginning at that address.

No matter where the memory is actually located, DOS sees only calls to legitimate DOS addresses when you try to access it. Just ordinary calls to very ordinary addresses between C000h and EFFFh. Some device, then—some form of memory manager—must in effect spin the lazy Susan to bring the actual block of memory that's called for back into the page frame. Having done its job, the EMM drops out of the picture until the next time it has to spin the lazy Susan.

Remember, no actual physical motion has taken place. It's an illusion in much the same way as call forwarding can intercept calls incoming to your home or office and invisibly reroute them to you, no matter where you are. All that matters is that information is exchanged and everybody (hopefully) is happy.

To Lotus users, this meant they could—at least theoretically—have incredibly *huge* spreadsheets, spreadsheets requiring several megabytes of data space. With larger spreadsheets you're usually working only with small portions at any given time anyway, and for such applications a page frame that allows for ready access to any selected part or parts of the data on a rotating basis is often all that's really needed.

This isn't to say that this is the ideal way to do it. All this juggling takes time. Ideal wasn't the issue, though—just the ability to do it. And expanded memory could do it. So as originally defined, expanded memory was intended

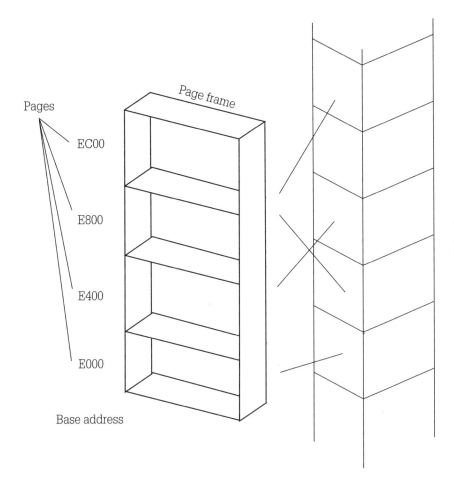

Pages

EC00

E800

E400

E000

Page frame

Base address

10-2
*This page frame is divided
into four 16K logical pages,
where the base address for
the frame is E000.*

solely to increase the memory available for an application's data space. The original 3.0 specification left much to be desired and was soon modified, and there was a short-lived 3.1 that included some additional features Lotus needed. A 3.2 EMS specification then emerged, taking some of the rough edges off of the earlier specs but adding little more.

When and how you use EMS expanded memory depends on several factors. The use of EMS memory to backfill conventional address space is completely invisible to software. However, when you move out of the conventional memory area to dip into the memory pool available through the page frame, it's a different world.

*Using
expanded memory*

Just because you add EMS memory to your machine doesn't mean any of your favorite programs are going to use it. These days, the odds are fairly good—but in many cases only if you have one of the later releases.

The use of any managed EMS memory other than to backfill conventional memory addresses requires that programmers make specific provisions for such usage in their programs. However, driven by competition, the demands of a more enlightened user base, and need for more memory, software developers quickly turned what started as a bandwagon into a steamroller that then set the pace for hardware development, pretty much until the introduction of the 80386.

In some cases it was an easy fix and in others not so easy, but it happened. At the time I wrote the first edition of this book, I had only a small handful of TSRs that would run happily above 640K. By the time I wrote the second edition, the numbers were reversed. And with upper memory becoming overcrowded these days, many of those programs (or their descendants) are today moving on into extended memory (where available) using DOS extenders. But *anyone* can have expanded memory—a number still support the use of EMS expanded memory as accessed though the page frame, either in addition to or instead of extended memory. Access through the page frame requires the following:

❑ The program has to be able to determine if expanded memory actually exists on the system.
❑ Assuming the program finds expanded memory, it has to determine if there is enough to meet its needs.
❑ Again assuming there is expanded memory, the program has to allocate expanded memory pages as needed.
❑ It has to get the available page-frame address(es).
❑ It has to actually map in those expanded memory pages.

Only after it has done all this can a program read, write, and execute data in expanded memory the same as if it had only conventional memory—which is where it loads and runs if unable to complete the previous requirements. But it's not done yet because it also has to have a mechanism for returning whatever expanded memory pages it used to the expanded memory pool before exiting—clean house so to speak.

The most important thing to see from all of this is that these requirements pose no restrictions on the actual program other than the normal rules of DOS. Where the program loads and runs—or more accurately, where it's allowed to load and run—and how it exits are in most cases all that necessarily has to change to utilize expanded memory.

I should point out, however, that the previous information includes only a bare minimum of functions a programmer must include to use expanded memory. It is by no means a complete list of the tools available to enhance the capabilities of software running in expanded memory. Anyone interested in investigating these in greater detail should consult the actual specification document.

Through the years, man's inventive nature has rarely let obstacles stand in his way for very long. Even as the PC began to slip its bonds and leave its "toy" image behind, programmers had found ways—many borrowed from the mainframe world—to make whatever actual resources they had available look and act like more.

This has been especially true in the case of memory, which, no matter how you slice it, is a finite resource with limits beyond which your hardware cannot go. As the size of programs grew, programmers were forced to look for solutions that would allow programs to run even though they were larger than the amount of space (RAM) available on a typical user system.

In the inventory of ordinary resources, though, you generally have two principle kinds of user memory. There's RAM, a volatile medium but the medium of choice for temporary storage, and some form of nonvolatile mass storage, these days generally a hard disk with a lot of megabytes—a lot more megabytes than RAM usually. And just as with a little clever programming you can make RAM look like a storage disk (RAM disk), you can turn that upside down and make part of your storage disk look just like more RAM— RAM you probably wish you had in many cases but often can't afford.

This led to the development of a group of expanded-memory emulators such as one incorporated in a product called Turbo EMS, which, although primarily a memory-management tool, billed itself as "the affordable alternative to expanded-memory boards." There were several such products on the market at one point, in fact. It was a gimmick and a poor substitute for the real thing—no more, though, than the virtual memory described in the next chapter that's the only way a lot of users get by with running Windows (and OS/2) today. Granted, virtual memory today is far more sophisticated than what substituted for the real thing in the EMS world, but then there were a whole lot fewer megabytes to move around in those days too, so it's a fair comparison.

Let me quickly point out, however, that EMS emulation does not necessarily mean swap-to-disk chicanery. The term *EMS emulation* is used today—and far more commonly in conjunction with the MS- or IBM/PC DOS EMM386.EXE EMS emulator (ver. 5.0 and later), which borrows extended memory and presents it to software—at RAM speed—as 4.0 EMS memory. So while those early emulators pretty much gave emulation a black eye, they're in the past.

EMS emulation today is more commonly just a matter of how whatever RAM you have beyond 640K is addressed—and then just part of it, based on what your applications need. It's a game the system plays with numbers, making what would otherwise be extended memory behave as if it were expanded memory—a juggling act, no more.

The stopgap that came to stay At most, expanded memory as it first entered the DOS scene was a stopgap measure, taken in desperation by an infant industry trying to define its legitimate place. But it was a turning point and the beginning of a movement no one could have foreseen or planned for. And without expanded memory, I think it's questionable whether the then struggling PC could have not only bridged the technology gap but provided the impetus that ultimately brought us 32-bit processing, extended memory, and all the other things we take so much for granted now.

This isn't a backward glance by any means, however. EMS expanded memory—the real stuff, or at least a darned good emulation—is alive and well. It still is the only way to break the 640K barrier on 8088 machines. And they're still selling 8088s. It's still used for mapping memory to upper address space on 8088s, 80286s, and even 32-bit systems with some memory managers. And, hey, even on a 486 with 16 megabytes of RAM I still run applications that use EMS expanded memory. It might not be the darling it used to be, but EMS expanded memory is going to be around for quite a while.

11 *Virtual memory*

Virtually every time you turn around these days someone's talking about virtual something or other. Before there were a whole lot of other virtuals, however, there was something called *virtual memory*. Just as it's possible to virtualize, i.e., create the illusion of having one or more entire and independent machines by skillfully manipulating system resources, particularly the CPU and memory, it's possible to virtualize specific resources within a real or virtual machine.

Many users have used RAM to create virtual disks (RAM disks) to great advantage for years. Compressed disks such as those created by Stacker or more recently by DOS itself are, in fact, *virtual* disks; they're special files residing on a disk that, when accessed by special device drivers, emulate the behavior of real disks. More recently, attention has focused more and more on using hard-disk space for the virtualization of RAM itself to satisfy the ever-increasing need for more. And now we've come full circle, using hard-disk space to make up for a lack of RAM.

Actually, it's something that's been done for years in one way or another, although the numbers have changed from kilobytes to megabytes, and the emphasis from virtualizing conventional to EMS expanded, and now finally to extended memory. We're still faced with the same old problem, though: never enough memory to go around. And through the years a number of ingenious schemes have been devised to get around the problem—and some that were less than ingenious but that in some, often crude, way served to fill a need.

What is virtual? In some ways virtual memory is generally better understood than the virtual machines looked at earlier—or rather, more users probably think they understand it, though few really do. Microsoft especially, in their zeal to sell us Windows, has promoted this newly-rediscovered wonder as if it was, perhaps, the greatest thing since indoor plumbing (see FIG. 11-1).

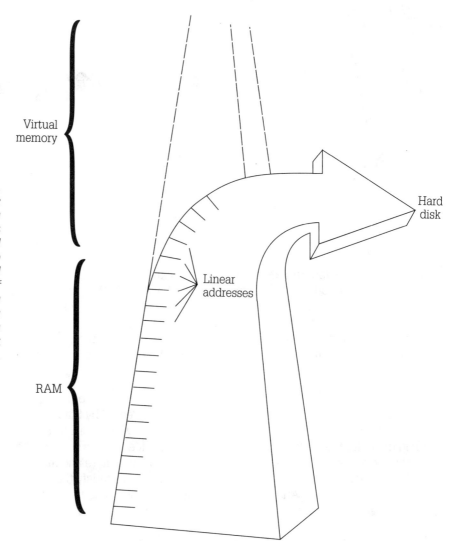

Virtual memory

RAM

Linear addresses

Hard disk

11-1

Software written to use virtual memory automatically redirects calls to address beyond limits of installed RAM to set space aside on hard disk. User may be aware of virtual memory use only by seemingly sluggish performance of system and excessive disk drive activity.

Windows 3*x* takes whatever RAM you've got, multiplies it by four, and that's what Windows in enhanced mode gives you to work with. But the more virtual memory you create, the more real memory it takes just to manage it, whether it's actually in use or not. That being the case, Microsoft has set a factor of four as the default value—a compromise at best between the seemingly insatiable demands of many Windows applications and the law of diminishing returns.

Still, if Microsoft had said you needed something like 8 megabytes of RAM and maybe even more to do the job effectively with Windows, they would have effectively limited their market to the small handful of users who—even at this stage—have that much RAM to work with.

And Windows isn't the only hog with a seemingly insatiable appetite for memory these days. Long before there was Windows there were DOS applications that, for lack of hardware resources, resorted to using virtual memory. And looking ahead, to run OS/2 effectively takes about twice as much RAM as it takes to do a decent job with Windows. And with Windows NT, 12 megabytes of RAM is barely enough to get up and running—never mind doing anything useful . . . The point is that everyone is doing it. Even with today's relatively cheap RAM, truly enough is rarely an affordable option.

But no matter how you look at it, you can't get something—memory or anything else—for nothing. Sooner or later it has to cost you something somewhere, and this one can cost you big time. Particularly if you don't really understand what's going on.

As originally implemented, "virtual memory" was pretty crude, being nothing more than a euphemism for swapping things to disk. Code, of course, can run only in actual RAM, not sitting on a disk. But aside from the time required to swap things back and forth, large chunks of data and, for that matter, even code that isn't actually being used at any given time can easily be swapped to disk and called back later when and if they're needed. You can often find the remains of these still cluttering your hard disk days or weeks or even months later—actual disk files in many cases, sometimes with .SWP or .TMP extensions, or in a worst-case scenario, lost chains and clusters when you run CHKDSK.

Early virtual

In fact, some applications put a fancy name on the very same crude swapping to disk that typifies the task switching you find even today in DOSs based on the Microsoft DOS 5.0/6.0 kernel. Some, but not all, applications tell you what they're doing. Others don't—and some aren't even neat about it, leaving your hard disk cluttered with the stuff they've swapped to temporary storage on your disk (which in many cases partially or even totally duplicates files on your hard disk).

This doesn't mean you're likely to bring up old data from an abandoned swap file some day when you least expect it. To prevent that happening, old swap files are never reused by later sessions. In fact, once you power down your system, the applications that created them forget them and can't even find them, let alone reopen them.

Even so, not all applications clean up their own swap-to-disk mess as they go along. Some do, of course, but others don't. DESQview, for example, leaves swap files on your disk when you run out of RAM and it starts swapping. Because these are never reused by later sessions, the batch file I use to start a DESQview session starts with the line:

```
IF EXIST D:\DOS\DV\SWAP*.DV DEL D:\DOS\DV\SWAP*.DV
```

Some applications zero-out their swap files but leave directory listings cluttering your disk. Appropriate lines can be added either to your AUTOEXEC or other batch files to dispose of old swap files left on your disk by other applications.

This, however, is virtual memory in its most elemental form—even today, an often necessary fact of life. And crude as it is, it's all we need a lot of times: a way to free some precious RAM at almost any cost.

You've come a long way . . .

Virtual-memory technology has come a long way since the crude, flat-out disk swapping we started with—not that most people would have noticed, judging from the old-fashioned way a lot of applications swap to disk. It's one thing when you have to do a swap in DOS—640K at most—and quite another when it comes to juggling several megabytes, often doing it repeatedly within a single application.

Windows, because of its reliance on virtual memory to even barely run on some machines, carries the fine art of memory virtualization about as far as anyone to date. While hard-disk games are still at the heart of memory virtualization, as implemented in Windows 3x it involves a number of other tricks to lessen the sting—tricks that don't easily lend themselves to use with ordinary DOS applications. It's indicative, however, of what you have to look forward to in the future as programmers are increasingly driven to embracing virtual memory.

A sidetrip to the dump

Windows really does some pretty neat things to get around the fact that nobody really has enough RAM to go around. One of the first things it does when memory is short is what the skipper of any sinking ship is going to do: start dumping overboard. This is actually a pretty slick mechanism as implemented in Windows, more so than most users understand. Figure 11-2 shows an analysis of system resources shortly after loading Windows, and you'll see that most of the memory used so far is considered disposable.

Disposable is stuff Windows can jettison and—at that moment anyway—keep running very nicely without. A function of how applications (and Windows itself) are programmed, disposable items can include code segments that aren't needed by whatever you're doing at the moment—not the whole program, but just parts you won't likely miss. Other disposables include such things as icons and dialog boxes. And if suddenly Windows or

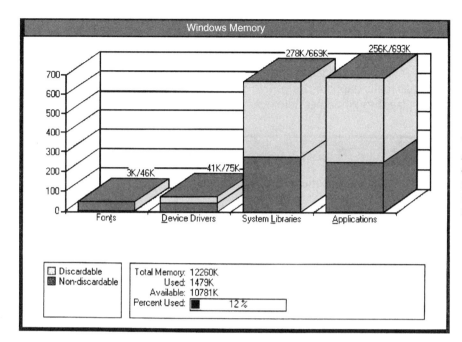

11-2
A fairly typical look at current Windows resources (Norton's SIW.EXE) reveals that most of what's loaded is disposable.

an application needs something that's been dumped, it knows just where to find it and reload it. You'll have to wait a moment—not even all that long in many cases—while it does.

This is actually a derivation of the old overlay scheme that predates DOS. Strictly speaking, dumping is *not* a function of virtual memory. It isn't virtual memory because nothing gets swapped out to disk; it's just written over by something the system needs more urgently. Dumping is, however, an important part of an overall strategy: it saves the time it would otherwise take to swap disposables to disk, and therefore reduces the time it takes to get on with whatever it is you're trying to do.

Referring back to FIG. 11-2, you'll note that Windows at that moment still shows something over 10 megabytes of memory as being available—which is a pretty good trick considering the machine in question had a total of only four megabytes installed, with the DOS and Windows kernels already taking their bite out of that. Whether you actually have that much that's actually usable in Windows can be problematical, though, I've found.

Is it even there?

Pardon the seeming contradiction of terms, but another problem with the humongous memory resources Windows reports, the bulk of which is virtual memory, is that you often have less to work with than you think. Working with real RAM, you always know what you've got going for you. If a program loads, it will most likely run; if there's not enough RAM to support it, it just won't load—or if it loads you can't open files.

When you start pushing Windows, asking it to put up all that memory it *says* it has, you might start running into trouble. I know I have, crashing the whole system on a number of occasions when I got too near the edge. Figure 11-3 shows an error message indicating you've run out of memory, but too late. What has really happened is you've crashed, managing to save only a copy of the display through rather heroic means.

11-3
A crash that was caused by over-committing.

After this happened to me often enough, I found that with the something over 12 megabytes of total memory reported on a machine with 4 megabytes of real RAM, if I exceed about 80% usage I was courting disaster. One time I did manage 91%—which should still have left me over a megabyte usable— before the house came tumbling down. But by and large I would caution against any more than about 80% usage as a general rule.

How do you know just how much you have left without making a career out of constantly checking your memory reserves? There are a number of utilities that do it unobtrusively, typically running as just icons down at the bottom of your screen, displaying constant updates of your reserves. One of the earliest of these is the memory view that comes as one of a set of utilities called First Apps from hDC. It's still one of the better ones around, and either it or something comparable should be an absolute must for anyone just squeaking by.

Still, based on that 4-megabyte system, 10 of the over 12 megabytes of memory reported by Windows probably seems like a lot of memory to most users. And it is . . . until you get used to the idea of having so much memory available and get a little careless about closing applications you've finished with. So be careful. Some of what you think is virtually there might not really be.

Waiting forever The biggest problem with virtual memory, no matter how skillfully it's implemented, is that it's slow; any disk access is painfully slow compared to working in RAM. And any time you have to essentially double the slower access times by swapping both to and from the disk, the wait can be significant.

To a hobbyist, a few extra minutes might not be important. To a businessman, though, those little respites can get pretty costly—far more than paying for the extra RAM it takes to make the difference in a lot of cases. Unfortunately, what we don't have at this point is a clever little TSR that pops up and tells you something like:

```
This operation will take 2:16 minutes to complete.
Completion time could be reduced to 0:16 if there were
sufficient RAM installed.
```

The next best thing is to just sit and watch the little light that tells you when the disk is being accessed—which you'll do a lot of if you're short on RAM and Windows has to do its juggle.

What's at issue here, then, is productivity. To the everlasting credit of Windows, OS/2, and NT—and properly written applications—it's often possible to "make do" with even the most meager resources. But merely making do is one thing; getting acceptable performance often quite another.

Unfortunately, unacceptable performance usually translates to a serious lack of speed. Just scanning a five-page document on a RAM-starved machine took 22 minutes—and I say "RAM-starved" because, even with twice the minimum RAM Windows has to have to run in enhanced mode, the disk-drive light was on most of that time, a prime indication that a lot of virtual memory is being used. Automatic spell checking and correction took another 25 minutes (while I watched the disk light do its dance), for a total of 47 minutes—call it 50 minutes when you include the time it took to load Windows and the program in the first place.

A good typist could easily have rekeyed the document in that amount of time, never mind the time it took to correct the errors that the software didn't catch. If that isn't enough to make you want to swear off of computers, I don't know what is.

When I ran the same job on a comparable 386 with 16 megabytes of RAM installed, the story was quite different. On that machine, scanning the same document took only 7:50 (again including time lost to manually change pages and restart the scanner, but in this case representing a more significant portion of the time). And without having to swap back and forth to disk, the automatic spell check and correction took just under six minutes, putting the total time at under 15 minutes.

Overdraft protection

What this all comes down to is a need to take a careful look at virtual memory, not only what it is but how you're using it. And what it's really costing you. With both operating systems and applications becoming more complex, you can expect to see more and more software that anticipates the need for virtual memory. It's inevitable and not necessarily all bad, but you have to put it in perspective. Every time a lack of adequate real RAM costs you 30 minutes—or ten or even five with any regularity—that translates to dollars lost if you're trying to run a business.

On the other hand, thinking you've got to rush right out and buy more megabytes of RAM every time you see the disk light flash when a program is running and you think it's using virtual memory is equally foolish. Even with 16 megabytes, I still come up short sometimes. Not very often, though, and certainly not often enough to spring for another 16 megs just yet. It's just something you have to keep an eye on as you add more applications.

Which brings me to the following point: rather than being the great benefit various software vendors and assorted snake-oil salesmen would have you believe it is, consider virtual memory as overdraft protection on your checking account. It really comes in handy when you're short, but it isn't something to depend on every day.

One of the biggest problems is that—unlike the bank—applications rarely tell you when you're overdrawn. They just tend to leave you twisting slowly in the wind, waiting, and waiting . . . and waiting. The more badly you're overdrawn, the longer you have to wait. And if you try to play a game of Solitaire to kill the time it just takes that much longer. One of the joys of virtual memory.

The curse The bottom line then is that *any* use of virtual rather than real memory, by virtue of the fact that it involves swapping blocks of data to and from a mechanical disk, degrades system performance. The greater the reliance on virtual memory, the more significant that degradation becomes—to a point where, on a fairly typical system with only two to four megabytes of RAM installed, throughput with some of today's more powerful applications might be reduced by a factor of three, five, or more.

Indeed, in a business environment where time translates directly into dollars, the cost of relying on virtual memory to make good any shortfall can, if not watched very carefully, quickly exceed the cost of adding enough real RAM to make the need for virtualization the exception rather than the rule.

Having said that—and hopefully gotten your attention—let me quickly point out that virtual memory *does* play an important role in the overall scheme of things today and *can*, if properly understood and used, be an invaluable adjunct to system resources.

It would be foolish, even in the extreme case cited previously, to rush right out and buy more RAM just because you need it for some job you do only occasionally. As in anything else, you need to weigh the cost against the anticipated return on your investment. As a general rule of thumb, though, I think it's fairly safe to say that in today's multitasking and graphical environments, if you have less than about 8 megabytes of RAM—real RAM—installed, there's nothing virtual about what the RAM you *don't* have is probably costing you.

Part three
Real-mode DOS

12 DOS in real mode

The introduction of Novell's largely protected-mode DOS 7 brings a whole new set of issues to deal with, although the issues have really always been there. At least since the introduction of the 80286—the clumsy DOS box in OS/2 1x that was intended for the 80286 was, in fact, a protected-mode DOS, though no one really noticed. As a practical matter, until now DOS has always just been DOS and protected mode was something abstract, something for the future, maybe.

Suddenly the future is now, and DOS is alive and well in both the real and protected mode. And because there is now DOS in both real and protected mode, you must—for the first time ever—understand both the differences and the implications. DOS applications should run equally under the auspices of real or protected-mode DOS (or DOS emulations). There are, however, a number of significant differences.

Protected mode, as discussed in an earlier chapter, is based on the use of what DOS—real-mode DOS—sees as extended memory. Extended memory begins precisely where the DOS you've always used—at least until now—ends. In fact, extended memory starts just one byte beyond the highest address an 8088 with its 1Mb address limitation can even deal with. FFFFh is the top of one megabyte (FFFFh plus 1 rolls over and becomes 10000h).

So completely aside from any other issues real vs protected mode might raise, as soon as you even mention extended memory or protected-mode operations, you're automatically excluding all of the millions of 8088/8086 machines that are in use. An 8088 or 8086 by design can run *only* in real mode, which means you *have* to use a real-mode DOS. And this, at least theoretically, includes any real-mode DOS going all the way back to DOS 1, though most application software today typically requires functions found only in DOS 3x or later releases.

Just because a machine has protected-mode capabilities (has at least an 80286 or higher CPU) doesn't mean that you need a protected-mode DOS. Nor does it mean that a protected-mode DOS is going to give you more than 1Mb of DOS space to work with, no matter how many megabytes of RAM you have installed.

Just as you're no taller or shorter in Paris or London than in New York, in real or protected mode the way DOS was written limits DOS now and forever to one megabyte of address space. Now and forever, *ad nauseum*. There are, of course, good reasons you might want to move to a protected-mode DOS (or protected-mode DOS emulation, as in OS/2 or Windows NT). But DOS is DOS is DOS is DOS.

Where the distinction blurs

At the risk of confusing the difference between real and protected-mode DOS, let me quickly point out the fact that real-mode DOS runs fine in protected mode. It's been done for years without a hitch. On 80386 and higher systems, DESQview runs DOS sessions in protected mode—it's running real-mode DOS on virtual machines, and that, by definition, puts those sessions in protected mode. The same with Windows 3x in enhanced mode.

Even in OS/2 2x, where DOS support is for the most part provided by a protected-mode emulation of the DOS environment, it's really not all that different, as evidenced by the fact that OS/2, in problem situations actually allows you to boot DOS sessions with whatever real-mode DOS you like. There, too, however, your real-mode DOS is actually running in protected mode (again on a virtual machine). The capability of running real-mode DOS under OS/2 doesn't extend beyond the actual real-mode kernel, with all functionality beyond 640 granted by resources controlled by OS/2.

The only absolute fact is that no DOS that's native to protected mode can ever run in real mode. Real-mode DOS, though, can be run in anything that looks like home with address space it *sees* as starting at 0000h. The distinction you must keep in mind is this, then:

❑ DOS is an environment, and as such can exist in any place that either is or emulates real mode—a block of address space that *appears* to run from 0000h to FFFFh.
❑ Protected mode is a specific place, specific in that it lies beyond one megabyte. Protected mode can be any place above one megabyte, right on up to 4 gigabytes. The one place it *cannot* be is on real-mode turf below one megabyte.

Hopefully, that clarifies the situation. Just a little anyway before we look at ubiquitous real-mode DOS, the DOS that can go anywhere—provided it doesn't try to take undue advantage of the hospitality of its protected-mode host.

We'll look more closely at DOS in the protected mode in part four of this book, and at that time, when it is more appropriate, I'll go into the pros and cons of a protected-mode DOS as well as emulations like those in OS/2 2.*x* and Windows NT. At that time I'll also explain what you must do differently when in protected mode to access seemingly the same features such as upper memory, the HMA, etc.

Whatever the benefits of protected-mode operation might be, and regardless of where DOS goes from here, there will always be a real-mode DOS as long as there are 8088/8086 boxes out there. And just as sure as God made little green apples, a lot of users will be running plain old real-mode DOS on Pentiums as well. And happily.

For now—and for this chapter—there are two new ostensibly real-mode DOS offerings, both generally following in the real-mode footsteps of MS-DOS 5.0. There are MS-DOS 6.0 and, from IBM, PC DOS 6.1.

It's amazing how two DOS products, both based on essentially the same underlying kernel code, can be so very different from a user standpoint. On the one hand is IBM's new PC DOS 6.1 with a bunch of brand-new IBM-developed utilities. On the other is Microsoft's Windows-oriented MS-DOS 6. And in between the two is a gulf at least as wide as formerly existed between the now discontinued DR DOS from Digital Research (now part of Novell) and MS-DOS.

A tale of two DOS 6s

Having brought up DR DOS, I must make a careful distinction here, for in that case, although most differences in similar functions were remarkably invisible—and, in fact, most users would never even have spotted most of the differences that did exist—the underlying kernel code was written by completely different teams. Now we're talking starting with the very same— or certainly very nearly the same—code, but implementing it in philosophically quite different ways.

One doesn't usually wax philosophic about operating systems, but then until now it has really never been an issue. This time around, however, it is. It is, in fact, *the* key issue users need to look at in deciding which DOS is the right one for their purpose: a DOS-user's DOS or a Windows-user's DOS.

Be that as it may, there are two new real-mode DOS releases. In alphabetical order, you have . . .

In a move that has attracted remarkably little notice in the computer press, IBM quietly changed DOS in its own way, and although the version marketed

IBM's PC DOS 6.1

by IBM is still largely based on code supplied by Microsoft, with version 6 there are a number of significant differences.

By eliminating a bunch of unnecessary PRINTF statements from the code (something of interest only to programmers), they made their DOS a little smaller, using some of the space they gained to provide special support for different operating platforms—which translates to a faster DOS, particularly on 386 and higher machines. This was accomplished largely by modifying the kernel so it senses what hardware it's running on at boot time, adapting itself accordingly. Int 10h calls, in particular, are very costly—several hundred clock cycles—on a 386 (and higher), and IBM figured out a way to intercept and fake them on these higher-level systems, leaving them as hard interrupts for lower systems that lacked the mechanisms that would benefit.

And in the interest of conserving precious hard disk space, they tweaked and pruned both the kernel and utilities, with an eye toward reducing not just the size but more importantly the number of *clusters* they required (in one case, a utility from DOS 5 blew past a cluster boundary for space to hold just 5 bytes, at the cost of 2019 that were wasted).

They've also done a number of things that have a major impact on the use of memory above 640K. In fact, beyond 640K the new PC DOS clearly has the edge at this point—and, unlike the old days, is a DOS designed to run not only on just IBM machines but any decent clone. In this release, even the 5K ROM stub that PC-DOS looked to for a BASIC kernel is history.

Here, however, it's important to understand the underlying marketing philosophy, the engine behind the change. And to begin with, IBM is not enamored with Windows—this has generally been acknowledged as being one of the major problems leading to the split between Bill Gates and Big Blue. IBM is not out bashing Windows, mind you, but IBM's aim has been to concentrate on creating a better DOS to meet the needs of the majority of DOS users.

And what do most DOS users need? More memory, of course, is at the top of everybody's wish list, and where can developers turn to find more memory for users? Above 640K, not only in the way UMBs are utilized but also in the HMA—an area that Microsoft doesn't use as effectively as it could. In fact, in IBM's new DOS they even manage to load more than just one program's code into the HMA—a feat that, as discussed elsewhere in this book, is generally impossible except in certain special situations. We'll look at that in greater detail later in this chapter, but for now let that suffice as just one indication of the lengths to which IBM has gone in optimizing this release.

And on the subject of optimizing upper-memory usage, too, IBM has gone a different route from that taken by Microsoft. Both IBM and Microsoft have included an optimizing program in their newest DOSs. The difference lies in who they looked to for technology they could license.

Neither IBM or Microsoft abandoned HIMEM.SYS and EMM386.EXE. Instead, both went out in search of something to help users utilize the mappable upper memory EMM386.EXE could make available on 80386 and higher systems. And whereas Microsoft licensed MEMMAKER from Helix, IBM went to Central Point, the PC Tools people.

The Central Point choice is interesting since, unlike Helix (the developers of Netroom), Central Point is not well known for their work in memory management. What they did have, however, was the technology required to take the memory provided by somebody else's memory manager and utilize it—more effectively than MEMMAKER, in fact, from several standpoints.

One of the most interesting and unique aspects of memory management in IBM's new DOS is that, recognizing that much of the world still runs 8088s, they've included four new IBM-developed drivers that, depending on what other hardware is available, can provide up to about 60K of usable upper memory on 8088s (and 80286s):

More memory for 8088s as well

```
umbcga.sys      1602    3-31-93   23:43
umbems.sys      1727    3-31-93   23:43
umbherc.sys     4272    3-31-93   23:43
umbmono.sys     1646    3-31-93   23:43
```

This should be of particular interest to many users, because it's an area Microsoft has always ignored, in this release offering nothing in the way of memory management for anything below an 80286—and no mapping capability even at that level.

Three of these, as you can see, are specific to various video modes—that is, they're specific to upper-memory address space as available with different video systems. These are all the more interesting because, unlike most other schemes that permit at least limited memory mapping to upper-memory address space on 8088s, you can even use 3.2 EMS memory (most require 4.0 EMS).

Building on this capability, then—one of the most intriguing things IBM has done in this release—they even came up with a way of using the SMARTDRV disk cache on an 8088 (driver available by BBS only), which is an especially neat trick since SMARTDRV is supposed to work only with extended memory, and 8088s don't support extended memory.

And all of this, of course, applies to 80286 machines that don't normally support upper memory as well. Of course, several third-party managers have provided memory-mapping support for 80286 and 8088 machines for several years now. Those, however, generally required machines to have specific chip sets (the chips that support the CPU with ancillary services), which in most cases tended to limit their use to high-end machines—at least to the high end of whatever hardware level you're talking about. The new IBM drivers sidestep that issue, providing users with a way of using 3.2 expanded memory, the kind even most of the older memory cards capable of providing expanded memory supported.

While this capability can result in a significant improvement in performance, however, it's generally a mixed blessing because the address space to which these drivers can map memory for use by TSRs or device drives is generally the same exact address space an EMS page frame would occupy. That pretty much makes it an either/or situation, forcing users to chose between having something loaded to upper memory or having EMS.

Often it's not an easy choice. Fortunately, with 6x it's not as hard a choice as it would have been with earlier DOSs—not now that DOS supports the use of menu-driven multiboot startup options. You can easily have one configuration that gives you upper memory for sessions that require more conventional memory, and another that allows a page frame and expanded memory for sessions where that's needed.

Center stage At center stage, of course, is RAMBOOST, part of the memory-management package IBM licensed from Central Point for optimizing the use of upper memory on 386 and higher machines.

After years of being a ho-hum and essentially following in MS-DOS's shadow, IBM has suddenly emerged as a power to be reckoned with in DOS in their own right—and not just for IBM machines, as was historically the case, but for anything that runs with DOS. In fact, for my money, I would rate IBM ahead of MS-DOS this time around—something I never thought I'd say. But I like PC DOS better for several reasons, with memory management just one area where their new DOS excels.

Of course, the most immediate and visible difference between these two new DOSs lies in the utilities they offer; Microsoft has created a situation where by default you can access some of their new utilities only through Windows, while, by contrast, IBM's new DOS, while doing nothing to discourage Windows use, is first and foremost still DOS.

There are still, of course, many similarities between IBM and MS-DOS in this latest release. After all, despite the apparently terminal rift between IBM and Microsoft, there are still contractual agreements in place whereby they're obligated to share certain bits and pieces of technology. Those parts—the DOS kernel, for example—are pretty much hidden from view, however. Even there, IBM has taken the basic DOS 5 kernel (which is the essence of any DOS) and enhanced it, resulting in a tighter, *faster* DOS. These differences are probably less obvious to the average user, though, than the utilities that give these siblings such distinct and different personalities.

Nowhere is the unique nature of PC DOS 6.1 more evident than in the arsenal of memory-management tools it provides—including some Microsoft apparently never considered, as in the case of several IBM-developed memory-mapping options it offers for 8088s and 80286s. As important as they might be to many users, I'll save them until later, though, and get right to the heart of the matter: the way PC DOS 6.1 manages memory on 386 and higher systems.

For 80286 and higher systems, IBM, too, has started with HIMEM.SYS, along with EMM386.EXE for 386 and higher machines—both developed from (and similar to) those in MS-DOS. Those subtle differences (mostly dealing with capatibility issues related to specific hardware) are not what sets PC DOS 6.1 apart from MS-DOS 6, however. What is uniquely different is a utility package built around RAMBOOST that automates the job of optimizing the use of upper memory.

IBM turned to Central Point Software (PC Tools) and licensed the upper-memory optimizing technology for this release from them—along with a number of other new utilities that differ from those offered by MS-DOS 6.

There are two parts to the Central Point optimization package, the first being a program called RAMSETUP, which lacks any counterpart in MS-DOS 6's MEMMAKER. RAMSETUP does as its name implies, installing HIMEM.SYS if no other memory manager is found. But more than simply adding a couple of lines to the CONFIG.SYS as MEMMAKER does in similar circumstances, it goes on to analyze what's going on on your machine above 640K. It goes looking for such things as network cards and other adapter boards that might be configured—possibly even hardwired—to use some block of address space. It not only looks for them, but it also marks them in a way that doesn't go away when you run (or rerun) its companion program RAMBOOST.

The analyst's couch

Here, for example, is the way RAMSETUP installed HIMEM.SYS and EMM386.EXE in the CONFIG.SYS on my test machine:

```
device=C:\HIMEM.SYS
device=c:\emm386.exe 256 frame=none ram x=a000-b3ff
  i=b400-b7ff
x=b800-c7ff i=c800-cbff x=cc00-ccff i=cd00-efff x=f000
  -f7ff h=64 a=7 d=32
device=c:\ramboost.exe load
```

Contrast that with the way MEMMAKER installed HIMEM.SYS and EMM386.EXE, starting with the same CONFIG.SYS on the very same machine:

```
DEVICE=C:\MS-DOS_6\HIMEM.SYS
DEVICE=C:\MS-DOS_6\EMM386.EXE RAM HIGHSCAN
```

All those *x*s and *i*s in the RAMSETUP installation mark specific blocks of address space RAMSETUP found—automatically—that EMM386.EXE specifically has to avoid (x=) or that are okay to map RAM to (i=). These are the ground rules, and when RAMBOOST runs to actually load things up there these indelible markings are observed—no questions and no mousing around.

Because of this power to analyze your system, RAMBOOST consistently succeeded on my test machine where MEMMAKER just as consistently failed and left me with a crashed machine and problems that could be resolved only by going in and manually editing my CONFIG.SYS to do inclusions and exclusions MEMMAKER had failed to do—which then screwed up the loading MEMMAKER had worked out. And this is what optimizing upper memory is—or should be—all about in my opinion.

A truly dynamic optimizer

One of the most interesting—and advanced—features of RAMBOOST is the fact that it's a dynamic optimizer—dynamic as opposed to most other ones, including not only MS-DOS 6's MEMMAKER but most third-party optimizers as well—that freezes a configuration as it was the moment you last ran the optimizer. Once installed, every time you boot/reboot your system, RAMBOOST checks, and if it finds any changes either in your CONFIG.SYS or AUTOEXEC. BAT file it automatically reoptimizes your configuration. You don't even have to think about it. It's a done deal. Consider the following MEM report:

```
Memory Type          Total =  Used  +  Free
Conventional          640K     63K     577K
Upper                   0K      0K       0K
Adapter RAM/ROM       344K    344K       0K
Extended (XMS)       9256K   6400K    2856K
Total memory        10880K   6807K    3689K

Total under 1Mb       640K     63K     577K

Total Expanded (EMS)                   640K  (655360 bytes)
Free Expanded (EMS)                    256K  (262144 bytes)

Largest executable program size        577K  (591232 bytes)
Largest free upper memory block          0K       (0 bytes)
IBM DOS is resident in the high memory area.
```

This report shows a significant improvement (121K) over 456K of conventional memory available with my standard configuration before running RAMSETUP with PC DOS 6.1—and this using just the default settings.

The actual difference in the amount of conventional memory I had available with IBM's DOS as configured by Central Point's RAMSETUP was minimal when compared with what I finally was able to get with MS-DOS 6 and MEMMAKER. What was more significant were the options that RAMSETUP allowed for custom configuration of upper memory. I could, for example, have marked the setup screen to include 36K in the ROM region without having to manually edit the CONFIG.SYS. I did, in fact, but it was too fragmented to help with the particular configuration I was using.

Even more important, it worked with the exact same startup files that choked MS-DOS 6's MEMMAKER and left me stranded in mid-stride, as you'll see a little later in this chapter. And in the interest of fairness, I repeated these tests on another machine of different vintage and origin with similar results. This isn't to say the results would always turn out this way, but in my situation, anyway, RAMSETUP won hands down.

So, even aside from having what I feel is a far more rounded set of utilities than its competition, just in terms of overall memory-management capability I would have to give IBM's new PC DOS 6.1 the nod over Microsoft's DOS 6.

Beyond upper memory

I'm intrigued by the attention IBM is giving to the HMA and to developing an API that will allow more than just one program's code or data to be loaded up there. There might be others working on this too, but IBM is the first to come to my attention—and I believe the first to actually do it as they have in their PC DOS 6.1.

Granted, the initial secondary usage is quite modest, consisting of only a few hundred bytes of data, but it's something everyone assumed couldn't be done, owing to the fact that DOS's only access to the HMA is through the 16 bytes that lie immediately below FFFFh, with the remaining 64K–16 bytes beyond the megabyte the DOS is capable of accessing.

At best, this can open up only a relatively small block. Loading DOS=HIGH typically uses something like 47K, leaving another 17K to go to waste, and anything else that loads up there must, then, require no more than that remaining space during the crucial intitialization phase. (I discussed the same problem earlier in this book in connection with upper memory; see chapter 9). Still, in this game every little bit can count, and IBM's attention to this area is surely noteworthy.

PCMCIA support

Unpronounceable as an acronym, this bit of alphabet soup stands for Personal Computer Memory Card International Association, and it represents a set of standards for a new breed of hardware that crept quietly in on little laptop feet. Laptops and notebooks, because of their diminutive size, don't afford the luxury of an open architecture bus such as we've always had with desktop machines. The need was always there, but not the space. So a scheme was devised whereby tiny little computers could have a special adapter slot built into them for retrofitting goodies that either wouldn't fit internally or hadn't been developed or anticipated by the OEM.

An offshoot of some of the early attempts at adding external plug-in modules for various things like games or printer fonts, this is a fast-spreading technology, already reaching beyond just ordinary computers, and bringing with it not only such things as new, miniaturized FAX/modems and nonvolatile memory cards, but even tiny hard disks.

As with the ISA, EISA, and other buses we're used to dealing with, increasing use of the PCMCIA standard has implications both above and below 640K in DOS, particularly since these devices can be plugged in or not, or swapped-out out to make room for other PCMCIA devices pretty casually—often in mid-session.

While until now few other than some of the better laptop and notebook computers make provision for the use of PCMCIA cards, support for PCMCIA devices has relied entirely on third-party drivers. With this new release of PC DOS 6.1, however, PCMCIA support becomes part of the package. The fact that MS-DOS 6 doesn't provide support for PCMCIA devices is interesting, particularly since Windows is one of the beneficiaries.

MS-DOS 6.0 I'm truly disappointed in MS-DOS 6.0—which seems to be nothing but the MS-DOS 5.0 kernel with a few bug fixes and a little less heavy-handed treatment of the A20 gate. Admittedly, MS-DOS 5.0 was a good DOS, and a tough act to follow—particularly on the heels of a very flaky MS-DOS 4.x that sent countless users fleeing back to 3.x. Version 5.0 was good—and it's still good. Which comes back to a question I raised earlier about DOS at the kernel level having gone about as far as DOS is going to go—at least in real mode.

Unlike several of the other new products discussed in this book, I had the final release of MS-DOS 6.0 rather than just the beta version authors usually have to work from (from which the discussion of most other products in this book were based on). Beta releases often have some bugs—which is why there are beta versions that go to selected sites for testing before the final products are released—but normally by the time the final product hits the street most of the bugs have been corrected.

I say that by way of prefacing my remarks about MS-DOS 6 because it had some bad bugs early on in beta. But the bugs and other problems I noted weren't fixed, however, with the result that MS-DOS 6.0 was still too flaky when released to warrant the hard disk space it took up once this book was finished. Certainly not, given today's alternatives.

Of specific interest to this book, Microsoft did add MEMMAKER to this release, for the first time providing a means of scientifically (as opposed to trial and error) and automatically optimizing the use of upper memory. In doing so, MS-DOS 6.0 certainly contributed to the demise of some lesser third-party memory managers that had little else going for them. It was a move that was long overdue, however, and IBM quickly followed suit, though taking a quite different tack. It also had the salutory effect of putting pressure on the surviving third-party memory managers to push the limits of memory-management technology still farther in order to maintain their traditional competetive edge.

Getting back to memory management as provided by MS-DOS 6.0, MEMMAKER didn't exactly pass the test with flying colors—the same test I put IBM's PC DOS 6.1 to, as well as various third-party memory manager/optimizer packages. And not even a very sophisticated test at that, I might add. I simply started with the CONFIG.SYS and AUTOEXEC.BAT files I use every day and let each DOS and third-party memory manager I tested see what they could do with them. There are two ways to run MEMMAKER:

❑ Express—the default method, intended for less experienced users (which is really what it's all about).
❑ Custom—which assumes at least some familiarity with upper memory and upper-memory issues, and expertise in dealing with them.

Since you shouldn't have to be a power user to benefit, I tried running MEMMAKER in the default express mode first. It went through all the motions and ultimately reported it had everything under control. However, the system crashed hard when I tried to reboot—and this after MEMMAKER, thinking it had done the job, closed the back door, leaving no way to get back in other than rebooting from a floppy.

Crash!

I undid the changes (manually) and ran MEMMAKER two more times with similar results. Ultimately, I did succeed, but only after manually editing the AUTOEXEC.BAT to change the loading sequence of two TSRs. But even then the results were questionable or misleading at best. In order to look good, it added the 64K page frame to the programs actually loaded into upper memory in order to claim even a modest 112K gain—which, if true, would hardly be spectacular, and this even with DOS=HIGH! Consider the following:

Before	**After**	**Net gain**
474,960	590,176	115,216

In fact, that's hardly better than you could expect to do with MS-DOS 5.0 and maybe an hour of trial and error (which was about how long it took with MEMMAKER). This is, in fact, poorer performance than I achieved on my own with HIMEM.SYS/EMM386.EXE and MS-DOS 5.0, as discussed in the 2nd edition of this book. And translated into a typical (for me) workday situation, the results were even more disappointing. When I tried running DESQview, the system MEMMAKER gave me allowed only 384K to run applications (with QEMM386, I typically have at least 576K—a difference of 192 kilobytes for applications running under DESQview). That was the result of using MEMMAKER in its default (express) mode.

Starting over with the original CONFIG.SYS and AUTOEXEC.BAT files but running MEMMAKER in custom mode produced exactly the same results as I had obtained in the express mode—even the same hard crash when I was finished—but with one notable exception. Even manually rewriting the AUTOEXEC.BAT to change the loading sequence didn't help that time; it still

Same song, second verse

crashed. And, again, the only way I was able to get back into the system was by rebooting from a floppy.

I was able to study the CONFIG.SYS and AUTOEXEC.BAT files as modified by MEMMAKER, and even if it hadn't crashed, it was evident the custom mode wouldn't have produced significantly better results. As you can see from the following CONFIG.SYS, it apparently hadn't even tried to load SETVER or my Stacker driver into upper memory, despite my trying to force the issue:

```
DEVICE=C:\MS-DOS_6\CHKSTATE.SYS /S:FR1 /10743
DEVICE=C:\MS-DOS_6\HIMEM.SYS
DEVICE=C:\MS-DOS_6\EMM386.EXE RAM HIGHSCAN I=B000-B7FF
BUFFERS=15,0
FILES=30
DOS=UMB
LASTDRIVE=F
FCBS=4,0
DEVICE=C:\STACKER.COM /P=1 D:\STACVOL.DSK
DEVICE=C:\SSWAP.COM D:\STACVOL.DSK
DEVICE=D:\OS\MS-DOS\SETVER.EXE
DEVICEHIGH /L:2,11104 =D:\WIN\MASTER\PCKRAMD.SYS
CONFIGFILE=D:\WIN\MASTER\PCKWIK.INI
DOS=HIGH
SHELL=C:\COMMAND.COM C:\ /e:512 /p
STACKS=0,0
BREAK OFF
```

On closer inspection of the startup files as optimized my MEMMAKER, the cause of the crash was also evident. Unlike RAMBOOST or most other state-of-the-art optimizing programs, MEMMAKER does not attempt to locate address space used by various adapter boards, exclude it, and work around it. While it included some wasted video address space I said it could use (I= on the EMM386.EXE line), there's no evidence of an *exclude* necessary to avoid conflicting with an adapter board—in this case, a Stacker coprocessor—that was sitting on a block of address space. Ignoring it, it had apparently tried to load something else there with predictable results. Again, I was able to manually edit to add the necessary exclusion, but this pretty much defeats the purpose since most users, lacking experience in dealing with such problems, probably wouldn't know where to even start to look for problems like this.

Admittedly, MEMMAKER would have had to do a lot better than it managed in express mode to come up with enough more upper memory to accommodate those two, but all of the third-party memory managers discussed in the following chapter did all that and more, leaving a very questionable Microsoft DOS 6.0 choking in their dust.

Comparing the failed custom-modified startup files with the express-modified files revealed some inconsistencies and flat-out errors, both in where MEMMAKER had tried to load one of the files and the space it had allocated for another. By simply substituting the corresponding numbers from the express-modified files, the system would at least boot without crashing, but c'mon guys, isn't that what MEMMAKER is *supposed* to do?

Giving DOS the proprietary edge

Since my standard configuration used a third-party disk cache (PC KWIK) rather than SMARTDRV—and a rather hefty one at that—I reran the test using DOS's SMARTDRV instead. As expected, I was able to substantially increase the amount of available conventional memory from 590,176 to 616,080 bytes, a net gain of about 25K overall.

Unfortunately, what should and does work are often two quite different things. First off, after running MEMMAKER (twice) for the new configuration, the reoptimized startup files crashed the system much as before. That time I was able to get a bootable system only by removing the TSR whose position in the loading sequence I had had to change (manually) in my earlier tests. That brought me up to 632,528 bytes, but when I then loaded the TSR to conventional memory from the command line, the figure came down.

And not only could MEMMAKER not manage to optimize the AUTOEXEC.BAT successfully with that TSR included, when I, in another test, attempted to load it high from the command line it crashed the system then as well. Neither IBM's PC DOS 6 or any of the third-party memory managers tested had any problem loading this particular TSR (SITBACK, an automatic backup program) into upper memory, but MS-DOS 6 did. And the fact that I wasn't even able to load it high from the command line would seem to indicate quite clearly that the problem was with Microsoft's DOS 6.0 rather than with the TSR.

MEMMAKER, interestingly, is not a Microsoft product but rather was licensed for MS-DOS 6.0 from Helix, the developers of Netroom, one of three powerful third-party memory-management packages featured in the next chapter. Superficially at least, MEMMAKER has much the look and feel of CUSTOMIZE, which is the Netroom equivalent. In my opinion, however, where MEMMAKER falls short lies in the fact that Helix's optimizing technology really assumes a memory manager—such as their own Netroom—that has some rather crucial features missing in EMM386.EXE.

To sum it up

Neither of these DOSs represent the ultimate in memory management. In either case, however, the new memory-management utilities will likely meet the needs of many users who, before this round of new releases, lacked the expertise or proper tools to use upper memory effectively and no choice except to turn to third-party products.

At best, though, even IBM's PC DOS 6 is probably at least two or more years behind the technology curve, with HIMEM.SYS and EMM386.EXE unable to keep pace—you simply cannot make a silk purse from a sow's ear, no matter who you are. A lot has happened in the past couple of years, and while these rival DOSs both have come a long way by finally offering automated upper-memory optimization, the technology—as always in this area spurred on by third-party developers—has done a quantum leap or two.

I think it's also important to put one other thing in perspective at this point as well. In an earlier edition, I stated flatly that it was possible to make as much upper memory available with HIMEM.SYS and EMM386.EXE as with third-party memory managers, that all that was missing was the means of locating mappable space and optimizing its use. The implication was that only something like QEMM's Optimize or 386max's Maximize was needed to put the memory management provided by DOS on par.

At the time it was true. To do so required considerable experience as well as information not readily available to most users, but the raw capability was there. That is no longer the case, however. As you'll see in later chapters, third-party developers have now devised and perfected exciting new memory-management technologies with capabilities far beyond those provided by either the PC or MS-DOS flavors of HIMEM.SYS and EMM386.

Perhaps the best advice today would be to pick your DOS—carefully and not just out of habit—and see which one does better for you. It might be enough to meet your needs. But if it isn't—if you still need more—it's there and you know how to find it.

13 *Third-party specialists*

For all the new memory-management tools the new IBM and Microsoft DOSs have added to their arsenals, they still lag, on average, at least one DOS generation behind the powerful and more sophisticated memory-management packages available from top third-party developers. Admittedly, given automatic optimizing, today's new DOSs are a quantum leap ahead of the last round—so far that several third-party offerings that were credible before no longer look particularly interesting. My guess is that some of them will simply fade away, eclipsed by, of all things, DOS itself.

That still leaves, however, several contenders that are far superior to any of the new DOS memory-management packages—including an interesting new entry from Helix, the developer Microsoft licensed MEMMAKER from. For my purposes, I've narrowed the field to three that represent, in my opinion, not only the pick of the litter, but distinctive management technologies—and in all three cases, technology that's new and really has no equal in the DOS offerings.

Interestingly, all three of these were quick to spot the "Achilles heel" in the multiboot configuration capability in IBM and Microsoft's new DOS releases. While both of the new DOSs now support the use of multiple boot-time configuration options, and both now also include utilities for optimizing the use of upper memory, neither MS-DOS's MEMMAKER or PC DOS 6.1's RAMBOOST are capable of optimizing the multiple configuration files DOS 6 supports. All three of the third-party memory managers discussed in this chapter already have that capability in their current releases, however—just one more reason why the real story beyond 640K still centers on third-party products.

Again, as in the past, two of the top contenders come from Quarterdeck (QEMM386) and Qualitas (386max and its PS/2 companion, BlueMax). Helix's new Netroom 3 is a sleeper—one I never thought was really that impressive in the past—that's coming on like gang busters in this last release, with a whole new way of doing business above 640K.

Blind justice It's tricky trying to evaluate different memory-management products because, in fairness, you really can't weigh them on the same scale. You need two sets of scales, in fact, or two sets of criteria.

To evaluate just the merits of a memory manager by itself against competing products, you need to work against a standard set of configuration files, loading—or attempting to load—the exact same set of TSRs and device drivers into upper memory. Given such a standardized set of conditions, you can see what sticks when you throw it at high memory, what doesn't stick, and what that leaves you to run DOS applications in. This is probably the fairest way of judging the power of the memory manager itself.

However, there are often ancillary programs in the package, proprietary utilities that, if used, replace conventional DOS functions or add-ons (or third-party utilities) in ways that significantly enhance the end result. In the case of 386max, in fact, the difference was an extra 61K of conventional memory when using Qcache (the Qualitas disk-caching utility) instead of PC KWIK. Netroom, too, provides its own proprietary cache, different from Qcache. And Quarterdeck supplies no cache at all. So you throw either the same third-party cache at all of them, which might not be fair to those that have their own, or none at all, which deprives you of both disk caching and a nice, in the case of PC KWIK, fairly high-overhead item to test them with.

So it's strictly a case of apples and oranges, out of which you'll hopefully wind up with . . . I don't know, grapefruit maybe.

Because of the great disparity in the numbers on the bottom line, here (as with the DOSs in the prior chapter) I've measured each against a standard configuration that used no ancillary utilities (such as disk caches), but rather strictly third-party utilities throughout. For comparison purposes, I ran PC KWIK with everything. PC KWIK takes up a lot more conventional and/or upper memory than most of the cache utilities that come with the DOSs or third-party memory managers—but then it does more too.

Having done that, wherever practical I then reran the test using the proprietary disk cache if there was one. In most cases, this gives you two quite different sets of numbers, neither set scientific but both based on real-world situations—which is really what it's all about.

What this says, then, is that as a practical matter there are no absolutes in this business. Often there are choices that must be made. For myself, I happen to like PC KWIK despite its greater overhead. If I was working only with what DOS provides I might think twice about it, but given a choice of third-party memory managers there are at least two that—even with everything else I run—can load that overhead into upper memory. If at some point something else comes along that needs the UMB space and winds up kicking 40 or more kilobytes of overhead back down below 640K again, then I'll have to take another look. But by then a lot of other things might have happened too.

Both of the new DOS 6s have given us a valuable new tool with their support for menued multiple boot configurations. And both of these same DOS 6s have also added automatic upper-memory optimizing to the package as well. What's interesting, however, is that both have overlooked the fact that the optimizing packages they've licensed are based on technology that predates DOS support for multiple boot configurations. As a result, neither the Central Point RAMBOOST licensed by IBM or Helix's MEMMAKER in MS-DOS 6 is compatible with the use of multiple boot options in your CONFIG.SYS and AUTOEXEC.BAT. If you try, either of these programs will read your entire CONFIG.SYS or AUTOEXE.BAT, multiple boot options and all, as one big file, and in all likelihood give you something that reads like a Chinese menu: one from column A, two from column B, and so forth. Which is fine for Chinese takeout, but it's not much help with DOS.

Optimizing with PC & MS-DOS 6x

Always looking for just such an opportunity, it didn't take third-party developers long to seize upon this situation. Qualitas was the first to release a new version of their memory manager, 386max 7.0, with the capability of maximizing individual configurations in compound DOS 6 startup files. Quarterdeck's QEMM386 version 7, released a few weeks later, also featured optimization support for compound DOS 6 configuration files. And while the customization routine in Helix's Netroom 3 didn't initially have this support, it wasn't long in coming. (Update files were initially made available by BBS to users who had purchased Netroom 3 before this support was included.)

There are, as might be expected, some differences in how these different optimizing routines go about the job of sorting out which TSRs and drivers go with what configuration, but all of them can do the job effectively, it seems, and that's what matters.

In any event, all of these three run rings around the memory management provided by either of the real-mode DOSs. All are good, but each is stronger in some areas than others, making it a tough call to say which one is truly best—impossible in fact, since what's best for me and the way I work might not be best for you.

386max   Completely aside from the issue of whose disk cache and other utilities to use, there are two quite different ways to look at 386max (see FIG. 13-1) and its PS/2 companion, BlueMax. One way is with an eye toward running DOS and only DOS and the other toward running Windows—either Windows by itself or, more within the context of this book, DOS sessions using Windows as a shell. In this chapter, we'll look at 386max version 7 from a strictly nonWindows user's point of view, saving memory management for DOS in Windows and just Windows for chapter 15. Bear in mind, though, that these DOS-specific features are relevant when working with DOS applications running under Windows as well.

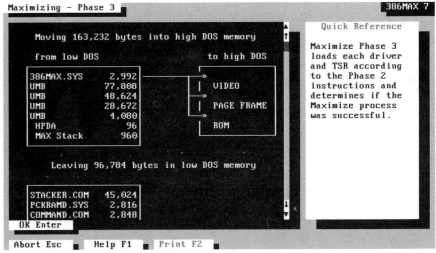

13-1

386max's MAXIMIZE gives detailed report of results obtained before altering your startup files. Here, unhappy with these results, I made some changes and next time did much better.

Qualitas was one of the first developers of a memory manager that could unlock the full potential of the then new 80386, and they're still one of only a couple of noteworthy third-party developers whose total commitment is to memory-management software. Quarterdeck, by contrast, was mainly interested in memory for DESQview and developed QEMM (and before that QEXT) mainly to support their multitasker; the fact that in meeting that need it became a leader in this area was really incidental to their story. Qualitas, however, does *just* memory management, and the mere fact they've survived in such a narrow sphere of interest is testimony to their leadership in developing new management technologies.

Having said that, however, let me also quickly add that, of the leaders in the field, Qualitas in some ways tends to be the most conservative. But with no other product line to cater to, they also do an excellent job of exploiting weaknesses in other systems with such special features as BlueMax's ability to shrink a PS/2's gluttonous 128K ROM down to a svelte 64K, freeing the rest for UMBs.

And in this release they've already added an important new feature for IBM and Microsoft DOS 6 users, including one that makes it possible to optimize (they call it *maximize*) the new multiple boot option CONFIG.SYS and AUTOEXEC.BAT files without having to disassemble them to deal with each part individually—and originally Qualitas was the only one that offered this important feature.

As with all of the better third-party memory managers, recovering as much of the ROM region for UMB use as possible is high on Qualitas' list of priorities, and their BlueMax version for PS/2s—discussed in detail later in this chapter—exemplifies their efforts in this area.

Even on more conventional machines where only the traditional 64K is reserved for system ROM, 386max has traditionally been more aggressive than its competitors, as shown in a screen taken from a typical 386MAX.PRO profile file (used by 386max when loading):

```
; This profile created automatically by INSTALL
RAM=CC00-CD00      ; MAXIMIZE ==> Protect RAM on adapters
SWAPFILE=C:\386MAX\386MAX.swp /S=8192 /T   ; INSTALL ==> Create an
                                           ; 8192 KB temporary DPMI
                                           ; swap file
NOWIN3             ; INSTALL ==> Do not install Windows 3 support code
USE=B000-B800      ; INSTALL ==> Recover RAM in MDA region
USE=F000-F100      ; MAXIMIZE ==> ROMSRCH recovers  4 KB.
USE=F200-F300      ; MAXIMIZE ==> ROMSRCH recovers  4 KB.
USE=F700-FE00      ; MAXIMIZE ==> ROMSRCH recovers 28 KB.
VGASWAP            ; MAXIMIZE ==> Relocate video ROM.
HPDAREG=80,0       ; MAXIMIZE ==> Move DPMI Host Private Data Area
                   ; to region 0 for 80 bytes
STACKREG=944,0     ; MAXIMIZE ==> Move Stack Overflow Protection
                   ; to region 0 for 944 bytes
```

While aggressive, this is a more conservative approach than that used by its strongest competitors. And note that this 36K is fragmented into three blocks, the largest of which is 28K, and all three are too small to be of more than limited practical use. 386max's major competitors have developed other ROM region strategies that I'll explore in depth a little later in this chapter.

ExtraDOS & other new extras

New to version 7 of 386max is a feature Qualitas calls ExtraDOS—one which, as the name implies, can free up as much as 20K more conventional memory than previous versions. To do this, 386max now has the ability to relocate COMMAND.COM, FILES, BUFFERS, LASTDRIVE, STACKS, and FCBS, etc. into upper memory. You might not realize it, but FILES, BUFFERS, LASTDRIVE, etc. are all overhead items. Each BUFFER, for example, uses 528 bytes, ten using up 5K of precious memory. And the savings add up pretty fast.

Although conceptually not new (QEMM has long supported relocating FILES, BUFFERS, and LASTDRIVE), it's new to 386max, and Qualitas has taken it still farther in relocating COMMAND.COM up there as well. It's little extras like this that you won't get with either IBM or MS-DOS.

386max was the first memory manager to incorporate DPMI (DOS protected-mode interface support), and now in version 7 integrates a full version of the 1.0 DPMI specification, including virtual-memory support. While this isn't crucial to most applications, it can be to DPMI-compliant applications that require more memory than is available on the system: Paradox 4, Lotus 123 v. 31, and Borland's C/C++ compiler to name just three.

In this release 386max also brings with it a RAM test utility called QMT, designed to detect unstable or defective system RAM that ordinary RAM checks (such as those run by the BIOS at boot time) often miss. This is a problem that's being seen more often, simply by virtue of the greater and greater amounts of RAM on one hand and the generally more crucial error handling of more sophisticated operating systems such as OS/2.

STACKS is an area DOS tends to be real finicky about, and it's an area few users seem to understand. The bottom line, though, is that poorly written or overly fussy TSRs can often crash a system by overflowing the stacks—either the default number of stacks DOS provides or some greater number specified by a STACKS= statement in the CONFIG.SYS. This isn't usually a major problem—in fact, I generally run with STACKS=0,0. 386max 7, however, has stack overflow protection. This feature—unique to 386max—cannot prevent stack overflows, but it can and does prevent stack overflows from bringing down the system.

Compressed drive support

The increasing use of disk compression, particularly now that all three DOSs offer it, has brought with it a number of new problems. Not the least of the problems is the sheer size of the drivers, which are typically something like 45K, and somewhat more than that during the initialization phase. If ever there was reason to use upper memory, this is it. Any good memory manager can probably manage enough upper memory to relocate such a driver, depending, of course, on how much other stuff you want to put up there.

One of the biggest problems with managing memory with some of the more popular disk-compression schemes—Stacker, for example—occurs when you compress your boot drive. When you do, the DOS kernel, a CONFIG.SYS (and generally AUTOEXEC.BAT), and the device driver(s) for the disk compressor must reside in their normal, uncompressed state on a portion of your boot drive that is *not* compressed. This is because, until the kernel and, after that, the device driver(s) for the disk compressor itself have been loaded, the compressed disk doesn't exist. It's there, of course, but as far as the system is concerned it's just one big, ugly, totally unreadable file.

Once the compression driver is loaded, that big ugly file becomes something the system recognizes as a disk, and (typically) at that point the system swaps drive designators so that the compressed disk becomes drive C:. The system then finishes the boot process, loading other device drivers (if any), TSRs, etc. from the compressed disk. Note, though, that you're in effect switching disks in the middle of the boot cycle. The CONFIG.SYS can be read only from drive C:, but right in the middle drive C: is suddenly replaced by something else. To continue booting, then, this new compressed disk drive C: must have a CONFIG.SYS that exactly matches the CONFIG.SYS on the uncompressed drive C: the system started from. And while the disk-compression software itself generally makes provision for keeping these two sets of startup files synchronized, it gets a little cumbersome, particularly when you start optimizing memory managers. 386max 7 provides special support to handle this situation.

As a quick aside, MS-DOS's DoubleSpace operates on a different principle and doesn't have this particular problem. There *is* an easy way around it: simply keep all files required during the boot cycle on an uncompressed portion of the disk and swap drive designators later. Or, as I do, use OS/2's Boot Manager on physical drive C:, using compression only on a separate drive D:. You still have that roughly 45K of overhead to deal with, though, and might have trouble loading it in upper memory with MS-DOS 6's MEMMAKER and HIMEM.SYS/EMM386.EXE.

PS/2 users in particular should take note of BlueMax, because it does make a significantly greater amount of memory available on those machines. Qualitas is, in fact, the only player in the memory-management game to date to produce a product specific to the PS/2's unique architecture. And BlueMAX now has been upgraded as well to include all the new features found in 386max version 7—although both of its chief competitors, QEMM with Stealth and NETROOM with cloaking, also have strategies that deal with it effectively.

Jor PS/2s only

There's good reason for having a separate PS/2-specific memory manager, although Qualitas is the only developer to date to do it. IBM, in designing the PS/2, set aside—and in fact has been using—an extra 64K of high address space (E000h to EFFFh) for system BIOS. There seems no apparent need for this in DOS, and in creating a memory manager specific to the PS/2 architecture, Qualitas manages to whittle the space the BIOS occupies back down to size, recovering more than half of the 128K area the PS/2 BIOS occupies for other uses.

By the way, Qualitas also now supplies QCache, a new disk-caching program with their memory managers. SMARTDRV.SYS, the default cache supplied with Windows 3, has been improved significantly, but QCache dynamically changes its cache size according to system needs. Creating a cache that's initially large to use all available extended memory, QCACHE then releases memory back to you as you continue to load applications that need more of it. This is similar to the way recent releases of PC KWIK operate, the difference being that QCACHE has fewer features, such as the integral RAM disk and spooler supported by PC KWIK. But it does have the advantage of being packaged free with memory managers from Qualitas.

Netroom 3 Netroom, as shown in FIG. 13-2, is the son of Headroom from Helix Software Company and has been around for several years, winning various awards. Until their release of 3.0, however, it hasn't really been up there with the biggies like Qualitas and Quarterdeck in my opinion. But suddenly Netroom has emerged as a formidable and extremely stable memory manager. What makes Netroom interesting is the new approach they've come up with to get around the BIOS problem and all those little chunks of upper memory that always look so tantalizing but are often so useless.

```
Customize v3.0
─────────────────────────────────────────────────────────────

An MS-DOS Multiconfig menu was found in your CONFIG.SYS file.
For CUSTOMIZE to properly configure your system, specify the
Multiconfig block you wish CUSTOMIZE to process.

     Startup Menu
     ────────────

     1.  NETROOM
     2.  QEMM
     3.  QEMM_STP
     4.  386max
     5.  Bare




   * Select a Multiconfig block to CUSTOMIZE, or press Escape
     to abort the CUSTOMIZE process.


Up/Down=Select   ENTER=Accept Selection   ESC=Cancel
```

13-2
Netroom's CUSTOMIZE, like all optimizers, allows you to single out any one configuration from new DOS 6x multiple configurations, leaving all others undisturbed.

Where Quarterdeck's QEMM386's Stealth swaps address space back and forth between the ROM BIOS and a page frame that overlaps most of the BIOS region, and Qualitas's BlueMAX squeezes the massive 128K BIOS IBM endowed the PS/2 with down to something much more manageable, Netroom *replaces* your old BIOS—both your system and video BIOS in fact (unless you're using SVGA modes, in which case it replaces only your system BIOS). After all, the BIOS is only a set of instructions, and software has been writing over bits and pieces of it almost from day 1. This just takes that process one step farther.

A free Helix bills this feature as a "BIOS upgrade," and essentially it is, which makes
BIOS upgrade it more interesting than might appear at first glance. There are a couple of fairly important issues here, though.

First off, the ROM BIOS on whatever machine you're running on was probably obsolete by the time it landed on your desk. In the case of significant new hardware—like the little 2.88Mb floppy drives—DOS upgrades typically include the interface support required to run them on older machines. Other than for less common bits of hardware—those requiring special installable device drivers in the CONFIG.SYS—this is all done invisibly. This stuff goes on continuously, though.

Unfortunately, there are BIOS issues other than just oddball hardware. I was having all kinds of trouble even running WIndows 3.1 (beta) until a BIOS maker I was talking to (Quadtel, now part of Phoenix) suggested that a whole lot of Windows users were having serious BIOS problems—a lot more than had any idea just what the problem was. Quadtel sent me special BIOS chip, and suddenly my Windows problems—or at least those that were related to the BIOS—disappeared.

The other issue is where the BIOS goes—what block of addresses it occupies. If it's your BIOS, you can sort of put it where you want to put it. And Netroom's cloaking feature puts it out into extended memory—all but a 4K stub of system BIOS (FE00h), plus another 4K stub (C000h) if the video is cloaked as well—as in the memory usage map shown in FIG. 13-3.

```
                    DISCOVER v3.00
                 Fri Feb 26 17:41:29 1993
       Copyright (c) 1990,91,92 Helix Software Company, Inc.
       _____

                              Memory Map
              Segment     0123 4567 89AB CDEF
       _____

              0x0000      ▓▓▓▓ ▓▓▓▓ ▓▓▓▓ ▓▓▓▓
              0x1000      ▓▓▓▓ ▓▓▓▓ ▓▓▓▓ ▓▓▓▓
              0x2000      ▓▓▓▓ ▓▓▓▓ ▓▓▓▓ ▓▓▓▓
              0x3000      ▓▓▓▓ ▓▓▓▓ ▓▓▓▓ ▓▓▓▓
              0x4000      ▓▓▓▓ ▓▓▓▓ ▓▓▓▓ ▓▓▓▓     V - Video RAM
              0x5000      ▓▓▓▓ ▓▓▓▓ ▓▓▓▓ ▓▓▓▓     B - BIOS ROM
              0x6000      ▓▓▓▓ ▓▓▓▓ ▓▓▓▓ ▓▓▓▓     ▓ - In Use
              0x7000      ▓▓▓▓ ▓▓▓▓ ▓▓▓▓ ▓▓▓▓     █ - Potential UMB
              0x8000      ▓▓▓▓ ▓▓▓▓ ▓▓▓▓ ▓▓▓▓     P - Page Frame
              0x9000      ▓▓▓▓ ▓▓▓▓ ▓▓▓▓ ▓▓▓▓     M - Mappable Conv
              0xA000      VVVV VVVV VVVV VVVV     E - EMS UMB
              0xB000      XXXX XXXX VVVV VVVV     X - XMS UMB
              0xC000      BXXX XXXX XXXX XXXX
              0xD000      XXXX XXXX XXXX XXXX
              0xE000      PPPP PPPP PPPP PPPP
              0xF000      XXXX XXXX XXXX XXXB
```

13-3
Memory usage map.

Of course, writing a BIOS these days is a pretty specialized business in itself, so for a suitable BIOS Helix went to Award, one of the better-known BIOS makers in the business. Because the Netroom BIOS is a software BIOS, the system boots up from whatever ROM BIOS chip you've got. But as soon as the machine is up and running far enough to read the CONFIG.SYS and load the Netroom manager, the software BIOS loads and from that point you run with it.

Performance plus

With Netroom's proprietary cloaked utilities installed—a RAM disk, screen accelerator, anti-virus, DPMI support, and their disk cache replacing DOS's SMARTDRV, the net conventional memory available went up another 12K (see FIG. 13-4). To me, the most significant number, however, is the 150K of upper memory that's still available—and not only simply available, but with no less than 117,312 bytes (114.5K) in one contiguous block.

```
                       DISCOVER v3.00
                  Fri Feb 26 13:40:42 1993
          Copyright (c) 1990,91,92 Helix Software Company, Inc.
```

| | | Memory | |
Name	Location	Size	

```
          80386sx running DOS v6.00
```

Conventional———————————————		655,344	(639.9K)
DOS	0000	9,664	
EMMXXXX0	025D	5,408	
DOS	03B0	3,408	
MM.EXE	0486	128	
ENVIRONMENT	049D	240	
Free		636,432	(621.5K)
UMB———————————————————————		32,720	(31.9K)
SETVERXX	B001	752	
CACHECLK	B030	6,112	
SB	B1AE	16,304	
DOSKEY	B5A9	4,144	
Free	B6AC	5,408	(5.2K)
UMB———————————————————————		125,648	(122.7K)
XLOAD	C151	704	
DPMI$	C17D	4,992	
COMMAND	C2B5	2,640	
Free	C35A	117,312	(114.5K)
UMB———————————————————————		61,424	(59.9K)
E:	F001	45,120	
F:	FB05	192	
SCRNCLK	FB11	896	
Free	FB49	15,216	(14.8K)

13-4
Memory usage map showing no less than 117,312 bytes (114.5K) in one contiguous block.

With that big a piece to work with, even DESQview manages to smuggle enough of its code into upper memory to leave up to 576K available for applications running under it. While that figure might sound low these days, it's exactly what I get on the same machine when using QEMM386 and Stealth. In fact, short of mapping over the video graphics area (A000h–AFFFh), it was the first time I had ever been able to run DESQview satisfactorily under anybody else's memory manager without reconfiguring the DESQview windows to use less than 576K—in some cases significantly less.

The unprecedented amount of *useful* upper memory Netroom now makes available by cloaking should be good news to network users, too. Most network drivers should fit nicely without using precious conventional memory. And even if they don't, they do.

Prior to the development of cloaking, Netroom had another strategy that gave the appearance of having more useful memory than you really had. Really a crude form of multitasking, Netroom could set up a virtual machine of up to 576K in size—it still can if you really need it, though rather than the recommended way to go it's now suggested only as a last resort.

Now you see it, now you don't

What the virtual machine trick did—or does—is give you a whole other bunch of space to load not only TRSs but device drivers to let them run, unseen, in the background. This didn't seem to work so well with pop-ups, and other than for network drivers I was never that impressed. However, there were and are some spinoff benefits.

The keystone of the NETSWAP virtual machine scheme was a clever utility called DEVLOAD, which loaded device drivers *after* the CONFIG.SYS had done its thing. DEVLOAD is normally used in a batch file in much the same way as DEVICE= in the CONFIG.SYS, and it can be a pretty handy one to have around even if you don't use the NETSWAP feature. I, for instance, hardly ever use a scanner—certainly not often enough to want to waste the space it takes to load the scanner driver every time I boot. With DEVLOAD, such a "sometimes" driver can be loaded from the command line, or even better, from a batch file that loads whatever application you're using with such a device.

If you use the new cloaking features, installation of the new Netroom takes longer than most other memory managers because you have to do it twice: once through (including customizing without cloaking) and then a second time to add the cloaking features and recustomize with them. I was pleased with the 624,352 bytes I had to work with after the first pass, but even more pleased to find that, even though I'd added several features including a RAM disk, as shown in FIG. 13-5, I had nearly 12K more to work with after I installed the cloaking features.

Installing Netroom

Netroom's setup program assumes that you already have somebody's memory manager installed, so you don't have to strip your CONFIG.SYS before installing Netroom. In fact, where specific inclusions and exclusions are found associated with whatever memory manager you've been using, the setup program automatically picks them up, carries them over, and tacks them onto the Netroom line when it rewrites the CONFIG.SYS.

Customize has finished optimizing your system's memory. The following table sumarizes the memory use (in bytes) on your system:

13-5

Customize screen showing almost 12K more to work with.

Memory Type	Before Customize	After Customize	Change
Free conventional memory:	624,352	636,544	12,192
Upper memory:			
Used by programs	69,644	81,856	
Reserved for Windows	0	0	
Reserved for EMS	65,536	65,536	
Free	150,128	137,936	-12,192
Expanded memory:	Enabled	Enabled	

The machine I ran it on—the same one used for testing all the memory managers I used when writing this book—didn't require a lot that was real fancy. Still, the "before" and "after" CONFIG.SYS and AUTOEXEC.BAT files give an interesting look at just what Netroom's setup program does. The following is CONFIG.SYS *before* installing Netroom:

```
DEVICE=C:\DOS\HIMEM.SYS
DEVICE=C:\DOS\EMM386.EXE RAM I=B000-B7FF
DEVICE=C:\DOS\SETVER.EXE
DEVICE=C:\STACKER\STACKER.COM /P=1 D:\STACVOL.DSK
DEVICE=C:\STACKER\SSWAP.COM D:\STACVOL.DSK
BUFFERS=15,0
FILES=30
DOS=HIGH,UMB
LASTDRIVE=Z
SHELL=C:\DOS\COMMAND.COM C:\DOS\ /e:512 /p
DEVICE=C:\DOS\SMARTDRV.EXE /DOUBLE_BUFFER
```

and this is CONFIG.SYS *after* installing Netroom:

```
DEVICE=C:\NETROOM\RM386.EXE AUTO
DEVICE=C:\NETROOM\VIDCLOAK.EXE /PMBIOS
DEVICE=C:\NETROOM\SYSCLOAK.EXE
DEVICE=C:\NETROOM\XLOAD.SYS -O
DEVICE=C:\NETROOM\XLOAD.SYS -SB001 C:\DOS\SETVER.EXE
DEVICE=C:\NETROOM\XLOAD.SYS -SF001 C:\STACKER\STACKER.COM
  /P=1 D:\STACVOL.DSK
DEVICE=C:\STACKER\SSWAP.COM D:\STACVOL.DSK
DOS=HIGH
DOS=UMB
BUFFERS=15,0
FILES=8
```

```
LASTDRIVE=Z
FCBS=4,0
SHELL=C:\NETROOM\XLOAD.EXE -SC151 C:\DOS\COMMAND.COM
  C:\DOS\ /p
DEVICE=C:\NETROOM\XLOAD.SYS -SF001 C:\NETROOM\DRIVECLK.EXE
  K=512 R=64 S=512 C=1
DEVICE=C:\NETROOM\XLOAD.SYS -SC151 C:\NETROOM\DPMI.EXE
```

Here is AUTOEXEC.BAT *before* installing Netroom:

```
@echo off
set dircmd=/o/p
PATH C:\DOS;d:\dos\batch;d:\dos\utility;c:\os2
prompt MS-DOS 6$_$P$_
d:\dos\sitback\sb
C:\DOS\doskey
```

and here is AUTOEXEC.BAT *after* installing Netroom:

```
C:\NETROOM\XLOAD.EXE -SF001 C:\NETROOM\SCRNCLK.EXE
C:\NETROOM\XLOAD.EXE -SB001 C:\NETROOM\CACHECLK.EXE K=2048
  WK=1024 WB=4 WD=54
@echo off
set dircmd=/o/p
PATH C:\DOS;d:\dos\batch;d:\dos\utility;c:\os2
prompt MS-DOS 6$_$P$_
C:\NETROOM\XLOAD.EXE -SB001 d:\dos\sitback\sb
C:\NETROOM\XLOAD.EXE -SB001 C:\DOS\doskey
```

Helix, interestingly, is the software developer Microsoft went to for an optimizer for MS-DOS 6, and MEMMAKER is, in fact, licensed from them. And the relationship is clearly evident from the similarity of MEMAKER prompt screens and some of those in CUSTOMIZE. HIMEM.SYS and EMM386.EXE together, though, have little in common with Helix's RM386.EXE memory manager and its companion utilities.

As interesting as Helix's new Netroom 3 is, however, it seems to be more finicky than QEMM386 or 386max. Or at least the CUSTOMIZE portion seems to be—once it was set up and running smoothly, I noted no stability problems. But it took more doing than I'm used to—plus several tech support calls—before I got there.

Quarterdeck (see FIG. 13-6) has traditionally been a leader in the area of memory management. They've had to be in order to support their premier product, DESQview. It was DESQview that brought true multitasking to the PC world as a practical reality—even while we still were running 8088s—thanks to a special kind of expanded memory (AST's EEMS) that ultimately became the model for today's LIM 4.0 EMS memory. It was Quarterdeck who first discovered and then exploited the HMA, that extra 64K DOS can use above 1Mb, and which Microsoft ultimately included in the XMS specification. And it was Quarterdeck who came up with the first automatic

QEMM

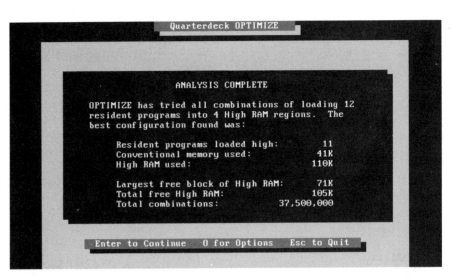

13-6
QEMM's OPTIMIZE is highly aggressive. Shown here checking some 35 million possible loading combinations, it will automatically suggest—and if you agree, try powerful Stealth options if initial results are not satisfactory.

```
                    Quarterdeck OPTIMIZE

                     ANALYSIS COMPLETE

 OPTIMIZE has tried all combinations of loading 12
 resident programs into 4 High RAM regions.   The
 best configuration found was:

       Resident programs loaded high:          11
       Conventional memory used:              41K
       High RAM used:                        110K

       Largest free block of High RAM:        71K
       Total free High RAM:                  105K
       Total combinations:             37,500,000


      Enter to Continue   O for Options   Esc to Quit
```

upper-memory optimizer—called OPTIMIZE—for the then still relatively new 386 machines. And MANIFEST is still probably the best DOS memory-analysis tool there is.

The driving force with this latest release of QEMM386 (now version 7), as much or more than any other factor, has been multitasking. They say that necessity is the mother of invention, and multitasking code requires a lot of memory. And since man cannot live by multitasking alone, you need more than just a lot today—and QEMM 7 does just that, providing as much as 250K or more of usable DOS memory beyond 640K on 386 and higher systems.

With the introduction of a new technology called Stealth in version 6, QEMM was actually able to better BlueMAX, Qualitas's PS/2-specific memory manager by mapping over almost the entire 128K block the ROM on this machine takes up (all but something like 1.6K, as opposed to the roughly 48K BlueMax shrinks it to).

And interestingly, there was an undocumented Stealth feature in that release (ST:P) that had the capability of moving system and video ROM into extended memory. This was somewhat similar to the cloaking feature that Netroom 3 now has, the most significant difference being that rather than introducing a new generic software ROM set, ST:P copies the existing system ROM to extended memory. The advantage to this is that the system still has the BIOS it was designed for. The bad news is that a relative handful of BIOSs don't take kindly to this treatment for one reason or another, so it remains an intriguing but yet undocumented feature—and one worth experimenting with—in QEMM 7.

That, in a nutshell, is the story behind QEMM386; today as always it's one of the most powerful and innovative 32-bit memory-management packages available.

Because of the continuing need for more and more memory above 640K, Quarterdeck has added a number of interesting new features to this latest release, not only for use with earlier versions of DOS but, in this age of specialization, features specific to MS-DOS 6 and to Windows 3x. And since it's special features such as these that set the better third-party memory managers apart from those provided by DOS's HIMEM.SYS and EMM386.EXE, I'll focus mainly on those extras here.

New in version 7

Of interest to all DOS users is a new "DOS-UP" feature that loads parts of DOS itself into upper memory. How much depends on which DOS version you happen to be using, but it usually amounts to at least 7K, and can run to as much as a 70K increase in the amount of conventional memory available to run DOS programs, certainly well worth the effort—which, by the way, doesn't even require any extra effort.

With QEMM's new Express Install option, it requires no effort at all, in fact. While QEMM still allows more experienced users to play "what if . . ." (even easier now with a "point and shoot" reconfiguration feature), less experienced users can automatically optimize or reoptimize their systems with a single keystroke, no experience needed. This isn't to say that the Express option will always do as well as you might with a little time and effort, but I think you'd be surprised how well it does.

DOS 6-specific support in general is more than simply specific to DOS 6, but specific to Microsoft's MS-DOS 6—not so much because of any preference but rather because the features QEMM caters to specifically in MS-DOS are quite different from equivalent features found in PC DOS 6.1. Also, PC DOS 6.1 was not released until after QEMM 7.

Specifically, QEMM 7 targets MS-DOS 6's DoubleSpace disk compressor, if installed, and relocates about 40K of DoubleSpace overhead to EMS expanded memory. MS-DOS 6's Vsafe (virus checking), Undelete, Doskey (one utility that QEMM automatically loads to upper memory in both IBM and MS-DOS) and Smartdrive are automatically loaded to upper memory. QEMM now supports the DPMI specification as well, although it also continues to support the VCPI specification for conforming software.

As discussed in greater detail in a later chapter when I look specifically at memory-management problems posed by Windows, the performance of Windows 3x as a shell to run DOS programs has generally been rather poor, with the size of DOS windows pretty much reflecting the amount of conventional memory available on the underlying system before loading Windows, a situation made even worse by the fact that, prior to DOS 6 releases that now have upper-memory optimizing tools, the majority of Windows users had nothing loaded high.

Up to 96K of added RAM for DOS in Windows

Even with upper memory in use, Windows wants to grab some address space it might not even use up there, reducing the effective size of DOS windows even on optimized systems.

QEMM386 has always had the capability of mapping any unused graphics video address space (VIDRAM), which, for text-based programs, typically includes the 64K immediately adjacent to what you usually have to work with as conventional memory (A000h–AFFFh) and with standard VGA and certain other displays still another 32K—and still contiguous to conventional memory—taking us all the way to B7FFh.

That amounts to 704K to 736K of *conventional* memory for DOS, enough for even the most demanding applications. You only have to add an Include statement (I=*nnnn-nnnn*) to the QEMM line in a CONFIG.SYS like this, taken from one of the new DOS 6 boot configurations on one of my machines:

```
[QEMM_no_graphics]
DEVICE=QEMM386.SYS INCLUDE=A000-B7FF . . .
```

As the configuration block name indicates, this configuration allows no graphics—and that includes any applications running in DESQview (or other multitasker) sessions. If any application you planned to run before rebooting required graphics support—say a Windows standard-mode session running under DESQview—you couldn't use this VIDRAM option. And of course you couldn't use such a configuration for enhanced-mode Windows.

Now with QEMM 7 you can configure QEMM to make this graphics video space available to text-based DOS applications running under Windows, while concurrently providing full graphics video support to Windows itself and any Windows (or graphical nonWindows) applications. Sort of like having your cake and eating it too.

And whether you use this VIDRAM in enhanced-mode Windows or not, QEMM has still another trick up its sleeve that can give you (typically) another 8K to 24K of RAM in DOS windows. Put it all together, and it doesn't get much better.

Stealth   One of the more exotic upper-memory-management schemes is Quarterdeck's Stealth technology. First seen in version 6 but significantly enhanced in this release, Stealth makes it possible to use the same address space for two things at *almost* the same time by switching back and forth between two functions on demand.

It's a little like the time-slicing that makes DOS multitasking possible. There, too, it's a trick of switching things—whole programs—in and out of what DOS sees as ordinary address space on a rotating basis so that the CPU can give a little of its time to all of them, switching back and forth so rapidly that the user never sees it happen. This is an overly simplistic look at what, in fact, is a highly complex subject, but the basic element is there.

The difference between multitasking and Stealth is that, rather than switching entire programs, QEMM386 simply maps over most of the ROM BIOS region, using that space for the EMS page frame as long as there are no calls to any BIOS services it has mapped over. Calls for any of those services, then, are trapped and held at bay while Stealth swaps the page frame out of the way and processes them normally. When finished, the page frame is swapped back in and things continue on their merry way until the next call for some BIOS function it's hiding.

Both QEMM386 with Stealth and Netroom 3 are pretty much recovering and reusing the same part of the F range and making it contiguous to what is (typically) the largest block of mappable address space above the video. The principle difference lies in how they do it; Quarterdeck takes the more conservative approach of keeping the entire existing system ROM available at all times, borrowing that address space only when no ROM calls are being processed (which frees that space for other use most of the time), as opposed to Netroom's more flamboyant approach of redirecting ROM BIOS calls to the surrogate (software) BIOS it has loaded in protected memory.

Stealth is only one part of QEMM386's bag of tricks. It's an option, and not everybody needs it—though I'm equally sure that there are more out there who do need and don't have it. And if you need it—if OPTIMIZE, QEMM386's companion optimizer, is unable to relocate all the likely candidates it finds up into UMBs by more conventional means, it gives you the option of letting it try a little Stealth as well.

There are two documented Stealth strategies available; the first is probably the easiest to understand, being the "frame" method (invoked by adding ST:F to the QEMM386.SYS command line in the CONFIG.SYS). In this mode, QEMM386 typically locates the EMS page frame in a 64K block starting at EC00h—which, to get a full 64K, overlaps all but the top 16K of the F000h–FFFFh block normally occupied by system ROM. In most cases, where Stealth is needed to get enough upper memory, OPTIMIZE takes care of it automatically.

Now everybody knows—or should know—that no two things can occupy the same space at the same time, whether you're talking computer addresses or two cars in a one-car garage, and here is Stealth encroaching on a rather grand scale. There are a couple of facts of life, however, that Stealth takes advantage of:

❏ No ROM BIOS calls ever use the page frame.
❏ No ROM functions ever use expanded memory.
❏ Once the system is booted—and this is the most important one—probably 99.9% of all programs use software interrupts when BIOS services are needed—which with today's programming techniques really isn't all that often anyway.

So what you have is an either/or situation, and Stealth's main job is to play traffic cop. It sits on top of the situation and, if an interrupt call is made requiring ROM BIOS services, it momentarily sets the page frame aside, allowing access to the ROM and restoring the page when finished. And it does all of it invisibly.

Overall, this not only can but often does make the net gain in the total bytes actually relocated into upper memory by Stealth significantly greater than the increase in the raw count of added address space. Unlike the bits and pieces of the ROM area that can be scavenged for use by almost any memory manager, here you're adding (typically) something like 48K of contiguous memory to a block that (except in the case of PS/2s) probably already had the 64K E block and very often the entire D block and part of C as well, giving all kinds of extra room for even the most rambunctious TSRs to thrash around in while initializing.

So if this is so, why not start the page frame at F000h and take advantage of the entire 64K? There are some BIOS functions near the top of the F range that are called directly, no interrupts involved, so they're nothing QEMM can intercept. This actually involves considerably less than the 16K of address space Stealth leaves untouched, but Quarterdeck has opted for a safety zone.

An alternate Stealth strategy, Move, as the name suggests, actually relocates things up there—the things being the ROMs themselves. Typically in this mode (invoked by adding ST:M to the QEMM386 line in the CONFIG.SYS) the system ROM found at F000h–FFFFh is moved to start at C000h instead, which, on VGA-equipped systems, puts it right on top of the video ROM. Here again QEMM386 intercepts interrupt calls and redirects them, making sure they're directed to the proper ROM.

So the EMS page frame (F000h–EBFFh) overlaps system ROM address space. In this case, though, most of the actual ROM has been made to appear in a different address block where, with a little more sleight of hand, it shares a block of address space with the video ROM. Consider the following:

```
QEMM-386 / Overview
    QEMM version        6.03
    QEMM status         There is High RAM.
                        Expanded memory is being used.
    Mode                ON
    Page Frame          EC00
    Stealth Type        M
    Stealth ROMs        F000: 64K
                        C000: 32K
```

The following additional data obtained with MANIFEST clearly indicates how much contiguous upper memory has been liberated, with all but just a little piece (FFFDh–FFFFh) of the 16K system ROM space remaining above the page frame scavenged, mapped with RAM, and now available. In other words, QEMM386, using Quarterdeck's Stealth technology is actually using 63K out of the possible 64K. This compares to something on the order of 24K–28K (typically) of system ROM address space—and that broken into at least two smaller, noncontiguous blocks—that can be safely mapped and used by more conventional memory managers.

```
CA00 - CBFF     8K   Unused
CC00 - EBFF   128K   High RAM
EC00 - FBFF    64K   Page Frame
FC00 - FFFC    15K   High RAM
FFFD - FFFF     0K   System ROM
     HMA        64K   First 64K Extended
```

Moving things around up in the attic is nothing new. All computers tried revectoring things with the memory-management software provided with early ChargeCards, but their efforts didn't prove successful in the long run and they subsequently abandoned the scheme. More recently, a memory manager called Memory Commander supported revectoring, providing a mechanism for moving the video up to higher addresses to push conventional memory limits to as much as 800K or more, but I found the performance trade-off to be generally unacceptable if pushed far enough to make it worth the while. Quarterdeck has taken a different approach, however, and Stealth seems to avoid the pitfalls that have plagued other relocation efforts.

Which of these two strategies is best depends on individual situations, and despite Quarterdeck's excellent OPTIMIZE program, for best results some experimentation on your part might be required. And there are hardware considerations that could dictate the use of one rather than the other—CPU upgrade adapters like the All Computers DX 486 (discussed elsewhere in this book) being a case in point. With that particular adapter, Stealth can be used only in the Move mode—and then only when an auxiliary Quarterdeck driver called HOOKROM.SYS is loaded first, as in the following example:

```
DEVICE=HOOKROM.SYS
DEVICE=ALL486.SYS
DEVICE=QEMM386.SYS ST:M . . .
```

In any event, Stealth is a tremendously powerful and proven technology, now looking even better in this latest QEMM version.

Note in the previous example that the page frame was located starting at EC00h. This is often not the best place for it, however. In fact, with Stealth I like to put it down at C000h. There, indeed, it maps over the video ROM—and on one of my machines a Stacker card as well—but Stealth can handle that. And look what that does for my system: a 190K unfragmented block of upper memory, running all the way from D000h to FFA5h, as shown here:

```
9FFC - B7FF    96K   High RAM
B800 - BFFF    32K   VGA Text
C000 - CFFF    64K   Page Frame
```

```
D000 - FFA5    190K   High RAM
FFA6 - FFFF    1.4K   System ROM
       HMA      64K   First 64K Extended
```

Note that I haven't even resorted to the undocumented ST:P parameter I mentioned earlier. Even without it, Stealth has mapped over all but the top 1.4K of system ROM as well as the video ROM. Although I've tried it on several machines and had no problem with it, given Stealth's almost incredible ability to pack everything I've been throwing at it into upper memory I don't really need it.

MANIFEST No discussion of QEMM would be complete without a look at Manifest, its companion memory-analysis tool (see FIG. 13-7). The first tool of its kind, initially introduced at the time Quarterdeck first gave us OPTIMIZE, it's the mother of all automatic optimizing programs and still by far the best in my opinion.

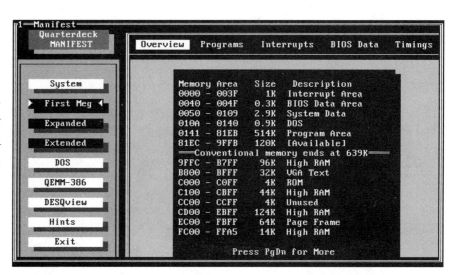

13-7
The first and still best analysis tool for memory, Quarterdeck's MANIFEST has been enhanced now to include network data.

In years gone by, Manifest—like all of the "also rans" from Quarterdeck's competitors—was useful only beyond 640K when using QEMM. It couldn't see what Qualitas or any of the other guys were actually doing up there—nor were any of theirs generally able to read other than their own proprietary mappings. This has always made it difficult to evaluate what different memory managers were actually doing on a comparative basis.

Lately, though, I've discovered that Manifest *can* see much if not all that's going on above 640K, not only with QEMM but with several of its competitors. Not all, but several—including most of those of interest to me at least.

Now for QEMM386 version 7, Manifest has been improved in other ways, adding expanded network and adapter support as well as the capability of letting you edit your CONFIG.SYS and AUTOEXEC.BAT files right from within Manifest—a particularly handy feature when dealing with multiple boot configuration files.

A DESQview primer

It should come as no surprise that Quarterdeck caters to DESQview in QEMM much as Microsoft these days is catering to Windows. The greatest difference is that Quarterdeck is far more subtle, endowing QEMM with the capability of giving all users—DESQview, Windows, and DOS users alike—the full benefit of its power.

DESQview (like Windows or any other multitasker) has a lot of code that must be loaded every time you run a DESQview session, and there are really only two places code can go: below 640K—in which case it puts a severe dent in conventional memory—or above 640K. It's hard to get away from putting some code below 640K, but to do it effectively takes some clever programming and close cooperation with the memory manager. Particularly when it comes to loading the bulk of the code above 640K.

Most people tend to think that DOS programs can run only in contiguous blocks of RAM. Fortunately, that isn't entirely true. It's true to the extent that most code is written with the expectation of being run in contiguous blocks of RAM and therefore makes no provision for finding any bits and pieces that aren't there.

Anticipating a fragmented upper-memory structure, DESQview has been written so it can be loaded—and run—in blocks that aren't contiguous. The break points, of course, must be at certain places in the code, and provision made to point to the next piece of the puzzle, wherever it is. But Quarterdeck has done it, and done it in a way that generally fits what bits of upper memory will, most likely, be available. Here you can see that cleverness at work in a Manifest excerpt:

```
===Conventional memory ends at 735K===
C800 - C803   0.1K   QEMM386
C804 - C832   0.7K   SETVER
C833 - C8DB   2.6K   PCKRAMD
C8DC - C8DE    0K    SUPERPCK Environment
C8DF - C8EA   0.2K   DV Data
C8EB - C967    2K    FILES
C968 - CBFE   10K    DV Data
CD00 - D800   44K    STACKER
D801 - E4A7   50K    SUPERPCK
E4A8 - EBFE   29K    DV Data
EC00 - FC0B   0.2K   DV Data
FC0C - FCB4   2.6K   LASTDRIV
FCB5 - FDFF   5.2K   DV Data
     HMA      64K    DV
```

This report, with DESQview loaded, shows bits and pieces of code scattered through upper memory and the HMA, contrary to what most users think is possible. However, by being able to break its code to run in smaller, noncontiguous blocks, DESQview enables QEMM and OPTIMIZE to load even large TSRs and drivers into upper memory. Note that this data was taken from a configuration that mapped the entire video graphics region as conventional memory using the VIDRAM option.

All this, and still enough usable upper memory for other TSRs and device drivers to qualify QEMM as one of the most powerful DOS memory managers around. With or without DESQview.

A bevy of beauties I've tried to crowd the essence of three of the very best, most powerful, and technologically advanced DOS memory managers available today into a single chapter. In so little space it's impossible to do justice to any of them. Yet it would be impossible in 20 volumes to say all there is to say, for every situation is a little different—enough that what's best for one machine with one configuration isn't necessarily the best for someone with a different mission. Even on the same machine.

There's no single program that's the best in every situation. In fact, I don't always use the same one, switching back and forth according to the best results I've attained for different kinds of sessions when I boot from real-mode DOS, thanks to multiple boot-time configuration options. (Prior to MS- and PC DOS, for several years, except when working with DR DOS, I used BOOT.SYS, a shareware boot manager that affords similar boot options with earlier DOS versions.)

If this were a beauty contest, these three would be the finalists. All three are beauties in their own right. Microsoft and IBM both made the semifinals of the contest this time around; for the first time, both of them are real contenders. My vote puts these programs in the finals, though. The final round is up to you.

14 Alternative strategies

In the beginning when we took our first, often faltering steps beyond 640K, life was relatively simple. Basically, the only option—and that only sometimes—was between conventional and, if we were lucky enough to have it, expanded memory. Now not only is there extended memory and something called the HMA, but everybody seems to have a different idea on how and when to use them.

Increasingly, as we're squeezed for more and more memory, squeezed on every side it seems, there seem to be more, new, and different ways to do whatever job we have to do. All too often, though, any gains are paid for in lost features and lost functionality. Which is not only ironic but a damned shame when in this age of mega-megabytes we can't squeeze out a few more lousy kilobytes. Help is on the way, however.

Lately—and increasingly—there has been a tendency to put the code for DOS device drivers and TSRs into extended (XMS) rather than conventional or upper memory. Let's face it: there's only so much upper address space. It's a finite resource whereas extended memory is virtually unlimited, and using it is an idea whose time has come.

The extended alternative

This is really what the cloaking in Netroom is all about. And in QEMM 7, Quarterdeck has managed to pack off all but about 1K of the roughly 250K of code to the inviting pastures of extended memory. These are just two examples that come quickly to mind. The problem until now has been that individual developers have pretty much just done their own thing—not carelessly, putting you at risk when running other software, but not really to help the next guy either. Netroom's cloaked utilities, for instance, will run, but try to run them using HIMEM.SYS or QEMM or some other manager and you'll get an error message that says:

```
RM386.SYS not loaded
```

I'm not faulting them for that. In fact, I'm sure there are some very good reasons why Netroom's cloaked utilities will run only when using Netroom. And the reasons likely have nothing to do with any proprietary attitudes on their part, but rather are simply a function of the way the code was written, anticipating certain conditions that only Netroom creates.

The problem was that until quite recently there was no standard way of dealing with the problems unique to loading device driver and TSR code into extended memory. None of the existing standards or specifications went far enough. Enter Novell (trumpets and fanfare please) with a new specification written not just for their own Novell DOS 7 but equally applicable to anybody's DOS and available to any developer to use *without fee or other obligation*. Enter the DPMS, and what certainly marks the beginning of a new chapter in the management of DOS memory beyond 640K, and hopefully the beginning of a new era.

Novell & the DPMS specification

Standing for DOS protected-mode services, everything a developer needs to take advantage of this API is in a software developer's kit (SKD) available from Novell. Earlier in the book I talked about the VCPI and DPMI DOS-extender specifications without which we wouldn't have such things as Windows, DESQview, or many of the larger applications that we tend to take for granted. Unfortunately—or fortunately, depending on your point of view—that's just what the VCPI and the DPMI are for: large and even larger applications. In many cases, that technology, by its very nature, makes it too cumbersome for utility programs and TSRs.

The purpose of the DPMS specification is not to try to burden us with still another "standard" but rather to provide a somewhat scaled-down set of services more suited to the needs of smaller chunks of code. The several functions of the DPMS can be summed up basically as:

❑ Allocating extended memory.
❑ Managing protected-mode descriptor tables.
❑ Handling the transition between real- and protected-mode execution.

In essence, it defines a client-server software architecture where the client program calls the DPMS server—typically located in upper memory, as shown in FIG. 14-1—to perform the necessary memory allocations and mode transitions.

Making this even more attractive is the fact that existing TSRs and device drivers can, in most cases, be ported with very little effort on the part of their

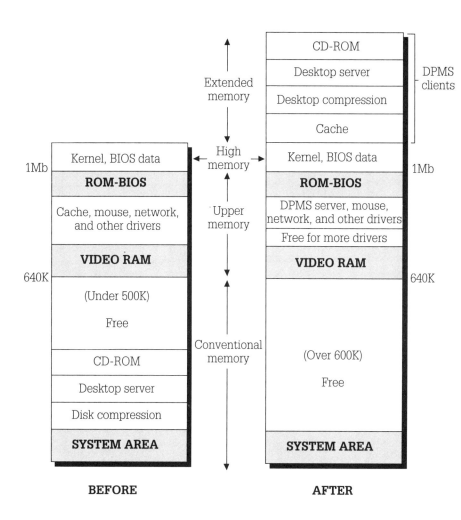

BEFORE

AFTER

Extended memory

High memory

Upper memory

Conventional memory

1Mb — Kernel, BIOS data

ROM-BIOS

Cache, mouse, network, and other drivers

VIDEO RAM

640K

(Under 500K)

Free

CD-ROM

Desktop server

Disk compression

SYSTEM AREA

CD-ROM

Desktop server

Desktop compression

Cache

Kernel, BIOS data — 1Mb

ROM-BIOS

DPMS server, mouse, network, and other drivers

Free for more drivers

VIDEO RAM

640K

(Over 600K)

Free

SYSTEM AREA

DPMS clients

14-1
Block diagram shows how DPMS can relocate greater part of device drivers and TSRs in extended rather than upper or conventional memory.

developers to take advantage of the advantages of DPMS operations—and at no loss of existing functionality—because DPMS clients are created as real-mode 16-bit .COM or .EXE programs. And if you run these programs and drivers on a system that doesn't support the DPMS specification (virtually any 80286 or higher system with extended memory and a DPMS server driver loaded does), they'll run just like they always ran: in conventional or, with luck, upper memory.

It's basically a winning ticket either way. And even if you're using MS- or PC DOS instead of Novell DOS 7, the free-standing DPMS server driver I was working with left only a 1K footprint loaded into upper memory. Not only will DPMS work with almost anybody's DOS, but it will work with almost anybody's memory manager as well. Regardless of how well Novell does in the marketplace with their new DOS, this could be one of the most important contributions to memory management of late. Now, if developers will only take advantage of it . . .

PC KWIK & secondary memory management

For the past several years, PC KWIK has been one of the most effective memory managers around. Now with versions for both DOS and Windows, PC KWIK is not a memory manager in the ordinary sense, but it's capable of utilizing memory like no conventional memory manager can or does. And more than simply having memory, using what you've got is really what it's all about.

The reason most users don't associate PC KWIK with memory management is that memory management is only secondary, a by-product of its primary function: disk caching. PC KWIK supports disk caching plus an optional RAM disk plus a print spooler plus a screen accelerator plus a keyboard accelerator, as well as some other options if you use the entire package.

The thing that initially set PC KWIK apart and ultimately set the pace for other cache developers to try to follow was the dynamic way it operated on a space-available basis. In other words, beyond some nominal minimum size, it borrowed whatever else there was that wasn't being used to build a bigger cache. And it would give back most of the cache and any RAM disk and spooler RAM it wasn't using at the moment any time another application came along and needed it.

If·you've got a lot of unused RAM, PC KWIK will quietly take up to 16 megabytes and put it to work as a cache (and RAM disk, spooler, etc.) if you want all the whistles and bells. But PC KWIK can also work with very little extra RAM. It isn't fussy—in fact, the less spare RAM you have, the more important it is to make the most of it. But the more you have to work with, the more PC KWIK can do for you.

The ability of PC KWIK to shrink or expand the size of the cache in mid-session is not, in itself, remarkable. These days even MS-DOS 6's SMARTDRV.EXE can, although on a much more limited basis, automatically shrink the size of the cache, as determined by the InitCacheSize parameter, to a smaller size (WinCacheSize) when Windows loads, anticipating Windows' greater need for RAM. There, however, unless these values are specified by the user, SMARTDRV does it on an arbitrary basis, as shown:

Extended Memory	InitCacheSize	WinCacheSize
Up to 1Mb	All extended memory	Zero (no caching)
Up to 2Mb	1Mb	256K
Up to 4Mb	1Mb	512K
Up to 6Mb	2Mb	1Mb
6Mb or more	2Mb	2Mb

There are some other caches that can shrink when system needs increase as well. An even closer comparison can be found in Novell DOS 7's new dynamic cache or in Qcache, the proprietary cache supplied by Qualitas with 386max, or CACHECLK.EXE, part of Netroom 3. These programs do much the same thing as PC KWIK as far as adjusting their size dynamically according to other system needs. There are also several other third-party disk-cache programs that can dynamically change the size of the cache according to other demands on system resources, keeping virtually all your available RAM at work at all times.

What puts PC KWIK in a class by itself is the fact that it's more than just a cache. It is, in fact, a whole suite of utilities, a suite in which all the main components—the cache, RAM disk, and print spooler—all participate in the continuous dynamic allocation/reallocation process, from the moment PC KWIK installs until you power down.

The first thing PC KWIK does when it installs (the driver loads from the CONFIG.SYS) is quietly assume control of all the free RAM you have (up to 16 megabytes) beyond 640K. This, of course, is *after* the primary memory manager—HIMEM.SYS, QEMM386, or what have you—has allocated memory for the HMA and mapped memory to UMBs, and after any device drivers, etc. loaded *before* PC KWIK have taken what they need. Before you even load your applications (or multitasking shell like DESQview or Windows), PC KWIK is in control of your memory reserves, and everything that's loaded from that point on draws from the pool that PC KWIK is managing.

When you boot

Without PC KWIK, all management functions are normally performed by the primary memory manager, with all available unused memory simply part of a pool that's available to any and all applications on a first come, first served (as long as it's there to serve) basis. If you have more than just a few megabytes of RAM available, then, a goodly part of it is likely sitting idle for at least a part—if not all—of most sessions.

By contrast, PC KWIK typically scarfs up the whole pool and immediately puts it to use. And if you really want to see a disk cache do its thing, you'll really see it if you have a fair amount of RAM to spare. This doesn't mean that a cache of 16Mb is going to be 16 times as effective as one that's 1Mb in size. Other than for extremely small caches, the relationship is not linear, usually reaching a point of diminishing returns rather quickly after the first megabyte or two, depending on the kind of work you're doing and the number and size of disk reads/writes, etc. (Actually, it isn't even truly linear with small cache sizes, but rather only seems to be nearly linear in some instances.) Regardless of the relationship, bigger is better, and given that, pressing every bit of unused RAM into service helps.

To accomplish its goal, once loaded, PC KWIK maintains an ongoing interactive relationship with the primary memory manager. It has to, because while it can in many cases allocate the memory an application needs directly from the pool it has to manage, there are situations when PC KWIK must work in conjunction with the primary memory manager. A case in point would be if PC KWIK was configured to cache in XMS extended memory and you started an application that requires EMS expanded memory. PC KWIK cannot emulate expanded memory, and in that case must turn extended memory back to the primary memory manager for conversion.

This, of course, assumes a primary memory manager such as QEMM386, Netroom, or 386max—one capable of delivering (or emulating) EMS expanded memory when needed. This wouldn't work with an XMS driver such as HIMEM.SYS unless EMM386.EXE, the EMS emulator, was loaded too. It does demonstrate the symbiotic nature of the relationship that must exist, however.

Disk caching   Probably nothing else you do when configuring your system is as vague as disk caching. Most users know that disk caching can make their systems run a little faster and some understand that it's a form of data buffering, but far superior to DOS buffers (too many DOS buffers, in fact, can actually slow your system down).

Almost any caching speeds things up, and most premium caches throw out benchmark numbers as an indication of how much they speed disk I/O. PC KWIK claims access speed increases from 300% to 1700%, but since it's really impossible to relate them to real-world access times, numbers like this tend to lack real meaning.

PC KWIK goes one step farther in the numbers game, however. During every session it keeps track of just how many times your system actually accesses your cached disk(s) and, on demand, displays that information plus the number of times it would have gone to disk without disk caching (see FIG. 14-2). This, at least, is a measure of the effectiveness of PC KWIK's disk caching: finite numbers in a field of vague.

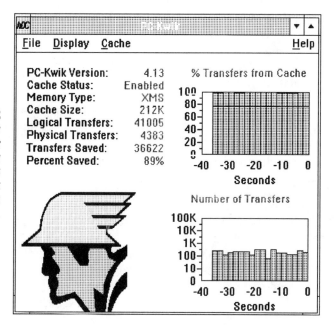

14-2
The benefits of using an efficient disk-cache program, where a relatively small cache (212K) has saved 89% of the disk read/write operations in a typical work session.

Make no mistake: the numbers are impressive. I would rate the example in FIG. 14-2 to be fairly typical, and anyone impressed by numbers has to be impressed. But even these numbers tell you very little; nowhere do they say that disk caching has saved ten minutes in the current session—or five, or even one. You can logically assume that it has saved time, but other than for the times you see the disk light on, indicating disk activity, it's hard if not impossible to quantify.

The beauty of PC KWIK's scheme is that you don't have to fret about whether disk caching is the most cost-effective use for RAM or if you should skimp on caching, leaving more of your most precious resource in the pool.

The PC KWIK RAM disk is equally intriguing. Of course, unlike the disk cache, the RAM disk can't give back any RAM that's actually being used. That would dump or at very least corrupt the contents of the RAM disk, whereas dumping disk-cache contents simply means your applications have to read the needed data from the disk again, assuming those same sectors are required. (No disk-cache contents are dumped until any pending writes are finished.)

It's there then it's gone

The PC KWIK RAM disk simply doesn't draw memory until it's actually needed. Here, too, the magic number is 16 megabytes, and given the fact the RAM disk doesn't actually use any of it until needed—and then only just what it needs—there's little reason not to go all the way. I don't, generally limiting the maximum size to something on the order of 1.5 megabytes—big enough to hold the contents of a high-density floppy (or a lot of .TMP files you don't need cluttering your hard disk).

Some days I use the RAM disk. Many days I don't though, but that's what makes the way it's done in PC KWIK so perfect. Otherwise, the option really wouldn't be that viable in many cases. But as long as it costs nothing (in terms of RAM) except when actually being used, it's pretty nice to have a RAM disk handy.

The same is true of the PC KWIK's print spooler. It, too, dips RAM from the pool only when actually needed, giving it back when finished. From a strict memory-management perspective, however, PC KWIK's other features don't play any significant role.

On systems that have enough UMB space available, PC KWIK automatically loads all of its code into upper memory. On systems that have EMS 4.0 expanded memory, about 50% of PC KWIK's code can be offloaded to expanded memory, minimizing the need for UMB space (or, as a last resort, conventional memory). While pretty sophisticated at one time, this is hardly state-of-the-art today and they are, I was told, looking into the possibilities of moving this one to extended memory as well.

In the meantime, the PC KWIK package has grown to include a number of utilities including Kwikboot, an alternative to the multiple boot configurations feature that is now a part of all the major DOSs and a special Windows package as well. The set piece of it all is still dynamic caching and a clever RAM disk (and matching spooler) that take only what they actually need at any given moment—and then give any back they're finished with. If that isn't a form of memory management, I don't know what qualifies.

There are other schemes as well. These just happen to be two of the best I know of at the moment. The important thing to keep in mind is that the management of memory does not—or at least *should* not—end with the choice of which memory manager you use. It isn't over until the fat lady sings, and if you have a bunch of fat utilities using up great gobs of upper memory, you likely won't be happy with the tune.

15 Windows 3x: torn between two worlds

Windows has finally emerged as the dominant graphical user interface (GUI) for DOS. Although plain-old, ugly DOS still outsells it, Windows has attracted enough of a following to assure it a place in the long-range scheme of things for many users.

However, Windows is currently torn between two worlds: the real-mode world, where it started, and protected mode, where it lives today but where it cannot go without real-mode support. Sort of like a space station orbiting the earth.

The discontinuance of real-mode Windows (beginning with version 3.1) has isolated Windows from the large 8088 contingent, so any discussion of Windows, then, is limited to 80286 and higher systems. Admittedly, as 3.0 demonstrated, Windows in 640K was pretty much a waste. So Windows now runs exclusively in the protected mode, even with its roots still firmly planted in plain ordinary old 640K real mode.

Aside from that, however, Windows raises a number of significant issues that fall directly within the purview of this book:

❏ The way Windows uses memory.
❏ The kinds of memory it uses.
❏ The way Windows manages that memory—all of it essentially beyond 640K.

And as long as Windows is a child of DOS, these issues will remain preeminent. In all three areas, Windows is sufficiently different from DOS to warrant separate discussion.

One flag, four kinds of memory

Windows, at various times and under various circumstances, can use or emulate up to four kinds of memory—and when those aren't enough, it has some more tricks up its sleeve. The four kinds include:

❑ Conventional memory (RAM only when loading)
❑ Extended memory (RAM)
❑ Virtual memory (emulation using hard disk space)
❑ Expanded memory (emulation using extended memory)

As a practical matter, with the demise of real-mode Windows (beginning with 3.1) you can really reduce that list to only two as far as Windows itself is concerned. Windows looks at what we call conventional memory as nothing but a launch pad. In fact, that's pretty much how Windows views the whole first megabyte.

Once loaded, then, conventional memory per se is not a factor (though users wanting to continue using DOS applications under Windows need to treat it as if it was), and expanded memory is provided only to support the use of nonWindows applications that require it—and then only on 32-bit systems running Windows in enhanced mode.

That brings you down to just extended and virtual memory, and Windows virtualizes memory only when running in enhanced mode (in standard mode, it just plain swaps to disk)—and then only when there isn't enough real RAM to go around. Once loaded, what Windows really wants and needs is nothing but extended memory. And lots of it. You provide the extended memory—any plain XMS memory manager will do—and Windows does the rest, even using some of it to emulate EMS memory (if needed by DOS applications when running in enhanced mode).

This doesn't mean that there aren't things you can do to make Windows use what memory you have more effectively. There are, especially if you run a mix of Windows and nonWindows applications using Windows as a DOS shell. In order to understand what can and can't be done, you need to understand a bit about the way Windows handles memory.

A matter of self interest

Windows really does its own thing when it comes to memory usage. Since real mode last saw the light in release 3.0, Windows really wants only extended memory. It doesn't matter whether you're running standard or enhanced-mode Windows. Once loaded from DOS, extended memory is all that Windows wants or needs. Nobody really has enough, so other than whatever minimal amount it takes to boot and load whatever device drivers are needed at the DOS level, Windows would like all the rest available to it as extended memory. No HMA, no upper memory, just more extended memory.

As long as you run *only* Windows applications, this is fine. But when you try to shell to DOS, suddenly you're back in the real world again and real-world rules, where the space for DOS applications is a direct function of how much conventional memory you had available before you loaded Windows—which, without DOS loaded in the HMA and DOS-level TSRs and device drivers loaded into upper memory—can get skimpy pretty fast. Not necessarily a whole lot worse than in a plain bare DOS environment that didn't use the HMA and upper memory, but . . .

Although Windows—particularly in enhanced mode—demands a far greater degree of memory-management sophistication than almost any other DOS-based application that comes to mind, Microsoft uses a decidedly bland XMS memory manager as its foundation: HIMEM.SYS.

Rather than taking Quarterdeck's tack of creating the most powerful memory manager they could conceive to meet the needs of DESQview (and now the even greater needs of DESQview/X), Microsoft has endowed the 32-bit Windows kernel (386KRNL.EXE) itself with the real power to manage memory. Even if you do install one of the premium third-party memory managers for use when you run Windows, Windows pretty much pipes the tune for almost everything you do inside of Windows 3*x*.

Let me quickly point out that once you leave real mode you *must* do things quite differently, and this is especially true of multitaskers or, as you'll see in the following section, any DOS or DOS emulation that's running in protected rather than real mode. DESQview, which is surely Windows' closest rival when it comes to multitasking on top of DOS, has to do all the same kind of juggles Windows has to do once it leaves real mode (which it does automatically on 32-bit machines). The difference is that it just isn't as conspicuous with DESQview.

Conceptually, there's nothing wrong with Microsoft's approach. However, as a practical matter it tends to box users into doing things that Microsoft wants to see done. In the case of users trying to run DOS applications under Windows, it can cost you as much as 200K (or more) of RAM and leave you with too little memory to continue using even those DOS applications that might suit you better than any available for Windows. Now the better third-party memory managers are all capable of getting around that problem— often, in fact, providing more RAM for DOS applications running under Windows (up to 736K) than you might have ever seen in a conventional DOS environment. More about that in the next chapter.

Still in a default Windows installation—just as in a default MS-DOS 6.0 installation—if Windows is found to exist on a hard disk, only those things Microsoft wants done get done to create a working environment that surely favors the use of Windows applications over DOS. And, unfortunately, most users are afraid to tamper with things, so as a practical matter most of the world dances to whatever tune the defaults dictate—the same holding true with almost any software.

The new MS-DOS 6 MEMMAKER utility does give DOS users with 386 and better systems a little more to work with than previous releases, of course. But make no mistake; Windows really doesn't want a bunch of other stuff in upper memory. In fact, Microsoft has MEMMAKER steer clear of it in case Windows might need it—a total of 24K that can and often does add up to a loss of considerably more than that in practice, given the peculiarities of upper memory use discussed elsewhere in this book.

The bottom line is that Windows needs a lot of extended memory—a lot more than most users have or even at this point in time probably even aspire to.

Given the ability of all the new DOSs to support multiple boot configurations and on-the-fly changes (see more detailed discussion in a later chapter), it's now much easier to serve your own interests if those interests also include nonWindows sessions. Unfortunately, however, there are a large number of users who lack the experience or technical expertise to properly avail themselves of this new (new to IBM and MS-DOS 6x) capability.

Left to its own, Windows wants all the resources you can give it and more. And HIMEM.SYS, a crude XMS-only driver, suits its needs perfectly—to a point that, with one notable exception (386max), Windows won't even install on a machine that has any another XMS driver installed unless you first let it replace your other memory manager with HIMEM.SYS. This doesn't mean you can't run Windows using other memory managers, such as QEMM386, but rather only that you can't install Windows under them. Once installed, you can switch to any XMS-compliant manager you want.

Because the Windows kernel, by design, assumes total control over all the system resources it sees, doing with them pretty much as it pleases, there's really little or nothing to be gained by using other memory managers. At least not when running *strictly* Windows applications. The biggest difference comes when running a mix of DOS and Windows applications, as you'll see a little later in this chapter.

Windows doesn't overtly bar you from using one of the more powerful third-party memory managers, mind you—or even from availing yourself more fully of the capabilities of HIMEM.SYS and its companion EMM386.EXE. It also doesn't overtly bar you from the use of upper memory for loading device drivers, etc., but only if a user knows there's more to life than what the defaults give you and is gutsy enough to go for it.

On the flip side of the coin, however, the Windows SETUP program, by automatically installing HIMEM.SYS if no acceptable third-party memory manager (386max being the only known exception at this writing) is found to be active when Windows is installed, is actually performing a considerable service for countless users by giving them—often for the first time ever—the use of sometimes as much as three or more megabytes of memory than they bought and paid for when they bought their computers. It never ceases to amaze me the number of users who buy systems that come with two to four megs of RAM but, for one reason or other, fail to install any memory manager. Many, of course, still live happily with 640K—even on 386s, and I'm sure 486s too. Windows can, beginning with 3.1, no longer live in real mode, so for those users Windows finally presses all that extra hardware into use.

I must, before we go much farther in this discussion, deal with the fact that there are not just one but two completely different Windows environments: enhanced and standard. (3.0 also had a real mode, but this was dropped in 3.1.) What many users don't know is that these aren't just branches of a single Windows program; they're completely different. Enhanced-mode sessions load from 386KRNL.EXE and standard-mode sessions from 286KRNL.EXE.

Nonidentical twins

The 286-compatible standard-mode kernel contains only 16-bit instructions, nothing that can't be executed by a 16-bit CPU. 32-bit CPUs, of course, can also read 16-bit instructions, so basically anything from a 286 on up can (assuming at least a meg or so of extended memory is available) run Windows in standard mode.

It is the 286 kernel that allows only nonWindows applications to be swapped to disk and absolutely no multitasking of nonWindows applications, no matter what. Also, the 286 kernel is not endowed with the power to create and manage virtual memory. And, of interest to users of DOS applications, it's the 286 kernel that's unable to emulate expanded memory and provide it to any nonWindows applications that require it (even when running standard mode on 386 and higher machines).

Exclusively for 386 and higher machines, Windows has an inherently faster enhanced-mode kernel written with 32-bit instructions. It's also, overall, a more powerful Windows, although the differences aren't entirely attributable to the 32-bit coding. Some are, like the much faster direct 32-bit hard disk access that the version 3.1 enhanced-mode kernel has added as an option (provided you also have a 32-bit bus and 32-bit interface card).

Regardless of the underlying nature of these differences, it's the choice of which of these two Windows kernels you use that determines how the systems resources—RAM and hard disk space especially—will be utilized. However, because the enhanced-mode kernel can run only on 80386 and higher systems, while the standard-mode kernel runs on 80286 and up, there is at least an indirect correlation between these two modes and memory management.

There is a *direct* correlation between which mode you're running and some memory-management issues, with the distinction becoming blurred by the fact that standard mode will run on 386 and higher systems, too—systems that inherently support more sophisticated memory-management techniques than the 80286 chips standard mode is meant for. And because of this, you have to break Windows memory management down still farther to include:

❑ Windows in enhanced mode (386 and higher systems only)
❑ Windows in standard mode on 80386 and higher systems
❑ Windows in standard mode on 80286 systems

Here again I should point out that Microsoft has never given expanded memory more than grudging acknowledgement despite the fact that their name is on it (LIM for Lotus, Intel, and Microsoft). Not until MS-DOS 4.0 did Microsoft provide any expanded-memory support, and then—as in Windows—only for 386 and higher systems via an EMS emulator, 386EMM.EXE, that can't be used alone but only in conjunction with an XMS driver such as HIMEM.SYS.

As for the ability to create and manage virtual memory, in its zeal to make the enhanced mode appear more glamorous than performance warrants, on loading, the enhanced mode kernel by default automatically assumes *four times* as much memory as is actually available on the system by assigning addresses to hard disk space to make up for the shortfall.

I discuss the pros and cons of virtualizing memory in greater detail earlier in this book, however, so I won't repeat them here. And the same applies to the relative merits of good, old-fashioned task switching as opposed to multitasking, so let's move on now to how best to deal with these various peculiarities, as they apply both to enhanced mode (386 and higher only) and standard mode (286 and higher).

DOS in Windows? Windows, among other things, allows you to run DOS applications under its auspices. It's a shell and, at least in the enhanced mode, a fairly credible one—provided you have RAM enough available so it doesn't have to virtualize or otherwise swap to disk. Most users don't, hence Windows' reputation for being so slow.

Windows isn't inherently slow, not even as a shell to run nonWindows applications. What it isn't, however, is generous; left to its own devices, it typically provides fewer kilobytes of usable working space for DOS than any of several other shells. MS-DOS 6.0 with MEMMAKER helps of course, though it's hardly aggressive in its search for mappable address space.

This is the point at which the serious user with TSRs and drivers that can be loaded in UMBs needs to start looking beyond even what MEMMAKER (or PC DOS 6.1's RAMBOOST) can provide, because this is where more powerful and aggressive memory management not only can but does pay off: not using

Windows for the sake of running strictly Windows applications, but when using Windows as a shell to DOS.

The deck is definitely stacked against you when it comes to running Windows in standard mode—again, particularly if you're still using and would like to continue using some or all of your DOS applications. Not only will Windows in standard mode not multitask any DOS applications—a communications package you'd like to keep running in the background, for example—but task switching will *only* swap DOS applications to disk, saving all the good stuff (RAM) for use by Windows applications whether they need it or not. And this no matter how much RAM is available.

Knowledgeable users can overcome the swap-to-disk problem—at least to some extent—by swapping to a RAM disk instead of a hard disk (assuming you have enough RAM to go around). However, you still can't run code that has been swapped out, not even to a RAM disk.

In fairness, there is some justification for Windows' inability to multitask DOS applications in standard mode. The 80286, for which standard mode is mainly intended, does not support the use of virtual machines—which is, of course, what DOS sessions run on in enhanced-mode Windows.

There are two major areas of difference between these two modes that are of crucial importance, however. The first is that, in enhanced mode, Windows runs on one or more—generally several—virtual machines rather than the single protected-mode environment in which it runs in standard mode. This by itself enables the multitasking of nonWindows applications running under the auspices of Windows in a way that isn't possible in standard mode.

The enhanced-mode Windows kernel is a lot more powerful in other ways as well when it comes to running nonWindows applications. Probably foremost in this area is support for nonWindows applications that require (or those that would at least benefit from) EMS expanded memory. The enhanced-mode Windows kernel is, as mentioned earlier, able to provide an emulation of EMS memory (borrowing from extended memory). This is totally apart from DOS's EMS memory support for 32-bit machines as provided by EMM386.EXE. EMM386.EXE doesn't even figure in the equation and need not even be included in CONFIG.SYS—at least not as far as running nonWindows applications under Windows is concerned. You do, of course, still need it if you want EMS when running directly from DOS (in or out of Windows).

The second most important difference between enhanced and standard mode is the fact that enhanced mode supports full 32-bit Windows applications, which standard-mode Windows—even running on full 32-bit machines—does not. Granted, there aren't a lot of them at this point, but given the advantages of 32-bit operations, this is increasingly where the action is.

In the enhanced mode, Windows does support the multitasking of nonWindows applications. It also supports virtual memory—also something not supported in the standard mode, though it is, as discussed elsewhere in the book, not as much a virtue as is often claimed.

Forget 640K In any case, you can forget about 640K. Beginning with version 3.1 and the death knell for Windows in real mode, Windows divorced itself entirely from the world below 640K. As far as Microsoft is concerned, anything below 1024K exists only as a boot platform from which Windows can launch forth into extended memory. And that means you have to have some form of memory management—which they willingly supply.

Windows, of course, provides only the rudimentary form of memory management required by Windows—either standard- or enhanced-mode Windows—in the form of HIMEM.SYS, which is also supplied with PC DOS, though there are some subtle differences. In order to gauge the effectiveness of Windows default memory management—in particular, the relative merits of third-party memory managers with Windows—you have to readjust your thinking.

As long as you continue running any DOS applications, there are, as you'll see, two distinctly different sets of criteria. They aren't mutually exclusive—or at least they needn't be. To prevent either from prevailing at the expense of the other takes some understanding of the issues, though.

In the DOS world, relocating 64K of TSRs and device drivers above 640K would immediately free at least 10%—usually more—of whatever part of 640K was available to run applications. If, for example, you had originally had 512K left over for your applications, an extra 64K would have jumped that to 576K for an effective gain of 12.5% more usable space. Relocating 128K would give you an effective gain of 25%—I myself have routinely run as much as 213K above 640K (including the HMA), so you're talking some really significant percentages.

Now say you're running Windows starting with 4 megabytes of RAM and, after setting up a decent cache and loading a couple of device drivers, Windows (standard mode) reports some 3 megabytes of RAM available. Even a 128K boost is going to amount to only an effective gain of roughly 4%, a pittance so small it's unlikely it would ever matter in the Windows scheme of things.

The bottom line, then, is that if you're running only Windows and Windows applications exclusively you might as well save your money and use HIMEM.SYS. And even now, with MS-DOS's MEMMAKER, any difference you might see when running Windows applications likely isn't worth the effort.

Read on, though, if you're not ready to scrap all that good DOS stuff you've got and want to keep on using it right along with Windows. There are a number of things you can do to significantly enhance the way DOS applications run in mixed-work sessions without compromising the performance of Windows applications either. First you need to understand some underlying truths, though.

Since I still run my share of nonWindows applications and demand a decent level of performance, I've spent a lot of time experimenting. And by and large I find the best system I can configure for just plain DOS is what I'm looking for in Windows: DOS loaded high (except when running DESQview, which can use the HMA to even greater advantage) and as many device drivers and nonWindows TSRs as possible loaded into upper memory.

Memory management in enhanced mode

Windows likes to set a couple of 12K blocks of upper-memory address space aside for its own occasional use—which, because of the the way they're situated, generally cost you considerably more than the 24K you might expect to lose. I've tried it both ways—letting Windows have that space and using it for something else—and frankly I can't see that it really matters.

Whether it will matter for you, however, depends to a large extent on whether you're using MS-DOS 6's MEMMAKER or some other memory manager that lets you chose—MEMMAKER just assumes you want to favor Windows if it finds a Windows installation on your hard disk (even of the OS/2 variety). In most other cases, optimizers tend to leave it up to you—at least if you look beyond the defaults.

You definitely want to load DOS=HIGH if using Windows as a shell for DOS. This all by itself can make a significant, sometimes crucial difference.

MEMMAKER is anything but aggressive (even when it says it's going to be) when it comes to finding upper memory to map on 32-bit systems for use by device drivers and nonWindows TSRs. If you don't have many to worry about, then MS-DOS 6 and MEMMAKER (or PC DOS 6.1 and RAMBOOST) might do all you need to do.

The bottom line—as always—comes down to how much conventional memory you have to run nonWindows applications under Windows. And this, of course, is an individual thing. Either you have enough or you don't; the difference is determined as much by what you run (how big your nonWindows applications are) and how well—or poorly—configured your system is.

If DOS and what it offers satisfies your needs, then fine; look no farther. If it doesn't, though, there are several excellent third-party memory managers I'll look at more closely in the next chapter, any of which can substantially increase your bottom line.

Deadly apps One of the more serious problems I've seen to some extent when running DOS applications under Windows stems from the fact that Windows running in enhanced mode, while providing an EMS 4.0 emulation for DOS programs that require it, apparently doesn't provide reentrant EMS services. What that means is that whenever a DOS application calls for EMS, Windows maps—or remaps—the available memory accordingly.

This is all well and good, so long as the initial process using EMS is allowed to execute until it terminates. If, however, in the middle of one process executing, another one requiring EMS is opened, Windows redraws the map—which suits the new process fine, but can leave the initial application twisting slowly in the wind with potentially catastrophic results.

Imagine, if you will, that the first process is a RAM disk or a disk cache that's using EMS, and it is suddenly looking at a map that's different from the one it started with. The application itself is probably not smart enough to spot the difference, but if you dump the contents of a disk cache somewhere where it isn't supposed to go you could wind up corrupting your hard disk (although I haven't seen this kind of doomsday scenario myself).

There is, as with most things, a way around such problems, but it requires special attention to the problem on the part of application programmers to assure that any preexisting mapping is restored—which many if not most responsible programmers seem to do.

Memory management in standard mode You might think that given the limitations of the standard-mode kernel in particular and 80286 systems in particular, memory management would be pretty much a "done deal," but it's anything but. If anything, running Windows in standard mode often requires more skill (or at least more savvy) than on 32-bit systems in enhanced mode.

First off, although not strictly a memory-management issue per se, is the matter of swapping to disk in lieu of using virtual memory. Swapping to/from disk is always painfully slow, and the only help for it is a faster swap disk . . . meaning a RAM disk. A RAM disk, of course, is going to detract from the amount of RAM your system has available to start with, and to be of much real value it should likely be two or more megabytes in size.

This brings me back to the subject of the last chapter; secondary memory management with something like PC KWIK: a "smart" disk cache/RAM disk package that can marshal system resources dynamically, shrinking or expanding the size of both the disk cache and whatever RAM disk you provide for on a basis of current demand and availability.

Another area that can be addressed only from outside of Windows (standard mode only) is the matter of expanded memory for nonWindows applications that require (or benefit from) it. Since EMS memory is not easily done on

80286 machines without additional hardware, the standard-mode Windows kernel (unlike the enhanced-mode kernel) makes no provision for it. It doesn't prevent the system from supplying EMS memory to nonWindows applications running under Windows, however, if you can supply it externally.

Basically, what you need is an expanded-memory card, the kind that used to be so popular a few years back. Such cards come with their own proprietary software drivers, which, unlike EMM386.EXE, are suitable for use on any 8086-compatible platform and can, at least in some cases, also deliver extended memory—which can be of considerable benefit on many older machines that (typically) support only about 4 megabytes on the motherboard.

Even with 4.0 EMS memory available, the standard-mode kernel (unlike DESQview) does not support multitasking for nonWindows applications. But it can, in many cases, make nonWindows applications run a whole lot better under Windows.

It's generally advisable to use the latest version of HIMEM.SYS you can get your hands on—which means that, for a user running Windows 3.1 under DOS 4x, a copy bundled in the Windows 3x package is surely the latest. It doesn't mean, however, that the latest HIMEM.SYS is really any better; HIMEM.SYS today works just like HIMEM.SYS has always worked.

Whose HIMEM.SYS?

All that really changes are the bug fixes—which change to try to keep up with hardware incompatibilities that keep popping up on certain new machines. Here again you run up against the myth of compatibility. As new machines with new incompatibilities appear, new fixes must be found. As a sidelight, it's interesting to note that while you might think the HIMEM.SYS in MS-DOS 6.0 has the same updated bug fixes as the HIMEM.SYS with PC DOS 6x, it isn't so.

In any event, simply using an older or different HIMEM.SYS is not inviting trouble—not if what you have works on your system. Remember the old adage "If it ain't broke, don't fix it," which in this case means if you're running with an old release of HIMEM—anybody's old release—and you aren't having problems, you're probably best off leaving well enough alone. At least until you get the urge to trade that old machine on something newer and and a whole lot faster—and who knows what else in the bargain.

From the beginning, one of IBM's most ambitious claims for OS/2 2x has been "a better Windows than Windows." I've found it to be much more stable than Windows and a very viable alternative to DOS/Windows, particularly release 2.1 (or later), with Windows 3.1-like enhanced-mode support. For this reason more than any other, I now run more Windows applications under OS/2 than I ever did under Windows.

Windows, à la OS/2 2x

OS/2, admittedly, requires more RAM than plain Windows—though not that much more. Anyone who thinks they're going to run Windows very effectively in the enhanced mode with just two megabytes of RAM is only kidding himself—as is anyone who believes OS/2 2.0 will run effectively in 4Mb. Both are capable of making up for quite a bit of shortfall in the RAM department by resorting to virtual memory, but again, as stated elsewhere in this book, you're only kidding yourself; unless you've got all day to sit and watch the little drive light on your disk drive, there's no substitute for RAM.

Memory management under OS/2

Most of the memory-management concerns I looked at earlier in this chapter and will explore in greater detail in the following chapters simply disappear in OS/2. As you'll see in greater detail in part four, on protected-mode operating systems, OS/2 does its own memory management for DOS and Windows applications. Yes, so does Windows, but with some major differences. Microsoft Windows is still a child of DOS, and DOS sessions under Windows— even in the enhanced mode—are a child process of an environment that itself is a child process of DOS, and like extra layers of government and government regulation at any level, you're hardly talking an ideal situation.

Microsoft is well aware of the problem, which is one of the reasons for Windows NT; a stand-alone environment beholden to no one and free of the excess baggage DOS represents in Windows. Windows needs to be divorced from DOS. Whether NT with its incredible demands for system resources that so far exceed all but an incredibly small percentage at the high end of today's installed hardware base is going to be the answer, however, remains to be seen.

For now, you need look no farther than OS/2 2x for immediate relief, relief that *is* compatible with a large percentage of machines in use today—everything from 386SXs (or even 286s with accelerator cards that replace the CPU) on up. And although OS/2 does require more RAM (a minimum of 4 megabytes) than ordinary Windows under DOS, it really isn't that much more. To run Windows really effectively on top of DOS you need eight megabytes of RAM, and with that amount OS/2 hums along really well.

DOS sessions under OS/2 are spawned as virtual machines directly by the OS/2 kernel, as are Windows sessions under OS/2. The only thing they have in common is their common host. There's no such thing as DOS under Windows under OS/2—nor standard-mode Windows under an OS/2 DOS session. You have DOS sessions under OS/2 and Windows sessions under OS/2, and since they never mix, the kernel can cater *exclusively* to the memory needs of each on whatever virtual machines it happens to be running on.

Therefore, configuring OS/2 for Windows couldn't be easier because not only is it automatic, but at no time do you ever have to compromise or make allowances for the fact that you want to run DOS sessions with all the whistles and bells: upper memory, expanded memory, an HMA, extended memory, etc. Adding some of the whistles and bells for DOS does take a little doing, but for Windows all you have to do is let 'er rip.

Unlike Windows running on top of DOS, there is just a single Windows kernel in OS/2. In OS/2 2.0 it was essentially a standard-mode kernel—2.0 couldn't run Windows applications that required the 32-bit enhanced mode. That changed in OS/2 2.1, however. Version 2.1 added a 32-bit graphics engine and, with it, a Windows kernel that supports 32-bit enhanced-mode Windows software.

Standard mode in OS/2?

Even in 2.0, the Windows support in OS/2 was drastically different from that provided in the Microsoft-DOS version. Even then, DOS applications could multitask concurrently with Windows (and OS/2) applications—none of the only-swap-to-disk limitations found in standard mode. OS/2 2x, running only on virtual machines, doesn't care who or what the client is. If it's up and running and not minimized, it gets full multitasking services from OS/2.

There are two kinds of Windows windows under OS/2 2x, but the distinction has nothing to do with standard or enhanced mode. It's entirely a matter of whether Windows applications load and run directly from the OS/2 desktop in their own private windows, or whether you run them from the Windows Program Manager. Having never liked the Program Manager (or even any of the third-party alternatives I've seen), I much prefer to open them directly from the OS/2 desktop—which has the added benefit of being faster since it doesn't have to load the extra layer of software for the Program Manager. So I hardly ever use the WINOS2 Program Manager (which looks and feels just like the Windows PM) except when installing new Windows software to my hard disk.

Despite the fact that OS/2 has attracted something like three million users as this goes to press and it's too soon to tell how much real impact, if any, Windows NT will have, Windows today is still very much an extension of DOS in the minds of most users. And that means you need to take a look at other things you can do for Windows in the DOS environment, particularly in the area managing resources beyond 640K.

16 *Windows' real-mode roots*

Windows, as established in the preceding chapter, pretty much does its own thing when it comes to memory management. And it can be pretty cavalier about it, particularly when it comes to running DOS applications. In point of fact, there's a lot that Windows users can do to make Windows run better. The first thing, of course, is to buy more RAM—and I cannot emphasize this point too strongly. However, there's a great deal you can do to enhance the way your system uses the resources you have, particularly when running a mix of DOS and Windows applications.

To gauge the role of upper memory usage in conjunction with Windows, you have to readjust your thinking. Ultimately, it all comes down to a matter of percentages, but in Windows the same raw numbers can have two entirely different meanings depending on whether you're talking just plain Windows or DOS sessions under Windows.

Playing the percentages

In the DOS world (and for DOS sessions running under Windows), relocating 64K of TSRs and device drivers above 640K immediately frees something like 10%—usually more—of whatever part of 640K was available to run applications. If, for example, you originally had 512K left over for your applications, an extra 64K would have jumped that to 576K for an effective gain of 12.5% more usable space for DOS. Relocating 128K would give you a gain under those circumstances of 25%.

However let's take Windows running in enhanced mode. After pumping up the amount of RAM the system actually has with a lot of hot air (otherwise known as virtual memory), Windows reports a total of 9200K available for Windows applications on a system with only four megs of real RAM—and that after taking a big chunk of real RAM DOS, a disk cache, and some other goodies (these figures from a machine in my office). Applying the same mathematics to this, 64K gained by relocating drivers to upper memory is only a drop in the bucket—less than 1%. And you're not even gaining that in terms of space Windows sees as being available.

In fact, that 64K is probably going to cost Windows something on the order of 256K, or about 3% of the space it thinks it can use (deducting the 64K it takes to map the address space from extended memory plus three times 64K in additional virtual memory it would have created). However, that's not necessarily a real loss because not that many Windows applications really need nearly 9 megabytes of real and virtual memory. It certainly is going to be a lot less significant than the extra 10% or more of conventional memory it frees for DOS applications.

The moral to the story is that if you're running *only* Windows applications, mapping UMBs is going to cost you some of the stuff Windows really needs: a little of your extended memory. However, to run a mix of Windows and nonWindows applications, you're probably better off using your UMBs and the HMA to the fullest possible extent.

This is an area where you have much more latitude and more control than most users seem to appreciate, but it's also one that takes some understanding if you want to do it right.

Catch 22 Interestingly, in standard mode where Windows doesn't use virtual memory, just plain old swap-to-disk, the reported available memory numbers drop significantly, reflecting the actual installed memory currently available if everything that's swappable is swapped to disk. On an absolute minimum (1Mb installed) system, in fact, the percentage gain achieved by using a better memory manager compared favorably with the DOS percentages.

There are several problems that rear their heads in this scenario, however. Standard mode, a 16-bit system, is really intended for use with a 16-bit processor: the 80286. You can run it on something higher, of course, but standard mode does impose some serious limitations, especially if you want to continue running some of your DOS programs (which standard mode won't multitask).

Let's assume for the moment that you have an 80286. Unless you have a machine that uses a C&T (Chips and Technology) supporting chip set, most of the better memory managers that boast the ability to map memory to upper address space will turn up their noses. Lacking a supported chip set, you might get by with mapping up to 64K with one of IBM's new PC DOS 6.1 8088/80286 drivers. There are also one or two third-party memory managers that support a wider range of chip sets, but the options are limited. (One of the best I've seen is UMBpro from Quadtel, which supports something like 20 different chip sets. However, the fate of this product was uncertain at press time in the wake of Quadtel's acquisition by Phoenix and the addition of better memory-management capabilities to the new DOS releases.)

The problem is that mapping memory to upper address space isn't something an 80286 can do. In general, it can be done only by adding memory-mapping support into the supporting chip set. However, simply having a chip set that will support memory mapping and having a memory manager that knows how to coax it to deliver that support are two quite different things. C&T seemingly came up with the first chip set that made it possible and soon commanded a large enough market share to make C&T chip sets the bandwagon to jump on. A number of other chip sets are now capable of supporting memory mapping on 286s, but have been largely ignored by most of the better third-party managers.

While all of the better third-party memory managers can easily run rings around HIMEM.SYS when you're running DOS applications under Windows, most do it as an afterthought—which is still better than the best MEMMAKER (or IBM's RAMBOOST) can do with HIMEM.SYS. Qualitas, one of the few third-party developers had not only survived but thrived strictly on the basis of their memory managers. And since the introduction of Windows 3.0, they've looked specifically for ways to enhance Windows, for running both DOS and Windows applications under Windows.

386max & family from Qualitas

386max (or BlueMAX for PS/2s) is, as of this writing, the *only* third-party memory manager the Windows 3*x* SETUP program will tolerate when installing Windows. Although other memory managers compliant with the XMS specification will work with Windows, Windows won't install in their presence. Rather, at least during installation, you must remove them (or let SETUP do it for you), reinstalling them later if you want (which really translates to they would rather you didn't).

While browsing through SETUP.INF, a 50K ASCII file that serves as one of the SETUP program's principle resources when installing Windows, I made an interesting discovery one day. I found a section for 386max, and under it a section for BlueMax, 386max's functional equivalent but optimized for use on PS/2s:

```
[386max]
    2:386max.vxd
    2:windows.lod

[bluemax]
    2:bluemax.vxd
    2:windows.lod
```

A further search revealed some references to HIMEM.SYS and EMM386.EXE. These were the only mentions of third-party memory managers, however. No QEMM, Netroom, QMAPS, or any of the others. Only these two from Qualitas.

Curious, I pursued the matter and learned that Qualitas has a special relationship with Microsoft. As a result, if SETUP should find either of these running on your system at the time you install Windows, it will automatically use whichever one it finds instead of HIMEM.SYS. And you don't even have to have the latest 386max/BlueMax release. Windows brings along a pair of VXD files (one for each) to update older versions to a level more compatible with 3.1 if need be.

Catering to Windows

Qualitas, more than any other player in the game I know, has, since 3.0, tried to cater to the Windows market from day one—though not at the expense of support for DOS users. Almost immediately after the release of Windows 3.0, they added special Windows features such as automatic instancing. With it, 386max/BlueMAX lets you run multiple sessions of nearly any TSR (one for every application you have running), which, under some circumstances, can cause problems. I can't say that I've ever had a problem with this—but then I'm not big on pop-ups. In any event, this feature, pioneered by Qualitas, is still unique to their memory managers.

386max also enables users to create virtual high DOS sessions under Windows, which adds still more flexibility to the Windows environment. And they were the first third-party memory manager to have publicly embraced Microsoft's DPMI (DOS protected- mode interface), although the significance of this is a bit obscure since it really doesn't seem much of an issue at the level where memory managers operate—you could easily run DPMI software—which Windows is—with memory managers like QEMM386.

In their new version 7.0, Qualitas has added still more of specific interest to Windows users. There are also new features for nonWindows users (discussed elsewhere in this book). But for Windows users only, they've added DOSMAX, WINSMART, and finally—a decent editor for Windows PIF files.

DOSMAX

One of the most intriguing features of version 7 is something called DOSMAX, which provides up to 736K of conventional memory in DOS windows under Windows, something no other memory manager has ever managed successfully. It does it by mapping memory to the video graphics region: A000h to A777h, and an extra 64K if the DOS applications involve the monochrome graphics region (A000h to B7FFh)—for a total of 96K.

This is intriguing for a couple of reasons. First off, of course, it addresses a basic flaw in Windows, which, by default, provides DOS windows that reflect the underlying DOS environment. These windows, particularly before the addition of optional automatic memory optimization to MS- and PC DOS 6, often left as little as 400K or even less for DOS applications running under

Windows. This was because, by default, device drivers and nonWindows TSRs were all loaded in conventional memory prior to loading Windows, significantly reducing the size of the environment inherited by Windows.

What is most intriguing is the fact that DOSMAX goes beyond the traditional memory-management role of merely providing memory to Windows and then letting Windows do with it as it pleases. It actually forces Windows to bend to *its* rules. And under DOSMAX rules, character-based DOS programs can have all or most of the video graphics region for use as additional conventional DOS memory, even though Windows itself must always have these regions free and available for its use to even load, let alone run.

What they're doing, then, is very cleverly manipulating the virtual DOS machines created by Windows. For a time, no other memory manager did this—it wasn't even possible with other multitaskers such as DESQview. DESQview sessions, for instance, can be set up using the video graphics address range as a means of providing additional memory to applications, but only so long as *none* of the applications that will be multitasked are graphical applications. Run even one graphical application in a DESQview session— say Windows in standard mode—and the entire session has to be configured with the graphics region left exclusively for graphics if that space was wasted on all other applications running in that session.

There are some multitaskers that virtualize the hardware more completely than DESQview—VM386, for instance—allowing individual virtual machines to be configured differently even to the point of having a mixed use of the graphics video range according to specific needs. And OS/2 2x DOS sessions can also be custom configured to use this area as well, when appropriate. In those cases, it's the operating system or environment itself that provides the capability. Windows doesn't, but with 386max 7 you can do it anyway.

Another Windows-specific feature in 386max 7 is Winsmart. While MS-DOS 6 for the first time provides the means of putting upper memory to work effectively (thanks to MEMMAKER), MEMMAKER, in addition to not being very aggressive in its search for mappable address space in general, automatically wastes 24K of space when configuring DOS for Windows—just because under some circumstances Windows might need it. Given the fragmented nature of upper memory, plus the fact that so many TSRs and drivers need so much more room to thrash around in during initialization than to run once loaded, this 24K loss can really cost you far more than just 24K.

Winsmart

And this isn't just a problem with MS-DOS's MEMMAKER, either. Other optimizers generally tend to be a little skittish about leaving extra high DOS space for Windows, questioning whether or not you intend to use Windows right up front. And Windows does do some peculiar things.

386max 7's WinSmart feature actually checks and dynamically determines the optimal amount of UMB space your Windows installation will require, automatically allocating that memory when Windows is loaded—but only when actually using Windows—regardless of DOS version.

Qualitas PIF editor Not really a memory-management issue in the same sense as DOSMAX and WinSmart, but of no small significance to anyone who has struggled with Windows' own crude PIF editor, 386max 7 has a new PIF editor for Windows. It's easier to use, having its own context sensitive help and even offering helpful hints, and it particularly addresses when to (or not to) change time slices and lock memory settings—areas most users need some help with.

Qualitas's new PIF editor also allows you to experiment and test new PIF settings without ever leaving the PIF editor. OS/2 2x offers similar functionality (but without the helpful hints) with its Settings notebooks, but this is the best I've seen for Windows.

For PS/2s only PS/2 users in particular should take note of BlueMax, because it does make a significantly greater amount of memory available on those machines. Qualitas is, in fact, the only player in the memory-management game to date to develop a memory manager specific to the PS/2's unique architecture, and all the new features found in 386max have been incorporated in a new BlueMAX release as well.

IBM, in designing the PS/2, set aside—and in fact has been using—an extra 64K of high address space (E000h to EFFFh) for system BIOS. There seems no apparent need for this in DOS (nor even in OS/2 2x, as was widely believed prior to its introduction), and in creating a memory manager specific to the PS/2 architecture Qualitas manages to whittle the space the BIOS occupies back down to size, recovering more than half of the 128K area the PS/2 BIOS occupies for other uses.

Quarterdeck's QEMM 7 Never one to be outdone, Quarterdeck's QEMM remains one of the most powerful all-around memory managers available. And beginning with release 7, QEMM has added special features tailored to the special needs of users running Windows (enhanced mode) as a shell for other than Windows applications. To overcome the relatively small DOS windows many users have when running Windows, QEMM is able to map the video graphics region of above 640K for use as conventional memory for any text-based applications you want to run—which can give you up to as much as 736K for each DOS application.

QEMM has always been able to map the video graphics range (A000h–AFFFh) and often another 32K beyond that (to B7FFh) as conventional memory. But until now, VIDRAM, as they call it, could be used only with text-based software. You couldn't use it with Windows because

Windows, being graphical by definition, had to use that address space for video graphics. You couldn't even use it for DESQview—which isn't a graphical environment—if any sessions you ran under it were graphical. There was no in-between once the operating environment was set at boot time to be either text-based or to afford full graphical support.

Now QEMM also has the power to map the video graphics region for text-based applications even while running under Windows, switching back to graphics mode—no mapping in that region—whenever you switch back to the Program Manager or to another graphical application.

This, coupled with QEMM's stealth technology (enhanced in this latest release) and a couple of other little tricks, are typically good for an extra 8K to 24K of upper memory when running Windows. This release has also added a new express option that, initiated by a single keystroke, not only automatically installs QEMM but optimizes the use of upper memory, no prior experience with upper memory required. All that—and now with full DPMI support as well—makes QEMM 7 almost unbeatable in the Windows arena.

Helix's new Netroom 3 also has features that are either Windows-specific or capable of doing things for DOS applications running under Windows. In the latter category, Netroom 3 has a utility called STRETCH (STRETCH.EXE), which, much in the manner of QEMM's VIDRAM, allows you to map the video graphics region for use as additional conventional memory for a total of 704K or 736K, depending on whether the monochrome graphics region (B000h–B7FFh) was included. As initially released, Stretch was not compatible with Windows, but following closely on the heels of 386max version 7 and QEMM 7, it was upgraded (v3.02) to be compatible with Windows. It obviously has to stand aside when Windows or any Windows applications are running, but it can kick back in when you return to DOS, giving text-based DOS applications running under Windows the benefit of this additional RAM.

Netroom 3 from Helix

Specifically for Windows (though again, not in the original 3.0 release) Netroom has a Cloaked Cache Monitor program for Windows. This has bar graphs that display an instant read and write hit ratio, the percent of the reads or writes found in the cache since the last bar was drawn in the graph. New bars are drawn every two seconds during disk activity. The numeric value below the bar graph is the total read or write hit ratio since the cache was started. From the monitor, you can also manually flush the cache and enable or disable write-caching by selecting the Enable Write Caching check box.

Also, Windows has an undocumented parameter that allows each DOS box to have its own, separate, upper-memory region. This allows you to have different devices and TSRs loaded into upper memory in each DOS box. To activate this feature, place the parameter `LocalLoadhigh=ON` in the [386Enh] section of your SYSTEM.INI.

This will, however, force Windows to load its translation buffers into conventional memory. To get around this problem, place the WINMEM.EXE file at the end of your AUTOEXEC.BAT, specifying how many kilobytes to reserve in upper memory for Windows. For example, the command WINMEM 36 will reserve 36K for Windows' use in upper memory, even if you have LocalLoadhigh=ON.

You can then run Customize to load this TSR into upper memory. After that, when you run Windows you can use the command DOS 5/6LOADHIGH (LH) to place device drivers and TSRs in upper memory. To load device drivers high, use the command LH DEVLOAD *device_driver_command*.

LocalLoadhigh=ON will operate correctly only if prior to starting Windows you had at least one upper-memory region with at least 12K free in it. If you didn't, you might receive an error stating that Windows has insufficient address space to start. If you get this message, you can't use LocalLoadhigh=On, so remove the line from your SYSTEM.INI.

This feature is recommended for advanced users only, because incorrect use of instanced upper-memory blocks can result in loss of data. Also, WINMEM is not useful and is not needed if you aren't using LocalLoadhigh=ON. It can be useful, though, and at this writing seems to be unique to Netroom.

For use with Windows, Netroom modifies the Windows SYSTEM.INI file—specifically the [386Enh] section. The exact changes will vary, depending on which Windows version you're using and which cloaking features are installed (applicable to Windows 3.1 only). In any event, if you ever go rooting around in the SYSTEM.INI file yourself (which is interesting even if you don't know what you're doing and don't plan to make any changes), you'll find remarks placed both before and after the changes CUSTOMIZE has made. Incidentally, a backup copy of the original SYSTEM.INI file is also saved to the Netroom directory as SYSTEM.UMB—just in case.

The most powerful new memory-management feature in Netroom 3, of course, is cloaking, which replaces up to 96K of system ROM (64K ROM BIOS plus 32K of video ROM) with its own software equivalents—which it loads in extended memory, leaving only an 8K stub behind. This results in a net gain of up to 88K of *contiguous* upper memory (at the expense of some extended memory), giving Netroom the power to relocate more TSRs and drivers into upper memory than any other memory manager on the market at this writing. And cloaking is compatible with Windows 3.1 (including Windows for Work Groups). It is not, however, compatible with 3.0, and any Windows users running 3.0 should take note of this.

This isn't to say that Netroom 3 doesn't support Windows 3.0. In most respects it does. But cloaking—which for my money is the whole reason for using Netroom—accesses specific functions that weren't anticipated in Windows 3.0.

There are some caveats for Windows users, particularly with respect to the UMB area Windows wants (B000h–B7FFh). In most cases CUSTOMIZE should be able to take this right in stride. If not, though, the documentation seems to cover the situation adequately.

This is another one of those places where using PC KWIK instead of SMARTDRV.SYS—Windows default disk cache—can pay big dividends, even bigger when you use PC KWIK's RAM drive as the swap disk for standard-mode sessions. The reason, as discussed in greater detail in a prior chapter, is the way PC KWIK manages whatever extended memory you have available, dynamically adjusting the amount of RAM available to your applications and the amount used for caching, looking first to the immediate needs of your applications but using whatever is left for caching and RAM disk usage.

A little secondary management

Qcache, the proprietary cache supplied by Qualitas with 386max, does much the same thing as PC KWIK, but only to a point. It does dynamically change the size of the cache according to other demands on system resources, keeping virtually all of your available RAM at work at all times. But it doesn't have the integral variable-size RAM disk feature that can be so beneficial, particularly when running Windows in standard mode.

While specific support for Windows (including a special Windows driver) began appearing in PC KWIK packages soon after the introduction of Windows 3.0, PK KWIK corp (formerly Multisoft Corporation) is now marketing a special Windows package called WinMaster, which includes not only the cache/RAM drive/give-back features previously described but an excellent set of Windows utilities as well. Included are several useful disk-management tools such as a disk optimizer (unfragmenter) that will, if you choose, automatically optimize your hard disk on whatever schedule you like, a disk compressor for archiving old files, and a set of icon-sized meters that can give you a continuous look at how your system resources are being used.

PC KWIK, of course, doesn't increase the amount of RAM available in DOS windows running under Windows. You still need a good third-party memory manager to pop things into upper memory and maybe one that can map the video graphics space to give DOS applications still more RAM as well. And there, the Qcache/386max combination, while not offering all the features, might prove a more cost-effective combination. It's something that certainly deserves some careful thought.

It's curious to note in closing that all the third-party memory managers that are able to provide as much as 200 or more additional kilobytes of RAM for DOS applications running under Windows do so by exploiting functions that are native to the 80386 (and higher) CPU. I was told, in fact, by one of the major memory-management developers, that this is not even specifically related to the DPMI (although all the major third-party memory managers

Polishing Windows

now support it) or to the Windows API, but rather is a matter of exploiting hardware features, making it something Microsoft could have done even in 3.0. In that light, why they chose not to provide better memory support for DOS applications running under Windows certainly raises some interesting questions.

Whatever the reason, there are, as you can see, a number of things that can be done just in the area of memory management to run Microsoft Windows more effectively. More so than working in a traditional DOS environment, the key lies in using better memory management than Microsoft (the Windows kernel) provides, keeping a tight rein on how your system is configured for the work you want to do, and determining how any memory you have is utilized.

In every case, I'm talking about steps that must be taken *before* Windows loads. After that, all bets are off.

17 *Optimum configurations*

It should be fairly evident by now that no matter whose memory managers you use or with what DOS, there's no such thing as one optimum configuration for all occasions.

Windows, particularly in 32-bit enhanced mode, does better with a different upper-memory configuration than, say, DESQview—assuming you use the same memory manager for both. Or as a true aficionado of high memory, you might prefer to use a different memory manager with Windows—386max with its special Windows provisions, for example.

DESQview generally does its best when teamed with QEMM386. But for DESQview power users, all DV sessions are not necessarily created equal. I have a couple of rather large DOS applications, for example, that do better with more than the 576K of conventional memory I can squeeze out for them in DESQview sessions under QEMM386. They happen to be character-based applications, though, so I can—when running them—have QEMM map the VGA video graphics area (A000h–B7FFh) as an extra 96K of conventional memory. Sometimes, however, I want to run a Windows session (standard mode) under DESQview. For those sessions I have to keep my muddy paws off of the video graphics area and, if multitasking with one of these hungrier DOS applications, make do.

I've already described three different startup configurations and the use of at least two different memory managers. And the more diverse the work you do, the longer that list can grow.

Then comes the day you want to try a different memory manager, but you don't want to mess up the configuration you have. There are many reasons for using the multiple-configuration options that both of the new real-mode DOS 6xs support. (Protected-mode DOSs also generally support customized configurations as well, but running on virtual machines they go about it in a different way.)

Once upon a time For a long time the only way to deal with multiple configurations was to boot from floppies that had different startup files. By putting a SHELL= statement in each floppy CONFIG.SYS, you could load COMMAND.COM from your hard disk (assuming you were using the same DOS version)—which automatically set the COMSPEC to point to the hard disk whenever DOS had to reload a copy of the command interpreter to overcome much of the sluggishness that goes with booting from a floppy. This also freed the A: drive for other things once you'd finished booting. This was how most of what I did was done when writing the first edition of this book, in fact. But it's a cumbersome system at best.

Interestingly, support for multiple configurations is not as new as most DOS users think. Digital Research (now part of Novell) introduced it in their DR DOS 5.0. And by the time of MS-DOS 5's introduction, Digital Research's DR DOS 6.0 had carried the technology to about the same state as in MS- and PC DOS 6—actually a little farther. Unfortunately, Digital Research, while having an excellent DOS (I still use some of their externals, even with PC- and MS-DOS) just never caught the public fancy.

In the meantime, someone came up with a pretty slick shareware utility called BOOT.SYS. And BOOT.SYS added to almost any Microsoft-based DOS version (it wouldn't work with DR DOS) allowed you to pick a customized startup configuration at the beginning of each session from a menu. Some of the earlier versions of BOOT.SYS had some odd compatibility problems with Windows 3x, but overall it was a tremendous help. I used it myself for some time—in fact, before the new DOS 6s added so many new features, I had planned to bundle BOOT.SYS (and some other utilities that have now lost much of their validity) with this book.

Now all of the new DOSs have support for multiple startup configurations built right in, and for my money it's the most significant new feature to be added. Once again, as has been the case so often in this business, third-party developers demonstrated a need by providing practical solutions, and the major players in the DOS game saw fit to add such features in subsequent releases. In this case, though, unlike in several other areas within the context of this book, the major DOSs measure up quite well. And yet they both fall disappointingly short.

While both of the new DOS 6s support the use of multiple boot configurations, neither of them provide the means of optimizing them to take advantage of upper memory—a rather curious oversight since this time around, for the first time, they provide some sort of optimizing utility.

Optimizing what you have

Always quick to seize an opportunity such as this, all of the major third-party memory managers developed optimizers that could handle these new multiple-configuration startup files, allowing you to optimize each startup option independently of the others.

Unfortunately, both IBM and MS-DOS look at the compound CONFIG.SYS and AUTOEXEC.BAT files (which are in reality multiple files) and, unable to differentiate, treat each file as a single configuration, trying to pack whatever is packable into upper memory—regardless of what belongs to which configuration. The result, typically, is a mess. To get around this, as discussed in a later chapter, you generally have to:

1. Rename your CONFIG.SYS and AUTOEXEC.BAT files (or copy them to a floppy or whatever you prefer that keeps DOS and/or the optimizing program from recognizing them).
2. Break out each section of your overall CONFIG and AUTOEXEC, temporarily renaming the ones you're working with as CONFIG.SYS and AUTOEXEC.BAT.
3. Run the optimizing program.
4. Rename the optimized files something else.
5. Repeat steps 2, 3, and 4 until all sections have been optimized.
6. Reassemble all the optimized sections back together as a multiboot CONFIG.SYS and multiboot AUTOEXEC.BAT.

By the time you go through all of this, you're probably going to wonder why you ever bothered in the first place. It's hard to imagine how both IBM and Microsoft slipped up on this and put out new DOS versions that supported the use of multiple configurations and endowed those versions with utilities to help you optimize upper memory, but failed to make those optimizers compatible with the multiple-configuration feature.

Well, it didn't take the third-party memory managers long to seize upon the opportunity to beat DOS at its own game. At this writing, all three of the major ones discussed elsewhere in this book have added the ability to optimize the individual portions of the new DOS 6x multiple-configuration files separately. There might be other ones that do as well, but the list at this point includes at least the following: 386max 7.0 from Qualitas, QEMM 7 from Quarterdeck, and Netroom 3 from Helix.

Thanks to third-party developers, therefore, it's not only possible but practical to optimize new DOS 6x multiple configurations, proving once again that you can have your cake and eat it too.

For aspiring power users

In the course of writing this book, I typically had boot configurations for as many as six different memory managers, with those broken down still farther to optimize performance for different kinds of sessions (Windows and nonWindows, for example). This is an extreme case, of course, but it does demonstrate the power of this new multiple-configuration feature in the new DOSs.

Let's take just one memory manager for now and see how, even there, the ability to choose whatever configuration best suits the session you're starting can pay really big dividends. Earlier in the book, I demonstrated how finely a system could be tuned and how much more memory you could have if running only character-based applications. Let's see what happens if you need to run Windows—or any graphical applications—sometimes.

The significant portions of a fixed-configuration CONFIG.SYS, in its original form, before being optimized, is as follows:

```
DEVICE=C:\DOS_BOOT\QEMM386.SYS RAM NOSH ST:F
   EXCLUDE=CA00-CBFF
DEVICE=C:\DOS\SETVER.EXE
DEVICE=C:\STACKER\STACKER.COM /P=1 D:\STACVOL.DSK
DEVICE=C:\STACKER\SSWAP.COM D:\STACVOL.DSK
DEVICE=D:\WIN\MASTER\PCKRAMD.SYS CONFIGFILE=D:\WIN\MASTER
   \PCKWIK.INI
```

Here is the corresponding section from the AUTOEXEC.BAT:

```
D:\DOS\SITBACK\SB
C:\DOS_BOOT\LOADHI /R:1 D:\DOS\QEMM386\FILES=40
C:\DOS_BOOT\LOADHI /R:3 D:\DOS\QEMM386\LASTDRIV=Z
```

Now here are the same CONFIG.SYS sections edited and optimized to take advantage of the unused VGA graphics region with QEMM386:

```
DEVICE=C:\DOS_BOOT\QEMM386.SYS RAM NOSH ST:F
   INCLUDE=A000-B7FF EXCLUDE=CA00-CBFF
DEVICE=C:\DOS_BOOT\LOADHI.SYS /R:1 /RES=736 /SQT=CA00-CBFF
   C:\DOS\SETVER.EXE
DEVICE=C:\DOS_BOOT\LOADHI.SYS /R:2 C:\STACKER\STACKER.COM
   /P=1 D:\STACVOL.DSK
DEVICE=C:\STACKER\SSWAP.COM D:\STACVOL.DSK
DEVICE=C:\DOS_BOOT\LOADHI.SYS /R:1 /RES=2704 /SQT=CA00-CAFF
   D:\WIN\MASTER\PCKRAMD.SYS CONFIGFILE=D:\WIN\MASTER\PCKWIK.INI
```

and, again, the corresponding AUTOEXEC.BAT:

```
D:\DOS\SITBACK\SB
C:\DOS_BOOT\LOADHI /R:1 D:\DOS\QEMM386\FILES=40
C:\DOS_BOOT\LOADHI /R:3 D:\DOS\QEMM386\LASTDRIV=Z
```

With the VGA graphics address space and optimized CONFIG.SYS and AUTOEXEC.BAT, the resulting memory utilization map will look like the one shown in FIG. 17-1.

```
First Meg / Programs
Memory Area    Size   Description
0E94 - 0E97    0.1K   COMMAND Data
0E98 - 0FBE    4.6K   COMMAND
0FBF - 0FC3    0.1K   [Available]
0FC4 - 0FD4    0.3K   COMMAND Environment
0FD5 - 0FE0    0.2K   [Available]
0FE1 - 13DB    15K    SB
13DC - 13E0    0.1K   COMMAND Data
13E1 - B7FF    656K   [Available]
====Conventional memory ends at 736K=====
C800 - C803    0.1K   QEMM386
C804 - C832    0.7K   SETVER
C833 - C8DB    2.6K   PCKRAMD
C8DC - C8DE     0K    SUPERPCK Environment
C8DF - C8EA    0.2K   [Available]
C8EB - C967     2K    FILES
C968 - CBFE    10K    [Available]
CD00 - D800    44K    STACKER
D801 - E4A7    50K    SUPERPCK
E4A8 - EBFE    29K    [Available]
FC00 - FC0B    0.2K   [Available]
FC0C - FCB4    2.6K   LASTDRIV
FCB5 - FDFF    5.2K   [Available]
```

17-1
Manifest report showing utilization of address space.

Given the amount of upper memory shown as still available—plus the HMA, which has also not been used at this point—this might appear to be a great deal of unnecessary trouble. There is method in the madness, however. I've set up this configuration with an eye toward running DESQview, which is pretty clever itself when it comes to using both upper memory and the HMA. It can, in fact, use almost the entire 64K HMA, while DOS, on the other hand, would waste nearly 20K. What happens when loading DESQview is shown in FIG. 17-2.

DESQview has some peculiar bookkeeping methods, so what is actually achieved with this configuration might not be obvious at first glance. The number at the lower right in FIG. 17-3 tells the story, though: 624K. It's called expanded memory—which is what it really is—but to DOS applications running in DESQview windows it's conventional memory, as much as 624K of it even after accounting for all of DESQview's rather hefty overhead.

If there's a lesson to be learned here, it's that it isn't over until the fat lady sings. Here it's only after the shell is loaded that you can get a true picture. There's an even more important lesson that might not be so obvious, however. DESQview is unique, especially in how it works with upper memory and the HMA. Windows, too, is quite unique in different ways—as are other shells—and it's only to the degree you know and understand their special

```
Area   Size    Description
0E94 - 0E97  0.1K  COMMAND Data
0E98 - 0FBE  4.6K  COMMAND
0FBF - 0FC3  0.1K  [Available]
0FC4 - 0FD4  0.3K  COMMAND Environment
0FD5 - 0FE0  0.2K  [Available]
0FE1 - 13DB  15K   SB
13DC - 13E0  0.1K  COMMAND Data
13E1 - B7FF  656K  [Available]
===Conventional memory ends at 736K===
C800 - C803  0.1K  QEMM386
C804 - C832  0.7K  SETVER
C833 - C8DB  2.6K  PCKRAMD
C8DC - C8DE   0K   SUPERPCK Environment
C8DF - C8EA  0.2K  [Available]
C8EB - C967   2K   FILES
C968 - CBFE  10K   [Available]
CD00 - D800  44K   STACKER
D801 - E4A7  50K   SUPERPCK
E4A8 - EBFE  29K   [Available]
FC00 - FC0B  0.2K  [Available]
FC0C - FCB4  2.6K  LASTDRIV
FCB5 - FDFF  5.2K  [Available]
(not shown: the HMA is not in use)
Area   Size    Description
0E94 - 0E97  0.1K  COMMAND Data
0E98 - 0FBE  4.6K  COMMAND
0FBF - 0FC3  0.1K  COMMAND Data
0FC4 - 0FD4  0.3K  COMMAND Environment
0FD5 - 0FE0  0.2K  DV Environment
0FE1 - 13DB  15K   SB
13DC - 1402  0.6K  DV
1403 - 99EF  535K  DV Data
99F0 - B7FD  120K  [Available]
===Conventional memory ends at 735K===
C800 - C803  0.1K  QEMM386
C804 - C832  0.7K  SETVER
C833 - C8DB  2.6K  PCKRAMD
C8DC - C8DE   0K   SUPERPCK Environment
C8DF - C8EA  0.2K  DV Data
C8EB - C967   2K   FILES
C968 - CBFE  10K   DV Data
CD00 - D800  44K   STACKER
D801 - E4A7  50K   SUPERPCK
E4A8 - EBFE  29K   DV Data
EC00 - FC0B  0.2K  DV Data
FC0C - FCB4  2.6K  LASTDRIV
FCB5 - FDFF  5.2K  DV Data
    HMA      64K   DV
```

17-2

What left so much upper memory and the HMA available in the optimized configuration takes on a quite different perspective after loading DESQview—note how it has used available spaces as small as .2K. The bottom line is that, with this configuration, you can load applications requiring as much as 624K into DESQview windows.

strengths and needs that you can customize your system, giving each the best your hardware has to offer.

Enough of that. Let's change the equation and see what happens when you optimize for Windows.

```
┌─4══Memory══Status═══════════════════════════════════════════┐
│                                                              │
│                    Total       Total       Largest           │
│                    Memory      Available   Available         │
│                                                              │
│                                                              │
│  Common Memory     15360       7880        7848              │
│                                                              │
│  Conventional Memory  639K     500K        498K             │
│                                                              │
│  Expanded Memory   6016K       2224K       624K             │
│                                                              │
└──────────────────────────────────────────────────────────────┘
```

17-3
The number at the lower right represents the size of the largest DESQview window possible, in this case 624K. Such peak performance is often impossible without the use of multiple configurations tailored to various regimes.

Opening Windows

Of course, the first thing you've got to do when running Windows is to keep your hands off of the video graphics area. Windows, being a graphical environment, can't even load—let alone run—if it can't use this area as it was intended to be used. With some of the new third-party memory managers like QEMM 7 and 386max 7.0, there are exceptions to this rule, but for the moment let's confine ourselves to normal Windows rules.

Until recently, you as a user could do little in terms of memory management for enhanced-mode Windows except provide it with a basic memory manager—and HIMEM.SYS is about as basic as they come. Until this latest round of releases from third-party memory manager developers—notably Qualitas and Quarterdeck—any additional memory management that was needed for enhanced mode was handled strictly by the enhanced-mode Windows kernel itself.

Actually, Windows either by itself or running only Windows applications doesn't benefit significantly from running on an optimized system, even with one of the later memory managers with special Windows features. The difference comes when you use Windows as a shell to run DOS programs. There, unless you're running on an optimized system, Windows might not give you enough memory to run them properly, or even to run them at all in certain situations, since what you get is just a hand-me-down of what your system had available before you loaded Windows—sometimes as little as 400K.

Therefore—and contrary to common misconceptions—running Windows on a tightly configured and properly optimized system can make a crucial difference. But aside from the fact that Windows (or any graphical application) must be able to access and use the graphics address space (typically A000h to B7FFh) for graphics and any other obvious considerations, optimizing is different because Windows itself often needs certain blocks (two 12K blocks) of upper memory, and needs for them to be set aside.

Clearly, the optimum system for Windows is not the same optimized system you created for totally nongraphical DESQview sessions. Windows doesn't need the HMA, so you can load DOS=HIGH if it (or something else) isn't there already. Otherwise, you can do things pretty much the same, as shown here (the first section is from the CONFIG.SYS; the second is from the AUTOEXEC.BAT):

```
DEVICE=C:\DOS_BOOT\QEMM386.SYS R:2 RAM NOSH ST:F EXCLUDE=CA00-
   CBFF
DEVICE=C:\DOS_BOOT\LOADHI.SYS /R:1 C:\DOS\SETVER.EXE
DEVICE=C:\DOS_BOOT\LOADHI.SYS /R:3 C:\STACKER\STACKER.COM
   /P=1 D:\STACVOL.DSK
DEVICE=C:\STACKER\SSWAP.COM D:\STACVOL.DSK
DEVICE=C:\DOS_BOOT\LOADHI.SYS /R:1 D:\WIN\MASTER\PCKRAMD.SYS
   CONFIGFILE=D:\WIN\MASTER\ PCKWIK.INI
DOS=HIGH
D:\WIN\MASTER\SUPERPCK CONFIGFILE=D:\WIN\MASTER\PCKWIK.INI
D:\DOS\SITBACK\SB
C:\DOS_BOOT\LOADHI /R:2 D:\DOS\QEMM386\FILES=40
C:\DOS_BOOT\LOADHI /R:2 D:\DOS\QEMM386\LASTDRIV=Z
```

Figure 17-4 shows how differently upper memory has been utilized when optimized for use with Windows—again the key is the R:*n* notations, indicating which upper-memory region each will be loaded into, with only one sizable but stubborn TSR (SB.EXE) down in conventional memory. The optimizer has loaded everything it managed to load high before into upper memory. The main difference is where it's loaded them this time.

```
First Meg / Programs
Memory Area   Size    Description
03C3 - 0467   2.6K    COMMAND
0468 - 046C   0.1K    [Available]
046D - 047D   0.3K    COMMAND Environment
0478 - 0482   0.2K    [Available]
0483 - 087D   15K     SB
047E - 9FFF   606K    [Available]
====Conventional memory ends at 640K=====
B000 - B02E   0.7K    SETVER
B02F - B0D7   2.6K    PCKRAMD
B0D8 - B0DA   0K      SUPERPCK Environment
B0DB - B7FE   28K     [Available]
C800 - C803   0.1K    QEMM386
C804 - C80E   0.2K    [Available]
C80F - C88B   2K      FILES
C88C - C934   2.6K    LASTDRIV
C935 - C9FE   3.2K    [Available]
CD00 - D800   44K     STACKER
D801 - E4B1   50K     SUPERPCK
E4B2 - EBFE   29K     [Available]
FC00 - FDFF   8K      [Available]
```

17-4
Manifest report showing utilization of address space.

You could use this same configuration if you wanted to run DESQview sessions with a mix of character and graphical applications—even Windows standard-mode sessions in DESQview windows. Clearly, though, no matter whose memory manager you use, there's no such thing as a "one size fits all" configuration. That's the complex part. Where it starts to get easy again is with the relatively newfound capability of choosing from among a group of different startup configurations at boot time—or sometimes changing them "on the fly."

While most of this chapter is based on multiple configurations as supported in both PC and MS-DOS 6x, Novell, in their DOS 7, has carried on in the tradition established by Digital Research, going back to their DOS 5 (which was concurrent with MS-DOS 4.0) and enhanced in DR DOS 6 (concurrent with MS-DOS 5.0).

Novell DOS 7

This feature has been further enhanced in Novell DOS 7, although the basics are similar to the multiple-configuration option in DR DOS. As shown in the CONFIG.SYS excerpt in FIG. 17-5, the structure is somewhat different, looking more like an ordinary batch file with labels rather than the bracketed block names found in the other new DOS releases.

```
?"Do you want to run standard configuration?" GOTO STANDARD
?"Do you want to run DESQview?" GOTO DESQview
?"Do you want to run a WINDOWS session?" GOTO WIN
:STANDARD
?device=a:\drdos\emm386.sys /BDOS=FFFF /F=E000 /AUTOSCAN=A000-FFFF
  /KB=1024 /USE=F800-FDFF /EXCLUDE=C800-CCFF
GOTO COMMON
:QEMM
DEVICE=C:\DOS\QEMM\QEMM386.SYS RAM ROM EXCLUDE=C800-CCFF AU DMA=32
DEVICE=A:\DOS\HIDOS.SYS /BDOS=AUTO
HIDEVICE=device
HINSTALL=TSR_program
GOTO COMMON
:WIN
.
.
.
:COMMON
?HIDEVICE=....
```

17-5
CONFIG.SYS excerpt showing multiple configuration options for Novell DOS 7.

Note that the question mark (?) precedes the command line. Also, all startup commands following the execution of the CONFIG.SYS need not be in the AUTOEXEC.BAT, but rather the SHELL command in each configuration can point to a batch file of any name you choose. There are other differences, with several new features added to DOS 7. They are well documented, and should require no further elaboration here.

Novell's DOS 7 also supports startup files that allow boot-time startup options. Question marks that cause DR DOS to pause and prompt for Y/N input can preface branching commands or individual loading options. Note how optional configurations can include both device drivers and TSRs not common to any other configuration.

Putting multiple configurations to work

Now that you have two configurations and have optimized them individually under DOS 6x, all you have to do is combine them in a single set of startup files. As mentioned earlier, this step is no longer necessary with any of the better third-party memory managers, but here, to help you understand the process, we're doing it that way. The new, combined CONFIG.SYS will look like FIG. 17-6.

```
[MENU]
Menudefault=No_Graphics,05
Menucolor=14,4
Menuitem=No_Graphics
Menuitem=Graphics
```

17-6

Using new DOS 6x Multiboot option, this combined CONFIG.SYS displays startup options (in color) at boot time, defaults to No_Graphics configuration after 5 seconds of no choice is entered.

```
[Graphics]
DEVICE=C:\DOS_BOOT\QEMM386.SYS R:2 RAM NOSH ST:F EXCLUDE=CA00-CBFF
DEVICE=C:\DOS_BOOT\LOADHI.SYS /R:1 C:\DOS\SETVER.EXE
DEVICE=C:\DOS_BOOT\LOADHI.SYS /R:3 C:\STACKER\STACKER.COM /P=1 D:\STACVOL.DSK
DEVICE=C:\STACKER\SSWAP.COM D:\STACVOL.DSK
DEVICE=C:\DOS_BOOT\LOADHI.SYS /R:1 D:\WIN\MASTER\PCKRAMD.SYS
CONFIGFILE=D:\WIN\MASTER\PCKWIK.INI
DOS=HIGH

[No_Graphics]
DEVICE=C:\DOS_BOOT\QEMM386.SYS RAM NOSH ST:F INCLUDE=A000-B7FF
EXCLUDE=CA00-CBFF
DEVICE=C:\DOS_BOOT\LOADHI.SYS /R:1 /RES=736 /SQT=CA00-CBFF C:\DOS\SETVER.EXE
DEVICE=C:\DOS_BOOT\LOADHI.SYS /R:2 C:\STACKER\STACKER.COM /P=1 D:\STACVOL.DSK
DEVICE=C:\STACKER\SSWAP.COM D:\STACVOL.DSK
DEVICE=C:\DOS_BOOT\LOADHI.SYS /R:1 /RES=2704 /SQT=CA00-CAFF
D:\WIN\MASTER\PCKRAMD.SYS CONFIGFILE=D:\WIN\MASTER\PCKWIK.INI
```

To make it easier to follow the moves, I've limited you to only two choices. As you can see, I've taken the entire contents from the two different CONFIG.SYS files you started with and combined them in a single file. I have, however, added a menu block at the top and a section header in square brackets to this piece of the menued CONFIG.SYS. I've also added a couple of embellishments—color and a default setting—but the basic formula is simply:

```
[MENU]
    Menuitem=block_name1
    Menuitem=block_name2
    Menuitem=block_name3
    [block_name1]
    [block_name2]
    [block_name3]
```

Block names can be as long as 125 characters—certainly long enough to be self-explanatory. The only caveat is that they must be tied together—as shown here—so DOS will see multiple words as single unbroken character strings.

The Menudefault and Menucolor items are exactly what they sound like; Menudefault is the more important because it allows you to select your most often used configuration as a default to boot automatically after some preset number of seconds. Both of these functions are adequately documented in MS-DOS 6's online help, though with PC DOS you'll have to go to the hard copy.

You can also use these block names as labels for subsections in the AUTOEXEC.BAT, but you're not done here yet. DOS still has some other tricks you can use, as shown in FIG. 17-7.

```
DEVICE=C:\DOS\SETVER
FILES=40
LASTDRIVE=Z

[MENU]
Menudefault=No_graphics,10
Menucolor=0,2
Menuitem=No_Graphics
Submenu=Graphics, Graphics: Select Memory Manger

[Graphics]
Menudefault=QEMM_graphics,5
Menucolor=0,3
Menuitem=QEMM_graphics
Menuitem=386max_graphics
Menuitem=Netroom

[Netroom]

[QEMM_graphics]

[386max_graphics]
```

17-7
Modified CONFIG.SYS file.

Two things are done differently here. For one, note that several commands common to all configurations are at the top of the file so DOS can execute them before it even sees the menu. You can put them at the end of the file, as well; that choice depends on just where in the loading sequence you want them to appear.

More importantly, note that there's a Graphics submenu. Choosing this one opens up another menu, in this case giving you a choice of memory managers to pick from. A subtle difference here is in the text that is displayed on screen. With an ordinary menu item, the block name is displayed exactly as shown. For a submenu, only the text following the comma is displayed, so the first menu you would see would look like the following:

```
PC DOS 6.1 Startup Menu

1. No_Graphics
2. Graphics: Select Memory Manager

Enter a choice:
```

Menu items appearing on the Graphics menu will, as with the menu item choice here, appear as the complete block name strings, where, if more than one word, they must be connected by a hyphen or underline so DOS will read it as a string. The use of submenus is not well documented, unfortunately.

Yes or no . . . The new DOS multiboot feature allows such arbitrary, on-the-fly choices from the CONFIG.SYS as well. All you have to do is put a question mark immediately following the DEVICE, SHELL, INSTALL, or other CONFIG.SYS command prefix, and each time you boot up that configuration DOS will pause and offer you a Y/N choice. For instance, I have a scanner I use only occasionally, and then only in Windows, so in a Windows section of my CONFIG.SYS I have this line:

```
DEVICE?=MSCAN.SYS
```

When I boot for Windows, at that point the CONFIG.SYS will pause, displaying:

```
DEVICE?=MSCAN.SYS [Y,N]?
```

Here, though, the use of a submenu might serve a better purpose because the scanner driver is fairly sizable and separate optimized configurations with and without the driver might prove a better option in the long run. Another place I sometimes use this feature is with a SHELL statement like this:

```
SHELL?=C:\4DOS\4DOS.COM . . .
```

Here, when prompted, a Y response will load 4DOS.COM, an extremely powerful alternative to COMMAND.COM; N loads COMMAND.COM by default.

This isn't a command you'll want to use except when necessary, because it doesn't support defaults and will just sit there waiting until you input a Y or N. I like to try to keep a default configuration that will boot to completion automatically unless I intervene.

Multiple configurations in the AUTOEXEC.BAT As long as you use the same block names to label sections belonging to the associated boot configuration, multiple-configuration AUTOEXEC.BAT files follow the lead established when you made your choice in the CONFIG.SYS. At that time, DOS 6x inserted a line like this in your environment:

```
CONFIG=block_name2
```

You then used the environment variable, CONFIG, to point to the label of that name in the AUTOEXEC.BAT. While I've seen several methods of doing that documented, probably the simplest is simply to insert a line in your AUTOEXEC.BAT at whatever point you want it to jump to the appropriate labeled section—which could be either at the top of the file or after some commands common to all configurations, as shown below:

```
goto %CONFIG%

:block_name1
commands
goto end

:block_name2
commands
goto end

:end
```

Note the use of the percent signs before and after CONFIG. This is a standard batch-file procedure any time you want to use the current value of an environment—whatever the current value is—in a batch file.

Since I usually have configurations using any of several memory managers, I use this same trick to set the prompt so it tells me which memory manager or configuration I'm using in that particular session. I use something like the following prompt command:

```
prompt $v using %CONFIG%$_$P
```

which, typically, displays a prompt like this:

```
IBM DOS 6.00 using NETROOM
C:\
```

More choices

New in both of the new DOS 6s is the CHOICE command, which, inserted in a batch file at any point that pleases you, allows you to choose from as many as 24 possible options. Actually, since you can use CHOICE more than once within a single batch file, the total number of options is virtually unlimited—but it's best kept down to a more manageable number.

Unlike most batch-file commands, CHOICE is an external command (CHOICE.COM) rather than internal to COMMAND.COM. Its use depends on one of DOS's most powerful but poorly understood (and therefore generally underused) features: ERRORLEVEL. Because the use of a poorly understood feature is the key to using this command, a brief discussion here seems warranted.

The term *errorlevel* is misleading because it doesn't necessarily mean an error has occurred. Rather, it's simply a mechanism many programs use to indicate the circumstances under which they were terminated. Typically, an ERRORLEVEL of zero often (but not always) indicates a job well done, but the numbers are arbitrary and can be almost anything the programmer chooses. In CHOICE, they simply a echo a number or letter typed in by the user when prompted to do so. So in this case, rather than being just an obscure by-product, the generation of ERRORLEVEL codes, representing up to a possible two dozen choices, is the sole purpose of the program.

Mercifully, this is a .COM file and quite small: only 1586 bytes in PC DOS and roughly 10% larger in MS-DOS. I say *mercifully* because, while it would be an easy exercise to write a comparable program in C, I doubt you would be happy with the amount of disk space it took up.

In a typical situation where CHOICE is used to create a menu within the AUTOEXEC.BAT (or any other) file—which is really about the only practical way to deal with more than just a couple of options—the command line might read like:

```
CHOICE /C:ABCDE   Choose one
```

Here are specified five possible choices, and when run the screen will echo:

```
Choose one   [A,B,C,D,E]?
```

Each of the choices will return a different numerical ERRORLEVEL, starting with 1 if the farthest left choice—A in this case—is selected. A series of IF ERRORLEVEL *nn* GOTO statements can then be used to jump to different subroutines within the batch file (or, using CALL rather than GOTO, transfer execution to some other batch file). When loading programs, with proper structuring you can get right to the point with something like IF ERRORLEVEL *nn program_name*.

A very simple Y/N use of CHOICE in a batch file might look like this, where the choice is whether or not to load a particular TSR (SB.EXE), this one defaulting to N after five seconds (note that no PAUSE command is used here since CHOICE pauses automatically):

```
choice /c:YN /t:N,05 Load Sitback?
if errorlevel 2 goto end
d:\dos\sitback\sb

:end
```

Or, if you feel like getting fancy, you can pretty-up the presentation, doing something like what's shown in FIG. 17-8. Here, for the sake of illustration, I've added .BAT after the names of other batch files this menu might execute, but as with any executable it isn't needed. These could all simply be the names of labels within the same batch file, as END surely would (or should) be.

Note that, when testing for the returned ERRORLEVEL, you test for the highest possible value first and then work your way down to 1. This is crucial! If you start from the bottom, *every line* starting with ERRORLEVEL 1 will execute until DOS reaches the value returned. In that case, you would always go to to WP for WordPerfect, no matter what.

```
:MENU
echo.
echo
echo
echo
echo              1: WordPerfect
echo              2: SuperCalc
echo              3: dBASE
echo              4: Exit to DOS
echo
echo
echo.
choice /c:1234 /t:1,10  Make selection

if errorlevel 4 goto END
if errorlevel 3 goto DB.BAT
if errorlevel 2 goto SC.BAT
if errorlevel 1 goto WP.BAT
```

17-8
"Prettied-up" CHOICE command.

I've also added a couple of other little goodies. The /t: parameter sets a default option, followed by a time (in seconds) before the default is executed. No PAUSE statement is needed since CHOICE does that automatically.

I assume the use of CHOICE in connection with AUTOEXEC.BAT, which is certainly one way to use it, whether part of a true multiple-configuration file or not. It isn't limited to that usage, however, and can be a valuable tool in many batch-file situations. And CHOICE.COM is interesting in that, unlike most DOS externals (particularly MS-DOS externals), it doesn't seem to be version-specific. I discovered that it was compatible with DOS 5, which means it's very likely compatible with at least some other versions as well—which is a handy thing to know.

Another trick I sometimes use to keep my AUTOEXEC.BAT from getting too long is to put the postCONFIG.SYS startup commands for each configuration in a separate batch file, simply inserting the name of the batch file at the appropriate place in the AUTOEXEC.BAT (instead of the actual command lines) so that control is transferred at that point and the rest of the startup conducted by one of these secondary batch files.

This, incidentally, is almost exactly the way Digital Research handled it in DR DOS 5 and DR DOS 6; the main difference is that DR DOS could bypass the AUTOEXEC.BAT entirely and go directly from CONFIG.SYS to an alternate startup batch file by including the name of that batch file as a parameter on the SHELL= line. Still, most of the good stuff got picked up in these new DOSs.

I might add that, as a precaution, I always make a backup copy of my current startup files before doing any tampering, reoptimizing, or whatever. This is something you should do in any case, but it assumes an even greater importance when working with the compound multiboot files DOS 6x supports. To avoid confusion in case I forget to delete old backups, I use the day's date as the extension for both the AUTOEXEC.BAT and CONFIG.SYS backup files.

In closing, I'd like to point out that the ability to customize DOS configurations is not limited to real-mode DOS. As soon as you move to protected mode things change, however. Using virtual machines, whatever customizing you do is generally just a function of configuring the virtual machine that will run specific applications. This is true even when, as in OS/2 2x, it's possible to boot a session of an ostensibly real-mode DOS in protected mode. That, however, is something I'll look at in the following section, where I discuss other features that are unique to DOS in the protected mode.

Part 4
Protected-mode DOS

18 Novell DOS 7 & beyond

Like Windows, Novell's DOS 7 is torn between two worlds: the real-mode world of its most immediate predecessor, DR DOS 6, and the protected-mode world of DR Multiuser DOS, with elements of both embodied in their new DOS 7 kernel—the only DOS that really qualifies as new this time around.

There had initially been some speculation—fueled by lack of any mention of real mode or 8088 use when first announced—that this would be the first strictly protected-mode DOS. These fires were further fanned by persistent reports that Microsoft's next new DOS release would be a full 32-bit protected-mode DOS (which will, according to some reports, be released at or about the same time as a new freestanding 32-bit Windows).

What has emerged is a new 16-bit DOS that, by still being a 16-bit DOS, neatly sidesteps the issue of what to do about the 8088s that keep on going and going like the Eveready bunny. It will, indeed, run in real mode on an 8088—but at the same time it brings with it a number of new features that can only conceivably run in protected mode. Yes, a 32-bit system would probably have some theoretical advantage over 16 bits. But as many Windows users have discovered to their disappointment, such things as 32-bit disk access are possible only with 32-bit interface cards running on a 32-bit bus.

The most obvious example of protected-mode features in Novell's new DOS, of course, is multitasking. DOS 7 multitasking is done on virtual machines, which, by definition, are in protected mode, therefore the DOS in multitasking windows is running in protected mode.

DESQview pioneered real multitasking using only EEMS expanded memory (from which the LIM 4.0 EMS specification was later derived) on real-mode 8088 (or higher) systems. With the advent of virtual 8086 mode, starting with the 80386, the use of virtual machines, all running in protected memory, became the multitasking environment of choice.

You don't have to look to multitasking in the conventional sense for the benefits of running virtual machines in XMS memory to become important. Not surprisingly, in view of Novell's dominant networking position, peer-to-peer networking—similar to NetWare Lite—is part of the package. And network drivers, no matter how cleverly you try to hide them, take up a chunk of RAM somewhere. But where?

The trick is putting that chunk somewhere it isn't going to hurt you. And in the course of doing that, as well as adding the several other sizable chunks of code required for multitasking, CD-ROM support, and a powerful dynamic cache utility, Novell developed a method for moving such things beyond the reach of ordinary DOS to execute in XMS (extended) memory. There was nothing new in this—at least in principle. Several of the DOS memory managers, in fact, do it; QEMM leaves only a 1K footprint in upper memory to point to something like 250K of code out in extended memory.

What Novell had done, though, beyond just simply coming up with yet another proprietary scheme for loading DOS TSRs and device drivers into XMS memory, was develop a formal API called DPMS (DOS protected-mode services) that was compatible with not only Novell DOS but virtually any 16-bit DOS. And they've made it available to all software developers to use—without license fees or royalties—with any software in this category.

While the implications are far-reaching (before long, we should start seeing the benefits in many of the TSRs and drivers cluttering our systems now), our first look at the DPMS has been in conjunction with Novell DOS 7 and its ability to deliver up to something like 620K or more of usable (conventional) memory even with all the DPMS goodies loaded—even configured as a server.

There are, of course, a number of other interesting features in Novell's new DOS, but for now and within the context of this book I will confine myself primarily to issues beyond 640K.

Memory management with DOS 7
As might be expected, Novell's DOS 7 has its own memory manager: EMM386.EXE. It's a one-size-fits-all package that includes not only an XMS driver (the equivalent of MS- and PC DOS's HIMEM.SYS) and EMS 4.0 emulator (which is all EMM386.EXE does in MS- and PC DOS), but the multitasking module and DPMI support all in one.

With the exception of the multitasking module, this is something comparable to the universal memory-management drivers from Quarterdeck and Qualitas. There's a reason for Novell's wrapping the multitasking module in the memory-management package, but I'll come back to that a little later. While there are many similarities between the memory-management package in Novell DOS and those from IBM and Microsoft, there are a number of gut-level areas where Novell's package is significantly different.

For one thing, while Novell provides tools comparable to Loadhigh for relocating TSRs and drivers into upper memory, they don't provide an optimizer like MS-DOS's MEMMAKER or PC DOS's RAMBOOST to make it any easier to work with. Outwardly, this might seem like a tactical error—and it might prove to be. In Novell's defense, however, since upper memory came into being, there has never been a DOS with less need for optimizing its use—at least in the conventional sense—than here.

The keystone of Novell's DOS strategy for managing memory is their new DPMS scheme for relocating the bulk of TSRs and drivers into extended rather than upper memory. Several of the most bulky items in Novell DOS 7—multitasking, networking, disk compression, and disk caching—all are written conforming to the new DPMS API (discussed in greater detail elsewhere in this book and later in this chapter). They automatically load their rather appreciable bulk into extended memory, leaving only relatively small footprints down below 1 megabyte (and that generally in upper memory). The DPMS driver itself (footprint of about 1K in upper memory) is not part of the memory manager, but rather is separate.

This is where it gets a little tricky, because you can use other memory managers with Novell DOS 7: QEMM, 386max, Netroom, whatever. Those three (and others) all have optimizing programs that, on the surface, would seem to make their use the more desirable option. They can be better, but not if you're going to use the new Novell DOS 7 multitasker. Remember? The multitasking module is part of the DOS 7 memory manager, and if you don't use Novell's DOS 7 memory manager, you don't use Novell's DOS 7 multitasker.

There's a logical reason for packaging the multitasker with the memory manager. In previous multiuser and multitasking Digital Research products, the multitasking module was intrinsic to the operating-system kernel—which, in those cases, was always a 32-bit kernel. This time we're dealing with a 16-bit kernel, though. And since multitasking can be done only on 386 and higher systems—machines with CPUs that support virtual 8086 mode—this extra overhead is the last thing you want to saddle someone running on an 8088 with.

Packaged as part of the memory manager, the multitasker overhead Novell DOS passes on to client windows is something less than 5K, typically leaving as much as 610K or a little more for any application running in a multitasking window. DESQview, on the other hand, imposes more like 50K of overhead on every DESQview window, with 576K about the best I can do short of mapping the video graphics region as conventional memory. Still, as so often is the case, it's a tradeoff. More on multitasking with DOS 7 later.

Another area where Novell's new DOS 7 does some very interesting things is in the HMA. With a little digging, I found that Digital Research's DR DOS 6 had managed to put code for more than just the kernel into the HMA—and the new DOS 7 really does a job up there. In one case I know of, Novell's DOS 7 used all but 700 bytes, wasting less than 1K of the 64K HMA. In addition to the kernel, DOS 7 had loaded the resident code for COMMAND.COM, SHARE, and KEYB, as well as buffers, and I understand that NSLFUNC will also load there (but not with only 700 bytes available).

The DPMS & new horizons From a memory-management standpoint, one of the most important features Novell has rolled out with their new DOS has nothing to do with EMM386.EXE, their new memory manager, or even their new DOS, at least not specifically. As discussed in greater detail earlier in the book, the DPMS is a new API that allows the bulk of TSRs—anybody's TSRs—to be loaded into extended rather than upper or conventional memory. And not just with their DOS but with anybody's DOS—on almost any machine that has XMS memory, meaning almost any 80286 or higher machine.

This technology, interestingly, is similar to the cloaking developed by Helix for use in Netroom 3 (and with features in QEMM). It isn't the same, however, with programs such as Netroom's proprietary cloaked screen savers unable to run except when using Netroom.

This distinction is especially important because Novell has made the DPMS available to all software developers without charge or license fee. This means that we should start seeing the benefits of this appearing in a number of TSRs and drivers fairly soon since the API is small and seems fairly simple to work with.

Novell, of course, has used the DPMS API to enhance several features that, without it, would require substantial amounts of DOS-addressable (1Mb or lower) RAM. These include:

❑ CD-ROM support drivers
❑ Disk compression
❑ Peer-to-peer network drivers
❑ Dynamic disk caching

These features alone on a typical system could chew up as much as 150K to 200K of RAM. But even with prerelease software, Novell's new DOS was able to provide as much as about 620K of conventional memory with all these loaded while still leaving upper memory for other things. And there were indications that the number might go even higher by the time Novell DOS 7 was released to the public.

So you have a DOS that can run in real mode on an 8088 that doesn't support extended memory, TSRs, and drivers that—in order to avail themselves of the advantages of the DPMS—require it. This is a problem only in that if there is no XMS memory, any TSRs or drivers written to support the DPMS have to load someplace else—which generally means down in conventional memory. As a practical matter this means you probably won't want to run more than one or two at most on an 8088—but, DPMS or not, you likely wouldn't want to anyway.

With the foundation in place, let's get down to business and see just what this means. Multitasking, one of the immediate beneficiaries of the DPMS, is one of the things that first caught my interest when Novell's new DOS 7 was announced, not only as a long-time multitasking user, but based on my experience with Digital Research's old Concurrent DOS and DR Multiuser DOS, which, even for a single-user environment, provided some of the best multitasking I've ever worked with.

Focus on the multitasker

The multitasking provided by Novell DOS 7 is, in fact, a direct descendent of the multitasking modules in those earlier products, right down to the use of all but a few of the same function calls. This is a full, preemptive multitasker, too, which means that even foreground tasks can be interrupted by higher-priority tasks running in the background to make the most efficient use of the CPU's time and services.

It's a powerful multitasker in other ways, as well. It doesn't suspend graphics applications when they're switched into the background—which means your graphics applications—even Windows sessions—can continue printing in the background while you do something else rather than tying up the system. And fast—it goes without saying.

Multitasking, you'll note, is not a DPMS client. The overhead gets packed off to extended memory, but this is handled directly by EMM386.EXE, of which it's a part. It doesn't matter how it gets there, though. The bottom line—how much memory you have to work with—is what's important, and leaving only about 5K of overhead behind the bottom line is really quite impressive.

It should hardly come as a surprise that networking was high on Novell's priorities with this new DOS—and this feature, too, is pretty much worth the price of the package, weighed against the street price of Novell Lite. Here again the role of the DPMS is significant, for network drivers tend to take up gobs of memory—so much, in fact, that Helix first made a real place for itself in the market with Netroom: a 386 memory manager that creates a separate, virtual machine to handle network-driver overhead rather than compete with other

Networking with Novell DOS 7

software in the standard DOS environment. With Netroom you had to know what you were doing, though, whereas with the DPMS version it's automatic.

DOS 7 provides peer-to-peer services that allow users to share not only files but work group resources with other computers. Support is provided for both server and client capabilities.

Configured as a server, a computer is able to share files and resources with other computers on a peer-to-peer basis. That is, as with Netware Lite, there's no dedicated server, making this a seemingly ideal solution for both first-time network users and existing work groups, while at the same time permitting access to a larger NetWare environment.

As implemented in DOS 7, the networking uses the same drivers, network interface cards, transports, and client utilities as a full-blown Novell NetWare network, so it's fully compatible by design. And for secure, efficient network management, DOS 7 provides an industry-standard SNMP agent, management information base (MIB), and diagnostic responder. These allow Novell DOS 7 workstations to be identified and administered from remote locations. And management utilities can be accessed through a full-screen DOS or Windows interface.

So the bulk of the overhead is relocated into XMS extended memory, only a modest footprint is left behind in upper memory, and as much as 610K or more of conventional memory is available to work with, even in multitasking windows. And there's more.

Dynamic caching with the DPMS

Little need be said about the DPMS CD-ROM and disk-compression support. On 80286 or any higher system, the bulk of the overhead just disappears. I did find one of the new DPMS utilities of more than passing interest, though: the new DOS 7 disk cache. I found it interesting because it's fairly easy to make a comparison with MS-DOS's SmartDriver.

Working with prerelease software, the 23K overhead left behind in upper memory by the Novell cache was more than twice that of SmartDriver (10K in the final release). The difference in performance belies the relatively modest extra overhead, however, because you're actually looking at a rather rigid cache (SmartDrive) on the one hand, as shown here:

Extended Memory	InitCacheSize	WinCacheSize
Up to 1Mb	All extended memory	Zero (no caching)
Up to 2Mb	1Mb	256K
Up to 4Mb	1Mb	512K
Up to 6Mb	2Mb	1Mb
6Mb or more	2Mb	2Mb

and a dynamic disk cache on the other (see FIG. 18-1). As you can see from the table, installed on a machine with 6 megabytes of extended memory, SmartDrive by default sets up a 2Mb cache that instantly and automatically shrinks to 1Mb as soon as you load Windows—whether Windows really needs this extra megabyte of RAM or not. Odds are it will, if not immediately, then at some point in the session. In the meantime, however, in order to assure the availability of XMS memory for other applications, at least 4Mb is going to sit there, all or most of it likely doing nothing a good part of the time.

```
NWCache R1.0  β12  Novell Disk Cache
Copyright (C) 1993 Novell, Inc. All rights reserved.
Copyright (C) 1985, 1990, 1992, Golden Bow Systems.
```

```
Cache size: 6000 kB (XMS)
Minimum cache size: 1536 kB
Buffered write drives: A B
Delayed write drives:  C E
```

```
Current options:
 /MLX         Program is loaded into low and extended memory (using DPMS)
 /BL=16       Look-ahead buffer is loaded into low memory, size is in kB
 /LEND=ON     Lend memory to other applications - 4464 kB available
 /DELAY=5005  Write delay is enabled, time is in milliseconds
```

```
Disk Usage Statistics:                    Error Statistics:
 Command Requests    #Done   Saved          0  Memory Manager Errors
 Reads:        67      10     85%           0  Disk Transfer Errors
 Writes:      104     103      1%           0  Errors Ignored by User
```

18-1
Novell's disk-caching program, NWCache.

Compare that with the DOS 7 dynamic cache that, also by default, has configured itself—initially at least—to use all 6 megabytes of XMS memory for disk caching. It, too, has a minimum size—here 1.5Mb—but you can configure it to almost any size you want by adding a command-line parameter. Even though in this case it, by default, has set a slightly larger minimum cache size, it's ready to lend back 4464K of cache RAM for use at *any* time—not just for Windows, but for any application that comes along.

Now a 6Mb cache isn't going to be three times better than a 2Mb cache. Once you pass a meg or two in size, the law of diminishing returns kicks in—to what extent and just where depends on the kind of work you're doing. Bigger is better, though, and the benefits far outweigh the few extra kilobytes of overhead you have.

And note the number of options you have as to where this cache, written to use the DPMS specification, can be run—depending on system resources.

There are four parameters to use (assuming they're supported by the available hardware):

/ML Loads the cache code into conventional DOS memory (no DPMS).

/MU Loads the cache code into upper memory (no DPMS).

/MLX Loads into conventional and XMS (using DPMS).

/MUX Loads into upper and XMS memory (using DPMS).

What's missing & where next?

For all of this, Novell's DOS 7 is the only current major DOS that doesn't provide some form of upper-memory optimization for use with other software. It's fine that DOS 7 uses the DPMS and automatically packs most of the overhead of SuperStor off to limbo in extended memory, but I happen to use Stacker and will continue to because of the OS/2 compatibility issue and the fact that I'm content with what I've got. And there are other things you just might want to load up there as well.

My guess is that there is a relatively small number of power users who really want to do this sort of thing and that, of the current crop, Novell's DOS 7 is the clear-cut winner in terms of memory management. Not only because of Novell's new DPMS API, but, even more, because it spans the gulf between the real-mode world we started with and the protected mode.

Which brings us to where we go from here. A colleague involved in the development of one of the new DOS 6s confided that, in his opinion, it was the last hurrah for real-mode DOS. Real-mode DOS will never go away as long as there is DOS, because there will almost certainly be 8088s around as long as there is DOS. But just as developers were once faced with the agonizing decision of whether to write 32-bit DOS extended programs or to saddle their DOS extended applications with the limitations of the 80286, today it increasingly makes sense to run with DOS itself up in protected memory.

Novell has hedged their bets in this release, giving us a number of protected-mode advantages in a DOS that can still serve the real-mode world—albeit within the constraints of real-mode operations.

And still the rumors persist about an all-new 32-bit DOS some say will be the next DOS release we see from Microsoft. Where that might take us no one knows for sure. In one way or another, however, the future of DOS clearly lies in the protected mode. And that future is already here . . .

19 DOS in OS/2 2.1 & Windows NT

At first glance it might seem inappropriate to include OS/2 2x and Windows NT in a book devoted to DOS, particularly a book dealing with issues beyond the native 640K scope of DOS. In point of fact, it's entirely relevant because OS/2 2x provides not only an excellent platform for running DOS applications in conventional memory, but also upper memory, an HMA, and the means for loading DOS (or what have you) to the HMA and TSRs and special drivers into UMBs. NT, too, provides for services beyond 640K for DOS applications in recognition of the fact that DOS compatibility is and will remain crucial to the success of any 8086-family operating system.

NT as a viable platform with more than limited appeal is still probably some two to five years off, as I see it, based on the relative few machines in use today that can, even if upgraded, properly support it. And just as it has taken OS/2 some years to "arrive," it seems unlikely that NT, an even more ambitious project, could truly have a major impact on the industry for several years.

This isn't just because it will probably take that long to smooth some of the rough edges that have a nasty habit of appearing, but—particularly in the case of NT—because it would make so much of today's installed hardware base obsolete, regardless of whatever benefits it might ultimately afford. And at this point we lack powerful new "killer" NT applications that run only with Windows NT as opposed to some that have been ported to NT from other platforms—to make us want to rush right out and buy the kind of heavy hardware NT has to have. I'll come back for another look at hardware issues NT raises later, though, concentrating in this chapter on its current support for DOS.

OS/2 2.1, on the other hand, can run on any machine that supports Windows in enhanced mode today, and with little more memory than the minimum required by Windows in the enhanced mode—as opposed to the 12 megabytes or more of RAM it now appears it's going to take to run NT. It has also been around now long enough to be familiar with.

In fact, OS/2 2.x's emulation of the DOS environment directly supports not only the multitasking of DOS and Windows applications, but both 16- and 32-bit applications written specifically for OS/2—either by themselves or intermixed. And seamlessly. A good part of this book—those parts not actually requiring the use either of one of the DOSs or DOS look-alikes like PC MOS—was written using XYWrite III+, my still-favorite word processor, running under OS/2 2.1, complete with all the whistles and bells I'm used to in plain DOS. And often while running a mix of OS/2 and Windows applications.

OS/2's DOS platform even allows some options for DOS applications none of the more traditional DOS multitaskers allow, not DESQview and certainly not Windows, to say nothing of a level of stability unmatched by multitaskers DOS users are probably more familiar with.

It isn't a perfect platform. Realistically, there's probably no such thing because what suits me might not suit you. OS/2 provides a seemingly ideal upgrade path, however, in that not only can you take your old, familiar applications with you, but you aren't penalized in the way Windows— particularly in standard mode—penalizes users who insist on clinging to DOS applications as long as they do the job at hand.

Still, for all the benefits, moving up to OS/2 requires more than just getting up some morning and saying to yourself, "Okay, today I'm going to do it," any more than that approach is practical with Windows NT or with any unfamiliar operating platform. To get the most out of any new operating environment— at least where DOS and and Windows applications are concerned—requires some understanding, a little planning, and a little effort on your part.

A better DOS than DOS

That was what IBM said they were going to give us—a better Windows too, they claimed. We had to wait until 2.1 for that, though, until they added full Windows 3.1 support, including support for 32-bit Windows applications requiring the enhanced mode.

It's in the world of DOS beyond 640K that OS/2 2.0 carves out a legitimate niche in this book. It has two reasons for being here in fact, being simply that protected mode by definition lies beyond one megabyte and that, even in that never-never-land beyond one megabyte, it emulates expanded memory, extended memory, and upper memory—even the HMA for DOS software that can use it. These are all beyond-640K concerns, but in a protected-mode environment we must address them in a different manner than with real-mode DOS.

One of the immediate advantages to running OS/2 2x (or other protected-mode systems) in DOS mode is that, not limited by ordinary DOS 640K restraints, memory management is not an afterthought. It's intrinsic to the operating system; everything you need is right there, just waiting to be put to use. And the same is true of multitasking. No add-ons are required (or even tolerated) for either of these functions, which, at roughly a hundred dollars (list) for a good real-mode third-party memory manager and even more for DESQview (including the cost of QEMM386) make OS/2 2.1 pretty much a bargain.

A cheaper DOS for power users

On the downside, unlike real-mode DOS, you *cannot* substitute a premium add-on manager like QEMM386, 386max, Netroom, or any of the managers for real-mode DOS to analyze your system and then set itself up automatically to maximize your use of OS2/DOS's equivalent of UMBs.

Outwardly this would seem like a backward step, particularly now that both Microsoft and IBM have added optimizing software to their DOS 6 packages. To an extent it is, but much less than you might think. The difference is that with OS/2 (and NT and Novell DOS 7) many services that require high overhead drivers or TSRs in DOS are provided by the underlying system kernel—or by drivers installed in the OS/2 CONFIG.SYS that then provide their services to any kind of session you run.

For example, accessing Stacker compressed drivers always requires a special device driver, regardless of whether you're running OS/2 or just plain DOS. If you use Stacker, though, and have the OS/2 version, once the OS/2-specific driver is loaded from the OS/2 CONFIG.SYS, any Stacker drives that you can access from OS/2 are also available to both real and emulated DOS session. In a plain DOS session, the DOS stacker driver eats up something like 45K and really needs to be loaded high, but when OS/2 hands it to you free it costs you nothing.

CD-ROMs are another high overhead item in DOS that costs you nothing under OS/2. In fact, it's typically a 50K+ overhead item in DOS—50K that has to either go into upper memory or take a big chunk out of conventional memory. Both OS/2 and NT deal with CD-ROM support outside of anybody's working space and as invisible to users as, say, support for floppy drives. And multitasking, generally a high overhead, add-on layer with real-mode DOS, is also handled invisibly by the kernel (not only invisibly, but generally better than by the add-ons).

The same, of course, isn't necessarily true of all devices or drivers, but by and large you're likely to have much less need of upper memory in DOS sessions under OS/2 than in stand-alone sessions. It's there, though, if you need it: not only UMBs but an HMA as well.

As extensively as I use upper memory—at least in real-mode DOS—I had no difficulty just throwing the few DOS TSRs I use with specific DOS sessions running under OS/2 in upper memory with arbitrary loadhigh statements, leaving my conventional memory free, my regular 640K and sometimes even more.

A 736K DOS environment

With the graphical environment supporting Windows applications handled by a separate OS/2/WIN function, OS/2 2.0 is free to cater specifically to the needs of character-based DOS applications, making more conventional memory available than most DOS users have ever imagined, let alone seen. It's just a matter of adding the address space normally used by VGA graphics. Since this graphics memory begins at A000h, it's contiguous to DOS's conventional 640K, giving you a net gain of 96K—an extra 15%.

Before any 386max and other hot-shot DOS memory-manager users jump down my throat, reminding me that you can do pretty much the same thing in DOS, let me hastily concede the point. 386max, beginning with release 7.0, does allow you to configure text-only DOS windows running under MS-Windows to use this extra 64K as conventional memory. No similar space is available to character-based DOS sessions running under DESQview if any applications running concurrently are graphical sessions, however. So this is sort of a gray area.

Under OS/2/DOS, you can have this extra 96K for your text-based applications unconditionally, and *still* run Windows applications—as well as powerful new 32-bit OS/2 apps—all concurrently. This isn't a perfect solution for all situations because some nonWindows graphic applications fall in the cracks. Still, it works well enough—and, more importantly, often enough—to be something that DOS users need to keep in mind. It's there, and you only have to open the settings notebook for the particular application you want, click on the DOS settings button (second page) and scroll down to the VIDEO_MODE_RESTRICTION and change the value to CGA or MONO as appropriate.

The OS/2 transition

Simply running DOS applications from the DOS prompt in an OS/2 DOS window is (with rare exception) exactly like running them from the DOS prompt in DOS. Provided you've migrated your AUTOEXEC.BAT to OS/2 (which OS/2 does for you during installation if you want it to), the DOS part of OS/2 will have the same path, environment, prompt, etc. as you had in ordinary DOS. That means that you can use even your old DOS batch files, if you like, to start DOS programs in an OS/2 DOS window, no modifications required in most instances.

And if those DOS applications need EMS expanded memory or XMS extended memory, no problem: OS/2 2x's DOS emulation will automatically provide up to 32 megabytes of EMS and 16 megabytes of XMS *per DOS application* if needed. This is all just part of the service OS/2 2x provides.

To this extent, then, running DOS applications under OS/2 is exactly like running them with real-mode DOS (with a few rare exceptions I'll deal with later). To a great extent, the same is true with regard to using familiar DOS internal commands such as DIR, COPY, and DEL, and externals such as FORMAT and XCOPY. *Most* of the familiar DOS commands are there, and for most of those that are, the syntax is similar if not identical to what you're used to. There are, of course, a number of exceptions, but most of these are in things that don't concern most DOS users anyway.

In some ways I think it's probably easier for users with only modest DOS (and/or Windows) skills and needs to transition to the OS/2 environment than for power users. OS/2's DOS emulation is just DOS, but DOS made easier because the operating-system kernel automatically does some of the things—like memory management—you had to configure for specifically in ordinary DOS.

When you want or need a little more, the situation changes, however, and you really need to learn a few new tricks. Once you get started, you'll really want to, anyway.

While the standard DOS emulation under OS/2 2x is truly excellent, there still are some DOS programs that are less than happy with it. There are, for instance, some programs that arbitrarily balk at any DOS later than, say, 4.01. Those are likely to balk at the OS/2 DOS emulation as well, returning an error message telling you it's the wrong DOS version. For those, you can simply boot a real DOS session from a floppy in drive A: of whatever real-mode DOS you like—or DOS 5.0 or later, with them listed in the SETVER table for those that can be fooled (the OS/2 emulation has no equivalent for SETVER at this time).

The other DOS in OS/2 2x

In my own case I have an automatic file-backup program (Sitback) for which there is not an OS/2 equivalent at this time. It's version sensitive, and a real DOS session solves the problem, with Sitback loaded from the image file's AUTOEXEC.BAT (loaded into upper memory at that). I also have an excellent DOS dictionary and thesaurus package, but it doesn't like the OS/2 DOS for some reason (it will run resident but not as a TSR), and, again, a real DOS session solves the problem.

Booting DOS from drive A: is an option that's provided for by the default COMMAND PROMPTS set, right along with Windows, windowed or full-screen (emulated) DOS sessions, and OS/2 of course.

Unfortunately, this is only the tip of a very poorly documented iceberg. You can, indeed, boot a genuine DOS session up at any time from within an OS/2 session, simply booting from a bootable disk in drive A: as the prompt suggests, but there are some limitations inherent in this approach. This complicates access to physical drive A: by other processes you might be running concurrently during such sessions. More crucial, however, is the fact that OS/2 does not tolerate the use of any memory manager other than its own, even in these real DOS sessions. There are ways around both of these limitations, however, making real DOS sessions not only a viable but often highly desirable option, though poorly documented.

First off, let's attack the drive A: problem. By changing one of the defaults you can change that to drive B: instead, but working from floppies is always slow. OS/2 is just as happy with a mirror image of a bootable floppy as with the original bootable floppy and even provides a means of creating such an image as a hard-disk file using a special command: VMDISK. Typically, starting with a bootable disk in some physical drive—I've used B: here just to prove that even as an image source drive you aren't limited to only drive A:— the command looks something like this:

```
VMDISK B: C:\OS2\MDOS\DOS_SESS\IBMDOS_5.VMB
```

That takes care of creating the mirror image file. What remains is to make OS/2 recognize the file—I called this one IBMDOS-5.VMB to distinguish it from image files of other DOSs I've been playing with. That requires going into the settings for the DOS from Drive A: object (using the right mouse button to bring up the screen shown in FIG. 19-1).

19-1

Accessing the settings for the DOS from Drive A: object.

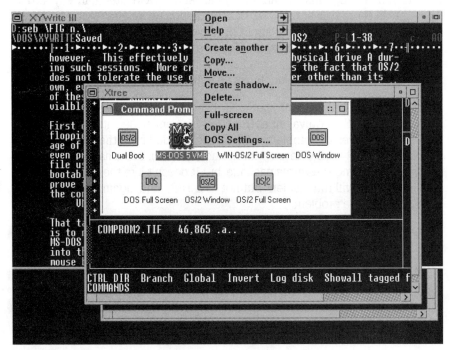

Moving on from that, open the settings notebook and the DOS Settings dialog, as shown in FIG. 19-2. You'll see that the full path to and name of the boot disk image file has been substituted for the DOS_STARTUP_DRIVE.

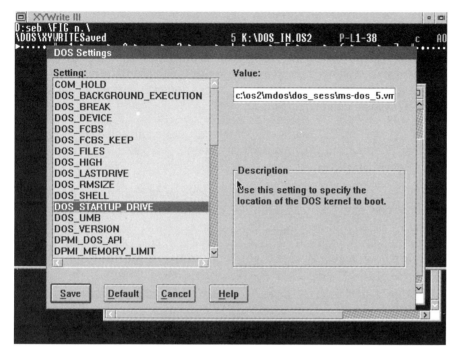

19-2
The DOS Settings dialog box.

A couple of interesting things happen at this point. For one thing, when you click on the DOS from Drive A: icon, the computer no longer even bothers to look at physical drive A. As far as this immediate DOS session is concerned, the DOS it's looking for is on logical drive A:, which is the image file. And, indeed, you can create or edit such necessary evils as a CONFIG.SYS and AUTOEXEC.BAT file on the image file by addressing them as being on drive A:—but only when that DOS session is the active session. Any other sessions currently running under OS/2, whether DOS emulation, Windows, or OS/2, are unaware of any of this and, to them, drive A: is available as physical drive A:.

Both extended and expanded memory are available in real DOS sessions, but only by linking those sessions to OS/2's own memory-management functions. To do that, a CONFIG.SYS (either on the bootable disk you're going to run in drive A: or the image file that is its surrogate) must have the following lines:

```
device=c:\os2\mdos\himem.sys
device=c:\os2\mdos\emm386.sys
```

These aren't the same device drivers you're probably familiar with. They aren't even full-blown, freestanding drivers, in fact, but at something over 500 bytes each provides the necessary linkage back to OS/2 to bring the functionality you would expect from these two drivers to your real DOS session, with the exception of UMBs. Overall, I haven't found that to be a problem, given the ability to tailor specific windows—emulated or real DOS—to the specific needs of individual applications.

Of course, once the DOS from Drive A: function no longer has any connection to physical drive A:, the command prompt is no longer valid. You can easily change this, however, by going to the last page of the settings notebook and changing the program name there. And, while you're at it, you can get rid of that ugly default icon and replace it.

DOS/Windows and OS/2 icons are not directly interchangeable, by the way, but the OS/2 forum on Compuserve has a couple of zip files for icon-conversion utilities.

There are a couple of caveats to keep in mind as far as running a real DOS session is concerned. For one thing, you can have only one real DOS but several emulated DOS sessions running concurrently. Your one real DOS session can run concurrently with one or more emulated DOS sessions (and a mix of Windows and OS/2 sessions), but one session of real DOS is all you get.

The shrinking image

In this day of monster hard drives, we tend to get a little careless sometimes, and image files suitable for booting real DOS sessions are a case in point.

When you talk about creating an image file of the contents of a bootable floppy and transferring that image to your hard disk, what you're really talking about is creating an image of the *entire disk*, not just the contents—empty space and all. Typically, with today's high-density disks, this can amount to 1.2 to 1.44 (or even 2.88) megabytes. In most cases, the actual files you need total only 150K, give or take, but VMDISK doesn't see files, it sees only whole disk images. And what it sees is what you get.

Remember the days when single-sided 5¼-inch floppies that could store all 180K of data were the rage? Today that's laughable, but it would be the perfect size to use for most image source disks. If you could find one, that is. All you have to do, though, is take an old 360K and reformat it as a 180K disk, transfer whatever DOS system files you want to it, and *voila!* You have a source disk that will give you a 180K image file, saving you a megabyte or more of hard disk space to use for something else.

Like a rock

Of course, one of the most crucial tests of any operating system is stability. DOS is pretty stable, but it crashes—sometimes several times a day, with all the weird things I have to play with. Usually it's just the application that crashes, but the result is the same. Windows crashes—again, often it's just a single application, but sometimes the whole works goes, leaving you either with a system that's completely hung or staring at a DOS prompt. When a multitasker goes, it's much more serious, however. It's intolerable, in fact, because it can cost you a lot more than just what you were doing in a single application.

I'm happy to report that, after using OS/2 extensively for well over a year, with the exception of one beta that, mercifully, was short-lived, I've found it to be the most stable operating system I've ever used, bar none—more stable than DOS, more stable than DOS with DESQview, and more stable than DOS with Windows.

The jury is still out on Microsoft's NT. I've still seen only a small part of the features, in part because in NT's first release they hadn't all been implemented, and in part because many of the features that are there require hardware that few users have—or need—at this point.

Windows NT

In general terms, however, if you know Windows you know NT. In fact, that's true to an even greater extent than knowing DOS and Windows puts you into OS/2. Other than for network services, with Windows NT the user interface is right out of Windows. Most of the default groups and icons in those groups are Windows. When it comes to installing DOS applications, changing properties, or opening the PIF editor, it's Windows 3*x*, plain and simple.

So DOS support in Windows NT is pretty much the same as DOS support in Windows. There are some notable differences, due to the fact that NT is designed to run on a variety of platforms other than the Intel 8086 family of CPUs (or clones)—for instance, DEC ALPHA and MIPS R4000 machines, which don't provide services that the operating systems we're used to provide, and which DOS applications have to have. To support DOS and 16-bit Windows applications, the NT kernel has to emulate these hardware services and that emulation, though better than was seen in early beta, has some flaws.

Beyond that, there are some other, more visible differences: NT handles DOS TSRs quite differently and, in fact, not very well in my opinion. And its use of virtual memory seems a little different—and certainly more aggressive than I'm used to. But then it has to be, given the fact that on a minimum system, installed by itself on a 70Mb hard-disk partition on a machine with only 16 megabytes of RAM and a 16.064Mb bare kernel, NT has to go to virtual memory before it even finishes loading the network and other device drivers. With so little hard-disk space to use as virtual memory—in my case only the remainder of the 70Mb required to install NT plus what it can grab on your D: drive—you can pretty much forget about having more than one application open at a time.

Assuming you have enough RAM to properly support whatever applications you want to run in NT, memory beyond 640K for DOS applications is comparable to what you have in MS-Windows running under DOS. The most notable exception is that NT loads DOS=HIGH by default. This, combined with the fact that there's often no other system overhead, such as network drivers, to be accounted for (as in Windows running on top of DOS), gives DOS windows a little more than 622K.

The virtual DOS machine

NT runs DOS sessions on what it calls virtual DOS machines (VDMs), as opposed to ordinary virtual machines. A VM and VDM are functionally the same, but there's an interesting difference. All the other virtual machines I've discussed in this book have been based on Intel (or clone) 32-bit processors, with a special virtual 8086-mode capability.

One of NT's primary purposes, however, is to bridge the hardware gap that currently exists between machines using 8086-family processors and those developed around RISC and other, generally incompatible CPU chips—chips that don't have a virtual 8086 mode, nor emulate the behavior of an 8086 chip in any way. Lacking hardware support for a virtual 8086 mode, NT has to emulate that support and, through software only, create an operating environment that other applications see as if it was DOS running on an 8086. In other words, it virtualizes the hardware that would normally virtualize one or more 8086-type CPUs. You can't get a whole lot more virtual than that.

It isn't only DOS applications running under NT that require the emulation of DOS running on an 8086, either. 16-bit Windows applications run on NT VDMs as well. In addition, NT also supports a 32-bit emulation of a DOS environment, though its use isn't well documented at this time.

Managing DOS memory in NT

Not surprisingly, NT provides a driver called HIMEM.SYS for the purpose of adding XMS support to the basic DOS emulation it provides on VDMs. This driver is installed by default in CONFIG.NT (the functional equivalent of CONFIG.SYS in DOS) and provides up to 16Mb of XMS memory for each DOS application. By default, DOS is loaded above 1024K (into the HMA) and RAM is mapped to available upper-memory address space above 640K.

Although the name is the same as DOS's XMS driver, NT's HIMEM.SYS is not a stand-alone driver. Since—as with other protected-mode DOSs or DOS emulations, memory management is a function of the underlying system kernel—this is really just an interface, a bridge to services provided by the NT kernel. With HIMEM.SYS installed automatically, XMS extended memory is available to DOS applications by default.

Unlike conventional DOS, NT provides no EMM386.EXE EMS emulator (or equivalent). However, ordinary Windows in the enhanced mode doesn't use EMM386.EXE or other user-accessible EMS emulators either, providing EMS to DOS applications that require it as a function of the Windows kernel. (Windows running in standard mode doesn't provide EMS memory, but users can provide it externally via expanded-memory cards.)

By default, NT doesn't provide expanded (EMS) memory for nonWindows applications that need it, but you can add EMS support by opening the PIF editor and editing the PIF files. Be careful not to set the value for EMS memory too high, however.

Using upper memory for DOS in NT

Although it seemingly had not been implemented at this writing, the DOS emulation in NT will support the use of upper memory for loading DOS TSRs or any DOS-specific device drivers you need. You'll recall that the DOS support in NT is equivalent to MS-DOS 5.0/6.0 and, as with OS/2, this distinction is notable when it comes to using upper memory.

NT does provide a DEVICEHIGH function, which, as in DOS, can be used to force the operating system to at least attempt to load device drivers into upper memory. For TSRs, it supports the LOADHIGH (or LH) prefix for commands. However, the NT emulation provides no mechanism (such as MS-DOS's MEMMAKER) for automating the task of loading things to upper memory. You're on your own and some trial-and-error experimentation might be required if you use many TSRs or DOS-specific device drivers.

How much upper memory you have available—how aggressive NT is in seeking out and mapping available address space—is uncertain at this point. However, again as in OS/2 and probably most other protected-mode situations, the need for upper memory is usually less than in real-mode single- or multitasking DOS situations because so many commonly used device-driver services installed for use by the operating system are passed along as freebies to DOS sessions. These services, like CD-ROM support, can on an ordinary DOS machine use up something on the order of 22K for the driver and another 35K just for the MSCDEX DOS extension.

NT, by the way, does not provide a mechanism for booting DOS sessions using other than the DOS emulation. In other words, there's no equivalent for the DOS from Drive A: feature in OS/2 that allows you to boot PC, MS-, or even DR DOS from within an NT session. This probably isn't a big deal because not many users need this feature very often.

NT also supports the use of OS/2x applications. That support is currently limited to character-based applications, and there are few true OS/2 apps that fall into that category. It's possible that later releases of NT will support graphical OS/2 applications as well—OS/2 didn't provide 32-bit graphical support for Windows applications prior to version 2.1 either.

When a file isn't recognizable

One of the most immediate considerations when moving to a more powerful environment is what file system to use. In the past this has never been a problem except when moving from Apple to DOS or vice versa. Now it's becoming a problem—or soon will be for anyone moving up from DOS. Regardless of whether NT or OS/2 is the way you go.

DOS does as DOS was written to do, using something called the FAT (file allocation table) system for saving files and data to disk. Fairly advanced when DOS first made the scene, today it's one of the technological dinosaurs that will linger on as long as there is DOS. It leaves much to be desired, however, and there are much better ways to do the job.

OS/2, in order to maintain compatibility, is able to read from, write to, and just generally live with hard disks (and floppies) formatted under DOS (as does NT). If it has to, that is. But both OS/2 and Windows NT were really written with more sophisticated file systems in mind: something called the HPFS (high-performance file system) for OS/2, and the NTFS (new technology file system) for NT. During the installation of either of these operating systems, you must make a choice whether to stay with the old FAT system or change over to the HPFS or NTFS.

There are two immediate problems when switching to either OS/2's HPFS or NT's NTFS, however. With OS/2, the first of these is that to convert to the HPFS you must reformat your hard disk—which means you'd better have real current backups of everything before you start. NT is a little more polished in this respect, and able to convert your existing disk "on the fly."

The NTFS is not without its peculiar quirks, either. One that still plagued it as of this writing was that, at least on my machine, I couldn't run NT with the NTFS installed. It would run with a FAT file system, but as soon as I took the option of converting to the NTFS, NT would no longer boot an operable system—and several reinstalls seemingly confirmed the problem.

Once you've converted to either the HPFS or NTFS, however, DOS can no longer read your disks. And that means that if you're not happy with OS/2 or NT for any reason—or you have a system crash that takes your operating system with it—you've got major problems. Here OS/2 seems to have the edge over NT because the kernel is small enough that it's possible to prepare an OS/2 bootable 1.44Mb floppy that, while incapable of running working sessions, at least makes it possible to retrieve HPFS files (as FAT files to floppies) if need be.

Still, if you need to run sessions under DOS (as I do) or exchange files back and forth between your laptop and other DOS machines, you might be better off sticking with your FAT system for now. Or at least keeping one hard disk (or partition) as a FAT "disk" for DOS files and software. That way, other than for a hardware crash that destroys your DOS files, you can generally boot DOS up from a floppy and at least access all your DOS files and software in an emergency.

This can create some unforeseen problems, though, because DOS, by its rather rude nature, tends to create a lot of what other file systems see as garbage on your disk. And the results can be rather frightening to say the least.

One of the biggest and most powerful arguments in favor of DOS users upgrading to OS/2 or NT as opposed to UNIX or some other system is that if you know DOS you already know OS/2, and if you know Windows you know NT. It's true that the command structure and syntax for these two systems is pretty much identical to those found in ordinary MS-DOS and Windows, but there are some holes in the argument and if you're not careful they can be real pitfalls.

In the area of disk management, for instance, DOS has CHKDSK.EXE. And indeed, in both OS/2 and NT you'll find CHKDSK.EXE, as well: same name and purpose, but functionally quite different—as logically they should be when you think about it.

In DOS, you have something called file attributes: R for read only, H for hidden, S for system, and A for archive. OS/2 introduced something called *extended attributes* and, without getting into a lengthy discussion of what they are exactly, suffice it to say that since they're something DOS doesn't use, the DOS CHKDSK command wouldn't recognize an extended attribute if it fell over it. But since they're important in OS/2, the OS/2 version of CHKDSK looks for extended-attribute problems with about the same zeal as it looks for lost chains, clusters, cross-linked, or truncated files. As a result, a FAT-formatted disk that looks perfectly clean to DOS—as in the case of the disk reported in FIG. 19-3—might be an absolute disaster zone as seen by OS/2's CHKDSK (see FIG. 19-4).

```
Volume MIXED OPSYS created 09-21-1991 12:00p
Volume Serial Number is E218-0815

  85106688 bytes total disk space
   1677312 bytes in 19 hidden files
    247808 bytes in 111 directories
  75984896 bytes in 2312 user files
   7196672 byes available on disk

      2048 bytes in each allocation unit
     41556 total allocation units on disk
      3514 available allocation units on disk

    655360 total byes memory
    559200 bytes free
```

19-3
DOS CHKDSK report.

In several cases I've seen, OS/2's CHKDSK found several *hundred* problems—many of them typically what OS/2 sees as attempts by DOS files to claim nonexistent extended attributes—on a disk DOS said was perfect. Which means that even if you stay with the FAT file system you can't just run the DOS version of CHKDSK before installing OS/2 and assume that clean is really clean.

The curse of familiarity

```
The type of file system for the disk is FAT
The volume label is MIXED OPSYS
The Volume Serial Number is E218-0815

Errors found. F parameter not specified.
Corrections will not be written to disk.

C:\BISEX UTILITY\VMAP.COM attempted to claim an extended attribute that
does not exist. The error was corrected.
C:\DOS\BUFFALO\ECHLPT.COM attempted to claim an extended attribute that
does not exist. The error was corrected.
C:\DOS\QEMM386\BUFFERS.COM attempted to claim an extended attribute that
does not exist. The error was corrected.
C:\DOS\QEMM386\EMS.COM attempted to claim an extended attribute that
does not exist. The error was corrected.
C:\DOS\QEMM386\FCBS.COM attempted to claim an extended attribute that
does not exist. The error was corrected.
  . . .
C:\WIN\WORD\WINDOWRD.EXE attempted to claim an extended attribute that
does not exist. The error was corrected.
C:\WIN\WATCHER.COM attempted to claim an extended attribute that does not
exist. The error was corrected.

Lost extended attributes were found.
Do you want to display them as files (Y/N)? N
SYS1359: 96256 bytes disk space would be freed

85106688 bytes total disk space
 1130496 bytes in 17 hidden files
  247808 bytes in 111 directories
75984896 bytes in 2312 user files
  450560 bytes in extended attributes
 7196672 bytes available on disk
    2048 bytes in each allocation unit
   41556 total allocation units
    3514 available allocation units on disk
```

19-4

OS/2 CHKDSK report.

The chicken or the egg? Unfortunately, you can't check a hard disk using OS/2's CHKDSK until you have OS/2 up and running. And even then the situation is further complicated by the fact that OS/2's CHKDSK *will not* check the disk the system was booted from. About the only practical way to check drive C:, then, is to boot up from an OS/2-bootable floppy in drive A:.

Ah, but here's the rub: you can't just transfer the OS/2 system to a floppy as you can with DOS because the system files aren't fixed as they are in DOS but rather customized on installation to suit the particular machine. In fact, you can't even copy OS/2 from one machine to another and expect satisfactory results unless, of course, the machines themselves are identical.

At this writing, there's an undocumented method in the IBMOS2 forum on CompuServe for making a bootable OS/2 disk that works quite well (but only on 1.2Mb or higher-density disks. It works quite well, and although it isn't recommended, I found that the OS/2 system installed on one of my machines was sufficiently portable to enable a floppy prepared from that system to be used to boot an emergency OS/2 session on another machine.

In any event, no matter how good the emulation, or even replication of the DOS environment is, there's more to moving up than meets the eye. And while familiarity is fine, it can also be a trap awaiting the unwary who think that they can simply wake up some bright morning and upgrade to another version of the same old real-mode DOS.

Part five
Future memory

20 The memory to manage

The question these days is no longer whether to upgrade but how soon and to what level. Hardware upgrades used to mark at least a fair degree of maturation, in terms of needs, skills, and attitudes about computers. Today, it's often a matter of survival in a changing world.

The pressure to upgrade is hardly new. It has always been there, fueled on the one side by new, more powerful application software, and on the other by the hardware vendors whose livings depend in large part on making last year's models obsolete. Still, until fairly recently you could pace your upgrades, break them into pieces you could manage financially: a new, more powerful motherboard this month, maybe more RAM next month, that badly needed, bigger hard drive three months or so down the line . . .

Gradual upgrades are still possible, but it's becoming increasingly difficult, not because things are moving that much faster though but more because the jumps are getting bigger. On the other side of the coin, prices for new hardware have been plummeting, including the price for entire systems that include not only faster, more powerful motherboards but hard drives in huge denominations.

Therefore, many of the options that were once attractive are no longer valid— or if they are, that validity is now conditional. Even in the short term. For that reason, we must now try to look a little farther down the road, lest we find ourselves trapped by shortsighted "opportunities."

By the same token, I don't think most of us will want to try to keep up with what's trendy or what the magazines are pushing. So let's try to put things in perspective, to look at things the way they are right now. Then we can look ahead and try to see the way they're going to be tomorrow so we can focus our priorities.

Down memory lane

Until now—or very recently—the driving force behind the need to upgrade has been the CPU: the speed of the 80286 over the old 8088, the 32-bit power and other benefits of the 80386 over the 80286, the built-in number-crunching capability of 80486s (except for 486SXs), and so forth. The CPU will—or should—always play a key role. Today, the choice of what CPU you need, though, is secondary in most real-world situations. For many users, myself included, the performance difference between a 33-Mhz 386 and even a Pentium would be negligible—let's face it, even an 8088 can process keyboard input faster than I type.

Today, the real prime mover in the industry is what this book is all about: memory. With DESQview, you can multitask two applications and support a modest disk cache (typically) with as little as 2 megabytes of RAM. Four is better, though, typically enabling you to multitask as many as three or even four applications (even including Windows in standard mode). Windows 3x in 32-bit (enhanced) mode can squeak by in two megs, but four—and preferably more—is decidedly better. OS/2 2.1 can run in something like 3 megabytes of RAM, but barely. I'd say a minimum of 8 megs there to do a decent job.

In any event, I think I'd call 4 megabytes of RAM about the entry-level minimum these days with DESQview. For Windows and OS/2, eight megabytes of RAM is what you likely need to really do the job. And if Windows NT is your thing, then you should start with 12 (but 16 is better).

Sixteen, I find, is what I want to run OS/2 2x on, too. While four megabytes will get you up and running under Windows or OS/2, as soon as you start doing anything you're into virtual memory (which isn't any better under OS/2 than under Windows).

Forget expansion cards

Unfortunately, it really isn't just a matter of going out and buying an expansion card if you need more than you can plug in on the motherboard. You can do it, but as soon as you isolate your memory from direct communication with the CPU, you slow all access to that memory down to bus speed (rarely more than 10 or 12 Mhz)—which is further slowed on 32-bit systems by the fact that, even with an EISA or other 32-bit bus, most expansion cards are limited to 16 bits. On most machines you can actually see a slowdown when the BIOS runs its RAM check when you boot and, after finishing its check of on-board RAM, goes out to check whatever else you've got.

True, in many cases most of us could live with slower access if that's all that was involved. Unfortunately it's not, because putting RAM that's crucial to system operations on the BUS also introduces some inter- and intraprocess timing problems that can be fatal—in fact with OS/2 you can almost bet on it (and contacts at IBM have pretty much confirmed that, based on reports from a number of customers). I haven't been able to try it yet with NT, but I would not expect it to take kindly to this kind of problem either.

To relieve the problem, you can go to plug-in disk-caching cards, plug-in RAM disks, external print spoolers, etc. There are a number of things you can do to offload overhead to save your motherboard RAM for system use. But no matter how you look at it, whatever amount of RAM you can or do have on the motherboard is a finite resource, and one not readily augmented by add-ons.

For these reasons (and the fact that motherboards today generally support more on-board RAM), the popularity of memory-expansion cards has fallen off significantly, with many disappearing from the market altogether. AST, once the leader in expansion board and expanded-memory technology has moved on, no longer even selling memory-expansion products but now focusing on total systems. Newer Technology, another pioneer in the area, while still maintaining a token position in the market, has redirected their main thrust to the Apple market. Expansion boards are still around, of course, but there are fewer of them. They still provide a vital upgrade link for many users, however. I have one in one old machine of mine, in fact.

Today, you should never approach the purchase of a new machine or motherboard with the thought that you can always add expansion cards if need be later on. At the very best, with the exception of proprietary expansion cards that provide full 32-bit direct access to the CPU through special socketing that's separate from the bus, expansion cards should figure only as a last resort—and then only after determining that their use is, in fact, recommended.

Motherboards in recent years have added socketing for more and more RAM. Particularly with 80386s, there was enough to meet all but the most demanding situation. High-end machines generally supported more than low-end models, but at either end of the scale there was generally enough socketing to let you add as much RAM as you needed. That is no longer true, however. And coming at a time when expansion boards aren't the viable option they once were, this is threatening to leave a lot of users stranded. And I'm not just talking older machines.

Reaching critical mass

Read the fine print and you'll see that most 32-bit machines being sold as this goes to press are barely up to running NT unless they're upgraded to the limit, so I'm talking critical mass.

How much RAM you can squeeze onto a motherboard depends on several things. In the first place, obviously, the number of SIMMS (or other memory modules) cannot exceed the number of sockets on the board. What isn't so obvious is the fact that there are still a few machines and upgrade motherboards for sale out there that don't support SIMMs larger than 1 megabyte. Smaller, yes, but larger, no.

The ability to accept SIMMS (or proprietary memory modules) of greater capacity than those for which boards—motherboards or expansion boards—were originally designed is a function of the number of address lines the OEM enabled when the board was manufactured. The standard inline memory module (SIMM) package has some 32 pins—the same number on a 256K SIMM (requiring 18 address lines) as for 16 megabytes (requiring 24). And even if the actual sockets have contacts to engage all 32 SIMM pins, it's more complicated (read that as *more expensive*) to design a board for 24 address lines than for only 18—or 20 (1Mb) or 22 (4Mb). So you often have socketing for address pins that simply dead-end at the board, ending any possible expansion at some very finite level.

For example, then, say you now have (or buy) a motherboard with four SIMM sockets. If those four sockets and the rest of the board are wired for only up to 1Mb SIMMs, you've got a problem—I know because I've got one like that. Even if you have eight 1Mb sockets, down the road you're likely to feel the pinch. Based on what I've seen so far, you'll never run NT. Today, anyone who buys a motherboard or system (or even an expansion card) that supports only 1Mb SIMMs is buying obsolescence, with socketing supporting four 4Mb SIMMs a questionable investment. You can buy it pretty cheap in many cases, but at any price obsolescence is no bargain if you're trying to make a living with this stuff.

Unfortunately, even in today's market 16 4Mb sockets is about the most you're going to see on most motherboards, with 8 far more common. Eight 4Mb SIMMs, of course, will carry you to 32 megs.

RAM upgrade economics

At some point, you have to consider another factor in the RAM equation that has slipped in quietly—the minimum increments allowable when adding RAM. Typically today you have to work in multiples of four—four, that is, of equal value: four times 1Mb, four times 4Mb, etc. But that's with a 32-bit system (it's a function of parity checking). Now with the Pentium and a 64-bit data path, you could be looking at a minimum of *eight* SIMMs at a time.

There are ways around it. AST, for instance, designs machines that use proprietary RAM modules that, combined with special BIOS support and other patented features, allow all kinds of upgrade options. I have one machine, an AST Premium, that can use 1, 2, 3, or 4 RAM modules, even allowing you to mix sizes of up to 4 megs each. Currently, it's running with 7Mb, with further upgrades to a maximum of 16Mb in 3Mb increments. You typically pay a little more up front for such machines, but given these and other options they afford, it can be well worth it in the long run.

There are also ways around this even with conventional SIMMs. In many cases, though, with 32-bit systems, upgrades can't be done with any less than 4 SIMMs at at time. The problem didn't start with 32-bit systems. It's just we really didn't notice it when we went from 8 to 16 bits—or to the 386SX, which generally behaves like a 16-bit machine.

This all has to do with bits, and a typical SIMM (or bank of RAM chips or other equivalent) has only eight available for data processing (in most cases there's also a ninth bit, but it's strictly for parity checking).

Eight data bits was all it took for the old 8088 machines because, even though it's sometimes referred to as a 16-bit chip, it really isn't; the 8088 is an oddball that actually has two back-to-back 8-bit processors, making eight the magic number for that chip. A single bank of RAM chips would supply eight data bits, so assuming the rest of the hardware was willing, an 8088 could be upgraded one 64K bank at a time—which even at about a buck per kilobyte was affordable as long as 640K was the outer limit.

Pieces of eight

An 80286 is a true 16-bit chip, and to do processing in 16 bits it needs 16 data bits of RAM to work with. SIMMs or RAM chips, still, provide only eight data bits per SIMM or bank of chips, so two becomes the magic upgrade number—which also then applies to 80386SX machines because that chip supports only 16-bit access.

Beyond the 386SX (still a 16-bit data path even though it's a 32-bit chip)— and for as long as we continue working at the 32-bit level—the magic number is four: 4×8 data bits = 32. Typically today, then, the RAM options look something like this for your basic, ordinary 386 or 486 with 8 SIMM sockets on the board:

1Mb, 4×256K	Not worth it unless you've got a bunch of
2Mb, 8×256K	old 256K SIMMs gathering dust
4Mb, 4×1Mb	About $180
8Mb, 8×1Mb	About $360
16Mb, 4×4Mb	About $650
32Mb, 8×4Mb	About $1300

Note the incremental jump, not only in on-board memory but in the price of reaching that last exalted level. In many cases, motherboards with 16 sockets won't allow any old multiple of 4 SIMMs at a time, but rather jump directly from 32 to 64Mb, raising the minimum upgrade cost of beyond 32Mb to about $1300 at reasonably recent mail-order prices. And I'm not even talking Pentium here, Intel's new darling with a 64-bit data path.

The result of all this can leave you with some rather agonizing choices. At one point— now history—I figured I needed 8 megabytes. With 8 SIMM sockets I could have managed for a while. But . . . if suddenly I'd found I needed more I would have had to *replace* at least four of my 1Mb SIMMs (and on machines that don't allow a mix of sizes, the other four as well). Taking into the account the money wasted on the SIMMS I would've had to replace, my upgrade cost would have been damned near the same as going directly to 16Mb to begin with.

The local bus Recently, a new bus called the *local bus* has come along. Intended to supplant rather than replace more conventional bus architecture, the local bus allows the CPU to directly address up to the full 4 gigabytes a 386 (etc.) allows. It's also seemingly possible to get around the problem of upgrading in multiples of 2, 4, or—in the case of the 64-bit Pentium—8 SIMMs at a time.

Imagine 4 gigabytes of RAM, and all of it directly accessible by the CPU. At least that's what one leading motherboard manufacturer (Hauppauge) told me was possible with local-bus architecture. While in theory this might be the limit, as a practical matter the reality falls far short of that in most cases. As this was going to press, ALR introduced a new local-bus machine that would support only a maximum of 128Mb of RAM. This is still a lot of RAM, but still only about 3% of the theoretical 4 gigabytes most 386 and higher CPUs support. So even using this technology, not all local-bus machines are on an equal footing by any means.

As of this writing, the local bus had been available for about a year, and while originally available only on high-end machines, local-bus technology was beginning to trickle down—the ALR machine previously mentioned was selling at $2,495 with 8Mb of RAM installed. Still, it will take some time for the local bus—even in more modest implementations—to have a major impact on the market.

According to industry sources, in that first year or so only some 2 million local-bus machines were sold out of a total of some 30 million—in other words, only roughly a 6% market share. But that's only 6% of *that* year's sales. Add that relatively small number of machines to the huge installed user base that predates local-bus architecture—a large part of which will still be in use five years from now—and you're really talking peanuts.

Various implementations of the local bus will continue to trickle down as costs come down. This will give it a bigger share of a market that, by then, will also be replacing more and more of the machines that predate local buses. And with that, the number of machines that are at least capable of achieving more than minimal performance with NT or with some yet unknown operating system could climb rapidly.

Still, it's clear that you can't just assume the new machine you buy today or next year will, in its newness, allow you to stuff in all the RAM it's going to take to run some of the software coming down the pipeline even now.

There's no question that technology is poised to make another jump: this time from 4Mb to 16Mb SIMMs (or some other modular package form). And soon. There's room for only a limited amount of socketing on any board, and it's not just a matter of trying to keep board sizes small. A number of design considerations come into play and, even for the near term, you need 16Mb RAM modules of some kind.

Technically, there isn't any reason you can't have 16Mb SIMMs even now. In fact, they already exist, and in a form that's essentially compatible with today's lower-density (up to and including 4Mb) SIMMs. This is the familiar SIMM package with 32 pins or contacts, two of which haven't been used to date. In keeping the the basic powers-of-two law that governs address pins, one extra pin (or contact) ups the ante from four to eight megabytes, the second extra pin doubles that again and, voila! 16 megabytes on just one SIMM.

The problem with this 32-pin extension of the present industry-standard SIMM is the same problem we have now, where standard 32-bit systems using standard SIMMs can be upgraded only in batches of four to meet the data/parity requirements of 32-bit CPUs. That's expensive enough even at todays tumbling prices for 4Mb SIMMs, but if you multiply that by a factor of four, by today's prices the smallest RAM upgrade increment possible using 16Mb SIMMs would cost something over $2000. Although this would put us directly up to 64Mb of RAM—which is looking better and better in the long term—it's well beyond the reach of the average user.

And that's for a 32-bit system. Now with the Pentium opening a 64-bit data path, we're looking at a whole new set of numbers—numbers that won't make anyone happy, except, of course, for vendors.

Given this, another modular RAM package design has been proposed that would increase the total number of contacts from 32 to 70. Such SIMMs—and they're being used to some limited extent even now—rely on a different mechanism for satisfying the data/parity requirements of the CPU. And assuming proper BIOS support, they allow SIMMs of different sizes to be intermixed with one-at-a-time upgrades.

There are two problems here, however. First, this is nonstandard in terms of today's thinking. The other problem, which follows closely from the first, is that manufacturers are now confronted with two different RAM options, each involving complex and costly motherboard design considerations that will surely affect their long term position in the market. And as of this writing there's no broad consensus of opinion as to which path to follow—at least not among manufacturers. And if they don't make it, we can't buy it.

Regardless of the outcome, once again, even more than the need for faster and more powerful CPUs, it's the need for more and still more memory that is the driving force. The only thing that's really changed is the size of the steps, and the next one is a whopper.

The memory does all the work

When I was a kid growing up in pre-TV Montana, the local radio station used to play a cowboy ditty with a verse that went "The shirt and the pants do all of the work, but the vest gets all the gravy . . ." It's sort of that way with computers when you stop to think about it. It takes all this memory—more every time you turn around it seems—but all anybody really talks about are CPUs: faster and faster CPUs, doublers for Intel 486s, RISC chips, etc.

In the mad scramble to keep manufacturing costs pared to the bone in order to maintain a competitive position in an atmosphere of plunging prices and declining profits, manufacturers don't really go out of their way to advertise RAM capacity. Rather than being in the main body of the advertising hype, it's usually mentioned somewhere only in the fine print. In order to remain competitive, most vendors seemingly have given little thought to increasing RAM capacity. Indeed, most 486s being sold at this point support only up to a maximum of 32Mb of RAM.

Thirty-two megabytes of RAM seemed laughable not too long back—back when most of us were living happily with only a megabyte or two beyond 640K. But it's no laughing matter now.

My rule of thumb says that to run any operating system effectively in today's work environment, you need *at least* four times the amount of RAM it takes to support the operating system—when you factor-in the demands of application software, effective disk-caching, and so forth. And I can tell you frankly that, even with 16 megabytes to work with, OS/2 2.1 winds up virtualizing enough to make me wish I had 32Mb.

So if it effectively takes a minimum of 8Mb to load an operating system; the rule of four demands a system capable of supporting *at least* 32Mb and preferably 64Mb of RAM if you're allowing for further expansion. Particularly in view of the fact that, on average, our need for more RAM has increased tenfold roughly every four years since the introduction of the first PC.

I don't mean to imply that future purchases should hinge entirely on how much RAM you can stuff on the motherboard. The CPU most surely makes a difference, for while there is no absolute, direct correlation between the size of the kernel and the number of instructions (lines of code) that must be processed to perform a given task, a relationship does exist. We aren't approaching critical mass; we're already there.

21 All that's past is prologue

From all indications, DOS is likely to outlive most of those who prematurely predicted its demise back even before most of us outgrew our 8088 PCs. It's still, despite its many flaws and foibles, the world's foremost operating system. Yet as DOS moves into its second decade, it has long since taken us where it was never supposed to go.

Never have there been so many choices available to us. But clearly, with those choices a whole new set of questions has come to bear. And at this point I think it's imperative that we all take a new look at DOS, at what it should be, and how best to reconcile it with this current crop.

DOS isn't on the endangered list by any means. They're still selling 8088 machines that do and always will require a real-mode DOS—and 286s that are only slightly less limited in terms of operating-system options. Even beyond that, DOS has too large a following.

Still, I think it's equally clear that few—if any—really powerful new 640K DOS-only applications will appear: nothing to compare with Lotus, dBASE, or any of the old standbys so many of us started with. Many new applications, yes. And countless upgrade releases for existing applications. As the dominant operating system, DOS will still be attractive to many developers because it still spells dollars, the fuel that ultimately runs this engine. But the emergence of much in the way of exciting new pure DOS applications seems doubtful.

Increasingly today, the trend seems more and more to write code that isn't specific to any one platform. Developers—Corel for example—are hedging their bets by writing new code that will run with OS/2 or Unix or NT. In some cases, it will trickle down to DOS—not really to DOS, but rather to protected mode.

For both today and the future, with DOS the real action is going to be beyond 640K, and most of it is going to be beyond 1 megabyte in extended memory, a place where DOS doesn't exist and plays no real role except for providing I/O services. And some of today's more advanced DOS extenders are even taking over some of those duties in order to bypass bottlenecks imposed by the 16-bit (and sometimes only 8-bit) services we're accustomed to.

Good old DOS. Except this is a different age with different needs. A different age, indeed, but remarkably DOS has kept pace, adapting, almost chameleon-like, to live in real mode or protected mode, in either instance taking old real-mode applications with it. Much of what has happened in the DOS world has been almost lost amid the hoopla over OS/2 and now NT. But DOS has never been in better shape.

Stop the world, I want to get off

There was a Broadway show by that name some years back. I missed the show, but increasingly these days I'm hearing the refrain from users as RAM requirements exceed the size of hard drives and hard-disk sizes make gigabytes seem far less awesome. Indeed, there comes a time for all of us to take a look at what we really need—or really want. Particularly at this time, when, more and more, we're torn between the diametrically opposed forces of the status quo and progress.

There's a comfortable logic that says, on one hand, that ordinary real-mode DOS—with just a little help—can likely take you any place you want or need to go, particularly with today's powerful DOS-extended applications, multitaskers, and even multimedia extensions. There's also a comfortable—and safe—logic that says "if it ain't broke, don't fix it."

On the other hand, with the high-end market reaching ever higher, making what was once high-end not too long ago now entry level—and at bargain prices—there are often compelling arguments to look beyond the world of DOS. Or if not beyond DOS, at least beyond the world of DOS as we've always known it.

Take hardware, for instance. There's a tremendous push to sell faster and more powerful machines, whether we really need new machines or not. But there's another group of vendors out there trying just as hard to sell old technology, often at bargain prices—happily reaping profit from the fact that there's still a market, and a good one, for even the lowly 8088.

As in most things, the truth lies somewhere in the middle, its precise whereabouts dependent on a lot of things, the most important single factor being you, the user. Let's face it, there are still a lot of users out there who are running DOS 3x quite happily on 8088 or 286 machines, many without the benefit of expanded memory. Many will, of course, move up at some point. But many won't. And if what you're using does the job you want it to and it does it in a way that suits your disposition, where's the need?

Software vendors don't like to hear this sort of thing. And hardware vendors surely don't because if none of us bought new machines until the old ones died, a lot of companies would be out a lot of money.

This isn't to say I advocate a "good old days" 640K approach by any means. The world has changed, and I wouldn't give up my 486 and multitasking, gobs of RAM and hard disk space for anything. And I've got some really great new 32-bit stuff I'd never want to do without again. But at some point I think we have to take a good hard look at where we're going, and then—and only then—try to figure out how best to get there.

No matter where it is we ultimately decide to go, today we have to look at DOS not as an operating system, but rather as a cheap-and-dirty launch pad to propel us out into what DOS can never even glimpse.

All a matter of perspective

The end of the first edition of this book left you looking down on DOS, down on the almost infinitesimal speck 640K would be viewed as from the lofty altitude of several gigabytes—like looking for an ant from atop the Empire State Building.

It's a funny thing about perspective, though. Standing close to the edge and looking down from the top is always just a little dizzying, a little terrifying. Standing, firmly rooted, looking up from where we are today—seeing where it is we can go beyond 640K from DOS—those gigabytes that once seemed so imposing now no longer look so big, or so very far away. Not so very far at all. Not even from DOS. It's all a matter of perspective.

A *Hexadecimal: the basics*

This is a book about addresses: computer addresses. Everything a computer does involves some block of addresses. Devices—printers, keyboards, monitors—are installed at addresses. Software installs itself at addresses. There are about a million of them, to be precise 1,048,576 unique, identifiable, absolute addresses—or, in simpler terms, FFFFh.

Yes, simpler. Much simpler than powers of and multiples of 2. You don't have to go deeply into hexadecimal—and I don't intend to here. But a few of the basics will make life easier. Back in TABLE 2-1, I took the 1,048,576 from the previous paragraph and converted it into 16 blocks, in hexadecimal notation.

We count in tens (the decimal system) because its easy—for us at least. Computers count in twos because that's all they have; each transistor (or equivalent speck buried in a chip) is either switched on or off, a zero or a one. But they do it a lot faster and better than we count in tens. So, like it or not, at some point you have to come to terms with it. But not necessarily by adding up long strings of twos.

Sixteens (2^4) give us, as you can see from TABLE 2-1, a convenient compromise—a bunch of impossible-to-remember decimal numbers on one side equated to a neat, uniform progression in hex on the other. You'll note that the first ten blocks (0–9) cover the entire 640K of conventional user memory available to ordinary applications.

So far so good, but we still need six more single-character somethings to bring the count to 16, so we use the letters A, B, C, D, E, and F. Now the count runs: 0,1,2,3,4,5,6,7,8,9,A,B,C,D,E,F.

Referring again to the Table, you'll see the progression in either notation is just a series of blocks of 64K—which really isn't nice, neat increments of 64,000, but actually 65,536. But in hex it really is a nice, neat, even number: 10000h. And that's really all there is to understanding hexadecimal. At least enough to start putting it to work.

Keep in mind that two address-numbering conventions are used, both apparently in hex notation with a mix of letters and numbers, but some with only four or five letters.

Even in hex it takes five places to show the whole of addresses to 1024 kilobytes (1Mb). To be precise, it takes 20 bits to point to any address in that range. However, the 8088 has only 16-bit address registers to work with. As a result, addresses must be broken up into components that can be managed by 16-bit registers. The result is a two-part address consisting of a four-character segment (xxxx) plus a second four-character offset group (yyyy), with the resulting address looking something like this:

xxxx:yyyy

To arrive at the full 32-bit address used in real mode from these two 16-bit numbers, add the two values, *offsetting* the second part in this manner:

```
  1111
+ 2222
 13332
```

Like rounding off any number for the sake of convenience, the segment address contains all of the information you need unless otherwise noted.

By the same token, I generally refer to blocks of memory—64K, for instance—in their decimal approximations, as is also common. Still, the most significant break points in DOS come at multiples of 65536 bytes—10000 in hexadecimal. So quickly, what is three times 65536? The answer is 30000 in hexadecimal, or if you drop a zero to reduce it to a four-place segment, 3000. You see, instead of complicating life it really does make it easier when dealing with computers.

B Mapping LIM 4.0 EMS memory

In accordance with the LIM 4.0 specification, all the better memory managers for 80386 and higher systems provide for mapping memory. However, there are a number of programs that have problems if they encounter mapped memory in specific areas they're programmed to try to use—including a number that, at least with certain memory managers, have difficulty dealing with mapped memory below 640K. In these cases, special allowances must be made when setting up the memory manager, usually by including some sort of specific EXCLUDE statement on the memory manager's command line in the CONFIG.SYS, as in the following example:

```
DEVICE=QEMM386.SYS ram rom EXCLUDE=C800-CBFF au dma=32
```

While in many cases other command-line parameters are determined and written to the CONFIG.SYS automatically by the installation program, such exclusions generally have to be added by the user. Information relative to the need for special-address exclusion should be part of the documentation for any program requiring such special treatment. However, if you observe any conflicts (for example, error messages during loading or the malfunctioning of any software that had been working previously), you might need to call for technical support.

Difficulties encountered by the failure to exclude specific address areas vary, in some cases resulting only in programs that can use high memory loading in conventional memory instead. In more severe cases, it can result in certain hardware or software failure.

The list in TABLE B-1 presents at least a sampling of programs known to have encountered problems under certain circumstances, and exclusions or other corrective measures taken to ensure proper operation. I've used EXCLUDE= and FRAME= in the examples and, while it's the syntax used by several memory-management packages, refer to the documentation for the specific manager you are using to determine the syntax to use. The specific address areas, if a problem does exist, should be constant regardless.

Table B-1
Programs that have
encountered problems under certain circumstances,
with appropriate exclusions and corrective measures.

Name	Special instructions
DC Windows Express	EXCLUDE=1000-A000 (under Windows 2.x or use WIN/N)
Deluxe Paint	EXCLUDE=1000-A000 (for versions 1 and 2)
Excel	EXCLUDE=1000-A000 (runtime version only)
Javelin	EXCLUDE=1000-A000
Pagemaker	EXCLUDE=1000-A000 (under Windows runtime 2.x or use WIN/N)
Paradox 3.0	EXCLUDE=A000-B000 (for monochrome or CGA systems)
Smartware II	EXCLUDE=1000-A000
SQL Windows	EXCLUDE=1000-A000
Stacker	EXCLUDE=C800-CBFF
SuperCalc5	EXCLUDE=1000-A000
SuperProject+	EXCLUDE=1000-A000
Word for Windows	EXCLUDE=1000-A000 (under Windows 2.11 and 2.1)
JLASER/SA	FRAME=D000 (versions of the JLASER/SA software prior to 4.14 only)
Ventura Publisher	FRAME=E000 (or below if the EMS page frame starts above E000)

There are also some programs that, while normally running in color mode, use the monochrome buffer area to access special characteristics of the VGA/EGA card installed. If these programs are used, the monochrome buffer area cannot be reclaimed as high DOS or as an EMS area without video problems resulting.

Of these, Supercalc 5 and Smartcom are probably the best known. In such cases, be aware of any statements on the memory manager's DEVICE= line that would include the B000 to B800 area. If found, those references should be deleted.

Additionally, a number of display adapters are known to require that special parameters be set when used in conjunction with certain memory managers.

When installing new display adapters—particularly special-purpose or high-resolution adapters—pay special attention to the documentation.

Beginning with release 6.1, PC DOS from IBM is also capable of providing mapping support for up to approximately 60K of upper memory on 80286 and even 8088 machines, using the EMS 3.2 memory provided by many older memory-expansion cards. This, too, is subject to any mandatory exclusions such as those in the previous list.

LIM 4.0 EMM advanced programming functions

Number	Function	Description
LIM 3.2 only		
1	Get Status	Tests whether the expanded memory hardware is functional
2	Get Page Frame Address	Obtains segment address of the page frame used by the expanded memory manager (EMM).
3	Get Unallocated Page Count	Obtains total number of logical pages of expanded memory present in system and the number of those not already allocated.
4	Allocate Pages	Notifies the EMM program it will be using expanded memory, obtains a handle, and allocates the required number of logical pages to be controlled by that handle.
5	Map/Unmap Handle Page	Maps one of the logical pages assigned to a handle into one of four physical pages within expanded memory manager's page frame.

Number	Function	Description
6	Deallocate Pages	Releases the logical pages of expanded memory currently assigned to the handle, then releases the handle itself.
7	Get Version	Returns version number of expanded memory manager software.
8	Save Page Map	Saves contents of page mapping registers from all expanded memory boards into an internal save area.
9	Restore Page Map	Restores (from an internal save area) page mapping register contents on expanded memory boards for a particular EMM handle.
10	(no longer used)	
11	(no longer used)	
12	Get Handle Count	Returns the number of open EMM handles in the system.
13	Get Handle Pages	Returns the number of pages allocated to a specific EMM handle.
14	Get All Handle Pages	Returns an array of active EMM handles and the number of pages allocated to each.
15	Get/Set Page Map (subfunction)	Saves and restores the mapping context for all mappable memory regions (both conventional and expanded) in destination array supplied by the application.

Functions added by LIM 4.0 EMS

Number	Function	Description
16	Get/Set Partial Page Map (subfunction)	Provides mechanism for saving partial mapping context for specific mappable memory regions.
17	Map/Unmap Multiple Handle Pages	In single invocation, it can map (or unmap) logical pages into as

Number	Function	Description
		many physical pages as supported by the system.
18	Reallocate Pages	Can increase or decrease the amount of expanded memory allocated to a handle.
19	Get/Set Handle Attribute	Allows the application program to determine and set the attribute associated with the handle.
20	Get/Set Handle Name	Gets the eight-character name currently assigned to the handle and assigns an eight-character name to the handle.
21	Get Handle Directory	Returns information about active handles and assigned names.
22	Alter Page Map & Jump	Alters memory mapping context and transfers control to specified address.
23	Alter Page Map & Call	Alters specified mapping context and transfers control to specified address. A return can then restore context and return control to caller.
24	Move/Exchange Memory Region	Copies or exchanges a region of memory from conventional to conventional, conventional to expanded, expanded to conventional, or expanded to expanded memory.
25	Get Mappable Physical Address Array	Returns an array containing the segment address and physical page number for each mappable physical page in the system.
26	Get Expanded Memory Hardware Information	Returns array containing hardware capabilities of installed expanded memory.
27	Allocate Standard/ Raw Pages	Allocates number of standard or nonstandard size pages that the operating system requests, and assigns unique EMM handle to them.

Number	Function	Description
28	Alternate Map Register Set	Enables an application to simulate alternate sets of hardware mapping registers.
29	Prepare Expanded Memory Hardware for Warm Boot	Prepares expanded memory hardware for "impending" warm boot.
30	Enable/Disable OS/E	Enables operating system developers to enable and disable functions designed for operating system use.

alternate register set   A single register set can point only to a single set of 16K blocks (logical pages) in expanded memory. To access more than 64K of data (under 3.2 EMS) or provide one set of 16K blocks to backfill conventional memory or access data in expanded memory (under 4.0 EMS), additional sets of pointers—alternate register sets—must be provided.

ASCII   American Standard Code for Information Interchange. A method of translating computer machine language to a user-identifiable character set.

beta test   A final phase of testing where a product is put in the hands of selected users for a period of actual in-use testing prior to general distribution.

BIOS   Basic in/out services, a set of instructions managing computer operations at the lowest level.

boot sector   A special disk sector reserved for information the computer needs in order to load the operating system.

boot manager   Program that allows the user to select which of several bootable partitions from which to start a session. As implemented in OS/2 2*x*, it allows for a mix of any 8036-compatible operating systems or multiple versions of same operating system.

byte   The basic unit of measure for computer memory. A character—such as a letter, number, or punctuation mark—uses one byte of memory. A byte is composed of eight binary bits.

conventional memory   Term applied to user memory that is generally below 640K but can under certain circumstances be increased to 740 or more depending on the type of display and video addresses used.

configuration   The grouping of hardware and software that makes up a computer system. This grouping includes the main console (display), any printers, the operating system, and any other applications and hardware.

data compression   A means of packing data to lessen the space it occupies for storage.

device driver   A piece of software that contains the specifications for running a particular device. When invoked, it activates and controls communications with the device.

DOS   Disk operating system. Sometimes used generically but in this book refers specifically to the Microsoft-based operating systems marketed as MS-DOS and PC DOS.

DPMI   DOS protected-mode interface. Microsoft specification governing the way DOS extenders and DOS extended software runs in protected mode.

DPMS   Novell adaptation of DPMI specification. Complies with DPMI but adds additional functionality. Intended primarily for load TSRs, device drivers, and other smaller programs into extended rather than conventional or upper memory.

Glossary

EEMS Enhanced expanded memory specification. An enhanced version of the earlier LIM 3.2 EMS. A superset of EMS, many features were incorporated in LIM 4.0 EMS.

emulate To behave or function the same as or better than another system (hardware or software).

executable file A file that contains machine-recognizable language that can be executed directly, without an interpreter.

expanded memory Nonlinear memory beyond 1 megabyte but accessible on a revolving basis in blocks made available by an expanded memory manager (EMM) at addresses within DOS's 1Mb limit.

extended memory Linear memory at addresses above 1 megabyte. Accessible and directly usable only with 80286 and higher processors, it can be used to emulate expanded memory.

gigabyte One billion (10^9) bytes.

hexadecimal The base-16 numbering system. Derived from the binary nature of computer logic (2^4), which cannot deal directly with decimal values.

high DOS memory Term used to refer to RAM mapped to unused address spaces above 640K but below 1024K. Also referred to as upper-memory blocks (UMBs).

high memory area The "extra" 64K available to DOS between 1024K and 1088K. Applicable with 286 and higher CPUs only.

kilobyte One thousand (10^3) bytes.

LIM Abbreviation derived from Lotus/Intel/Microsoft, used to describe the expanded memory specification (EMS) developed through a joint effort that ultimately included other companies as well.

linear memory Directly accessible memory made up of conventional memory (including upper memory from 640K to 1Mb) and extended memory above 1Mb for 80286 or 80386-based machines.

logical page A 16K block of memory. Under 3.2 EMS, it applied only to blocks (4K to 64K page frames) above 640K. Under 4.0 EMS, it can apply to any 16K block (with the base address a multiple of 16K) below 1024K.

low RAM *See* conventional memory.

megabyte One million (10^6) bytes.

memory module Compact plug-in memory device typically containing some group of RAM chips (typically 9). Class includes SIMMs (standard inline memory module), as well as other standard and proprietary groupings.

multitasking Running multiple applications simultaneously. With DOS, this is facilitated by using a multitasking or windowing environment such as

Microsoft Windows or Desqview. This capability is integral to protected-mode operating systems such as Xenix and OS/2.

nanosecond   One billionth (1/1,000,000,000) of a second.

overhead   The memory used by whatever software is loaded. The operating system requires a substantial amount of memory—overhead—and still more is added by any TSRs, drivers, etc.

page   One 16K block of information that can be electronically repositioned from expanded memory to conventional memory through the bank-switching process.

page frame   An area through which pages are switched in the bank-switching process.

page register   A memory location that acts as a point and locates a particular area in memory.

paged memory   Memory that's divided into 16K blocks called pages. *See also* expanded memory.

PCMCIA   Personal Computer Memory Card International Association. The abbreviation is most commonly associated with a specification defining standards for plug-in memory cards and other devices, primarily those intended for use with laptop and and other small computers that don't support conventional expansion buses (such as ISA and EISA).

perfect superset   Term used to describe some set of functions or commands that go beyond the limitations of the underlying system to provide additional services while maintaining absolute compatibility with that system. EEMS, for instance, was a perfect superset for the original LIM EMS specification.

port   The physical device that serves as a channel for peripheral devices to communicate with the central processing unit (CPU). It's also used to describe the process of adapting software code to run in other than its native environment.

print spooler   An area in volatile memory (RAM) set aside to take data that's being sent to the printer, thereby freeing the processor for other tasks. While not considered multitasking in the usual sense, it is to the extent that the user can go on with some other task while a job is still printing.

protected mode   A special mode of operation that allows addressing of up to 16Mb of extended memory with 80286 systems. Currently available in alternative operating systems such as Xenix and OS/2, it can also be used by the 80386.

RAM   Volatile memory. An area of memory in which code and data can be stored during processing.

RAM disk   An area of volatile memory (RAM) set aside for quick access of data. When data is placed in a RAM disk, a program can access it much more quickly than it could if it had to read that same data from a floppy or hard disk.

register   The pointer required to locate a particular 16K block of data stored in expanded memory.

register set   Collection of all the registers used by a particular program or application at any given time.

remapping   The ability to assign unused addresses (typically above 640K) to blocks of physical RAM so they appear to be at those addresses. Generally limited to 80386 systems where this is supported by the microprocessor chip itself.

ROM BIOS   Low-level basic in/out services loaded into memory during boot processes from read-only memory chips.

SIMM   Single inline memory module. A mini circuit board generally containing one complete bank of—typically nine—memory chips. This type of memory unit takes up significantly less space than individual DRAM chips in sockets, but requires special socketing.

Split Memory Addressing   A term used by AST to define the ability of their boards to allocate some memory to fill out conventional memory (up to 640K), allocating the rest to expanded or extended memory.

superset   Term used to describe some set of functions or commands that go beyond the limitations of the underlying system to provide additional services. *See also* perfect superset.

terabyte   One trillion (10^{12}) bytes.

time slicing   Commonly used technique for switching (dividing the attention of) a single microprocessor chip between two or more applications. Switched fast enough, it can give the illusion of simultaneous processing, or multitasking.

thrashing   Where the time slice allotted to an application using virtual memory in a multitasking environment is insufficient to complete read or write access. As long as that access remains incomplete, the heads thrash back and forth each time that application's time slice comes up—until the task is finished.

upper memory   Sometimes called *reserved memory*, this is any memory in the 640K 1Mb address range. It was originally used for system functions such as display memory, ROM BIOS, and various auxiliary functions. It now also includes page frames used by expanded memory and, with remapping (80386 only except with additional hardware support), relocation of various functions from conventional 640K.

Vdisk   IBM software product to create simulated disk drive in RAM.

volatile   Term used to describe memory that retains its contents only as long as it's receiving power to refresh itself. Common RAM falls into this category.

XMS   A memory-usage and management specification written by Microsoft and incorporating the work of others that defines a protocol controlling access to high (1024K–1088K), upper (640K–1024K), and extended memory on all computers using 80286 or higher chips.

Index

Other Bestsellers of Related Interest

WRITING DR DOS® BATCH FILES

Ronny Richardson

Boost the performance and increase the efficiency of the DR DOS operating system with this first and only book/disk package on batch file programming for DR DOS. After a complete batch file programming tutorial, you'll discover how to create your own batch files using DR DOS commands and the batch file utilities included on the FREE 3.5" companion disk. A screen compiler, a batch file utility kit, and a quick-reference summary of the DR DOS command language round out this thoroughly practical, easy-to-follow guide.

■ 464 pages. ■ 79 illustrations. ■ 3.5" disk
Book No. 052364-9 $32.95 paperback only

BUILD YOUR OWN 486/486SX AND SAVE A BUNDLE

2nd Edition
Aubrey Pilgrim

This hands-on guide makes it possible for you to build your own state-of-the-art, 100% IBM-compatible PC for about one-third of the retail cost or less with little more than a few parts, a screwdriver, and a pair of pliers. So don't shell out huge sums of money for a PC at your local retail outlet. This book will allow you to enjoy the speed and power of a 486—and still put food on the table.

■ 256 pages ■ 58 illustrations
Book No. 050110-6 $19.95 paperback
Book No. 050109-5 $29.95 hardcover

DOS SUBROUTINES FOR C AND ASSEMBLER

Leo J. Scanlon and Mark R. Parker

Fully tested and guaranteed to make programming faster and easier, this collection of subroutines will work on any IBM-compatible computer running DOS. It's a valuable source code toolbox that experienced C and assembly language programmers can draw on to save the hours or days it can take to create subroutines from scratch. Beginners will also appreciate this book because it's an easy-to-use source of pretested, error-free code that demonstrates the correct way to prepare programs.

■ 360 pages ■ 125 illustrations ■ 3.5" disk
Book No. 055022-0 $34.95 paperback
Book No. 055021-2 $44.95 hardcover

WINDOWS™ BATCH FILE PROGRAMMING

Namir C. Shammas

Here is a complete book/disk package that contains everything you need to create and run Windows-based batch files quickly and easily. In addition to expert programming tips, you'll find detailed coverage of the shareware product WinBatch—included on disk along with WinEdit, a shareware text editor—and the commercial package BridgeBatch. Plus, you'll find a step-by-step illustrated tutorial that shows how to input and output with batch files, construct highly interactive dialog boxes, manipulate text in files, and manage files, directories, and disk drives.

■ 384 pages ■ 147 illustrations ■ 3.5" disk
Book No. 056448-5 $32.95 paperback only

DR. BATCH FILE'S ULTIMATE COLLECTION

Ronny Richardson

Boost productivity, enhance DOS performance, and save hundreds of unnecessary keystrokes with this practical library of programs—no programming skills required. Assembled here and on the FREE 3.5" companion disk are over 120 of the most useful batch files available for creating and using keyboard macros, saving and reusing command lines, tracking down viruses in COMMAND.COM, and much more.

■ 440 pages ■ 146 illustrations ■ 3.5" disk
Book No. 052359-2 $29.95 paperback
Book No. 052358-4 $39.95 hardcover

NORTON DESKTOP® FOR WINDOWS® 2.0: An Illustrated Tutorial

Richard Evans

"Evans tells the reader virtually everything necessary to use the Norton Utilities . . . Recommended."

Computer Shopper on a previous edition
This example-packed guide gives you step-by-step, illustrated instructions for using each Norton Desktop library—including valuable troubleshooting advice and solutions to common problems. Evans, whose previous books on the Norton Utilities have sold more than 50,000 copies, not only shows you how to optimize the Norton Desktop Utilities, he also demonstrates the use of Norton Disk Doctor and Norton Backup.

■ 240 pages ■ 109 illustrations
Book No. 019883-7 $19.95 paperback
Book No. 019882-9 $29.95 hardcover

BATCH FILES TO GO: A Programmer's Library
Ronny Richardson

Ronny Richardson, respected research analyst and programmer, has assembled this collection of ready-to-use batch files featuring over 80 exclusive keystroke-saving programs. These fully developed programs—all available on disk for instant access—can be used as they are, or altered to handle virtually any file management task.

■ 352 pages ■ 100 illustrations ■ 5.25"disk
Book No. 4165 $34.95 paperback only

UPGRADE YOUR COMPUTER PRINTER AND SAVE A BUNDLE
Horace W. LaBadie, Jr.

With this timely guide, you'll explore the affordable upgrade opportunities available for several popular printer makes and models, including Apple LaserWriters, the Hewlett-Packard Series, HP DeskJet, Canon Bubble Jets, Okidata, and others. You'll also look at added font and graphics capabilities, spoolers and buffers, printer sharing and network boxes, interface converters, and caching drives, as well as software solutions such as PostScript and others.

■ 288 pages ■ 245 illustrations
Book No. 035837-0 $19.95 paperback
Book No. 035836-2 $29.95 hardcover

EASY PC MAINTENANCE AND REPAIR
Phil Laplante

Keep your PC running flawlessly—and save hundreds of dollars in professional service fees! This money-saving guide will show you how. It provides all the step-by-step instructions and troubleshooting guidance you need to maintain your IBM PC-XT, 286, 386, or 486 compatible computer. If you have a screwdriver, a pair of pliers, and a basic understanding of how PCs function, you're ready to go to work.

■ 152 pages ■ 68 illustrations
Book No. 4143 $14.95 paperback
** $22.95 hardcover**

BUILD YOUR OWN COMPUTER ACCESSORIES AND SAVE A BUNDLE
Bonnie J. Hargrave and Ted Dunning

Here are step-by-step, easy-to-understand instructions for 27 useful network management and computer diagnostic devices. Page after page of practical guidance for building accessories make complex, time-consuming computer network operations easier and faster. Plus, you'll find a special section on the tools necessary for basic soldering and cabling operations . . .information on how to read circuit diagrams and schematics . . . a list of component suppliers . . . and estimated total costs for each project.

■ 376 pages ■ 222 illustrations
Book No. 026381-7 $19.95 paperback
Book No. 026380-9 $29.95 hardcover

HIGH-PERFORMANCE C GRAPHICS PROGRAMMING FOR WINDOWS®
Lee Adams

Take advantage of the explosive popularity of Windows with the help of computer graphics ace Lee Adams. He offers you an introduction to a wide range of C graphics programming topics that have interactive and commercial applications. From software prototypes to finished applications, this toolkit not only explores graphics programming, but also gives you many examples of working source code.

■ 528 pages ■ 224 illustrations ■ Includes coupon for supplementary C graphics for Windows programming disk
Book No. 4103 $24.95 paperback
** $34.95 hardcover**

ENHANCED BATCH FILE PROGRAMMING
2nd Edition
Dan Gookin

Create powerful batch files that automate your system, boost productivity, and improve efficiency with this guide—now updated for DOS 5 and Windows. It's packed with programming tricks, over 100 special utilities, and a working copy of the bestselling batch file compiler Builder—on two FREE 5.25" disks.

■ 368 pages ■ 92 illustrations ■ Two 5.25" disks
Book No. 4099 $34.95 paperback only

GLOSSBRENNER'S GUIDE TO SHAREWARE FOR SMALL BUSINESS
Alfred Glossbrenner

Now, in as little time as one hour, you can use a personal computer to keep track of your customers, ride herd on your inventory, and run your business with a degree of control you may have only dreamed about. This valuable book/disk package clears away the misconceptions surrounding today's computer jargon and products, offers solid advice on how to select IBM-compatible hardware, and reviews and recommends dozens of today's hottest shareware programs—all at the lowest possible prices!

■ 432 pages ■ 64 illustrations ■ 5.25" disk
Book No. 023543-0 $27.95 paperback
Book No. 023542-2 $37.95 hardcover

WRITING AND MARKETING SHAREWARE: Revised and Expanded
2nd Edition
Steven Hudgik

Profit from the lucrative shareware market with the tips and techniques found in this guide. If you have new software ideas, but are not sure they'll be competitive in today's dynamic PC market, this reference will show you how to evaluate and sell them through shareware distribution. Plus, you get a 5.25" disk—featuring a shareware mailing list management program and a database with over 200 shareware distributors—through a special coupon offer.

■ 336 pages ■ 41 illustrations
Book No. 3961 $18.95 paperback only

THE ENTREPRENEURIAL PC
Bernard J. David

Put the expensive home PC to work for you. You will learn about the profit-making potential of computers in typing, word processing, desktop publishing, database programming, hardware installation, electronic mail, and much more. David uses detailed, real-life examples to describe some of the more popular avenues of entrepreneurship for the home PC owner.

■ 336 pages ■ 50 illustrations
Book No. 3823   **$19.95 paperback**
                          $29.95 hardcover

BASICs FOR DOS
Gary Cornell, Ph.D.

Use this book as your hands-on tutorial for the popular BASIC programming language. It's the most comprehensive guide available on using GW-BASIC, BASICA, and especially the new Microsoft QBasic being shipped with DOS 5.0. Whether you've just decided to break away from prepackaged programs or are already a veteran at testing and debugging, you'll appreciate the programming skills that Gary Cornell describes.

■ 448 pages ■ 66 illustrations
Book No. 3769   **$21.95 paperback**
                          $31.95 hardcover

Prices Subject to Change Without Notice.

Look for These and Other Windcrest/McGraw-Hill Books at Your Local Bookstore

To Order Call Toll Free 1-800-822-8158
(24-hour telephone service available.)

or write to Windcrest/McGraw-Hill, Blue Ridge Summit, PA 17294-0840.

Title	Product No.	Quantity	Price

☐ Check or money order made payable to Windcrest/McGraw-Hill

Charge my ☐ VISA ☐ MasterCard ☐ American Express

Acct. No. _____ Exp. _____

Signature: _____

Name: _____

Address: _____

City: _____

State: _____ Zip: _____

Subtotal	$ _____
Postage and Handling ($3.00 in U.S., $5.00 outside U.S.)	$ _____
Add applicable state and local sales tax	$ _____
TOTAL	$ _____

Windcrest/McGraw-Hill catalog free with purchase; otherwise send $1.00 in check or money order and receive $1.00 credit on your next purchase.

Orders outside U.S. must pay with international money in U.S. dollars drawn on a U.S. bank.

Windcrest/McGraw-Hill Guarantee: If for any reason you are not satisfied with the book(s) you order, simply return it (them) within 15 days and receive a full refund.

BC